The
Economics
and Politics
of Race

The Economics and Politics of Race

AN INTERNATIONAL PERSPECTIVE

Thomas Sowell

QUILL
New York

Library of Congress Cataloging in Publication Data

Sowell, Thomas, 1930–
    The economics and politics of race.

    Originally published: New York : Morrow, 1983.
    Includes bibliographical references and index.
    1. Race relations—Economic aspects—Cross-cultural
studies. 2. Race relations—Political aspects—
Cross-cultural studies. 3. Ethnicity—Economic aspects—
Cross-cultural studies. 4. Ethnicity—Political
aspects—Cross-cultural studies. I. Title.
[HT1531.S68   1985]   305.8   85-6341
ISBN 0-688-04832-3 (pbk.)

Printed in the United States of America

First Quill Edition

1 2 3 4 5 6 7 8 9 10

BOOK DESIGN BY ANN GOLD

TO MARY FRANCES

PREFACE

An international perspective on race and ethnicity means much more than a compilation of minority experiences in different countries. It means an opportunity to test competing beliefs and theories in a way that cannot be done in any given country. For example: How much of any minority group's economic state depends upon their own culture and how much upon the way they are treated by the larger society around them? While there are ways of trying to puzzle this out for a given country,[1] current group characteristics can themselves be depicted as products of "society" in the past, leaving us with a chicken-and-egg dilemma.

An international perspective permits an examination of a given racial or ethnic group in a wide variety of societies—Germans in Brazil, Australia, and the United States; Chinese in Hong Kong, Indonesia, and the Caribbean; Jews in Spain, Iraq, and eastern Europe. If society is the dominant influence, we would expect to see fewer similarities between Brazilian Germans and Australian Germans than if the German cultural imprint remains strong wherever Germans settle in the world.

Moreover, an international perspective makes possible a closer look at the vague and ambiguous concept, "society." Is *society* or the *environment* where people are currently living? Or does it include their ancestral lands, or perhaps other lands where they may have settled for centuries in between—as in the case of ethnically Chinese refugees from Vietnam now living in the United States, or "the wandering Jew" in a variety of countries over the centuries?

Once environmental explanations of group behavior begin to take on this expansive concept of "society," then the notion of a given country's causal or moral responsibility for current conditions is correspondingly changed. If the economic performance of the Chinese greatly exceeds that of the Malays in a number of countries (including Malaysia), then to what extent should a given society consider itself responsible for those statistical differences between them (often described as "disparities" or "inequities")? If the people of Japan economically outperform the people of Mexico, to what extent are income differences between the Japanese and the Mexicans in California a product of American society?

The study of economics and politics together likewise provides more insights than considering them separately. The operation of the marketplace often produces a very different reality from the perceptions conveyed through the political process. The market may say that a given group's skills are valuable benefits to the larger society while politics is condemning them as parasitic bloodsuckers. Nor is it possible to escape these conflicting conclusions by saying that it is all a matter of how you choose to look at it. There are concrete empirical differences in what follows if the group is expelled—as has happened to various groups many times in history. Expelling a parasite produces very different effects on the rest of society than expelling a vital part of the economy. At many times and places in history, nations have acted politically as if they were doing one of these things, only to discover later economically that they were doing the opposite.

Nowhere is man's inhumanity to man more tangible or more heartbreaking than in racial or ethnic differences. It is tempting to dismiss it all as mere irrationality. Yet even insanity must be studied logically, if it is to be understood and effective policies followed. Even if we do not fully understand the underlying sources of group frictions and hatreds, we may nevertheless gain some insights into what kinds of social arrangements reduce or increase discrimination, violence and other overt expressions of hostility.

We need to examine not only the facts but also the conceptual framework within which we look at facts. We need to reconsider to what extent terms like "racism," "exploitation," or the "Third World" are both clear and useful.

This book has benefited from a variety of influences. The resources and freedom provided by the Hoover Institution has permitted me to take up this topic and explore it at leisure, even though I came here with the intention of writing on an entirely different subject (Marxian economics). My colleague Alvin Rabushka has been preeminent among those who have generously given of their knowledge, advice, and other help. It should be unnecessary to add that they share no responsibility for my errors, shortcomings, or conclusions.

THOMAS SOWELL

The Hoover Institution
August 19, 1982

CONTENTS

PART I

History

CHAPTER ONE

The
Role of
Race

Race has affected all kinds of human relationships for thousands of years, and in all parts of the world. Strife between Africans and East Indians has erupted into varying levels of violence from Uganda to Guyana to Trinidad.[1] The "overseas Chinese" have been victims of mob violence and brutal expulsions in countries from southeast Asia to Mexico.[2] Racial strife between blacks and whites, as in the United States, is part of a world-wide pattern.

These antagonisms have not been limited to groups that fall into different divisions of the human species into Caucasian, Negroid, or Mongoloid races. The levels of group hostility and group violence *within* each of these divisions has at least equalled that among people who differed more visibly in skin color, hair texture or other physical features. The most ghastly example of racial fanaticism in history was the Nazi extermination of millions of defenseless men, women, and children who were so similar to themselves in appearance that insignia, tattoos, or documents had to be used to tell the victims from their murderers. The *apartheid* of South Africa today is based on sharp differences of race and culture, but in a larger context of human history, degrees of biological or cultural difference have had little relationship to the degree of strife, repression, or violence.

Contemporary black and white Americans, for example, have lower levels of antagonism than exist in all-black and all-white nations such as Burundi or Northern Ireland. The atrocities committed against the Chinese minorities in southeast Asia—including "the boat people," whose traumas shocked the world—indicate that Asia too has not escaped the tragedies associated with racism, or the anomaly that much of it occurs among people who are biologically very similar. The history of Africa has likewise been full of depredations, subjugation, and massive enslavement among peoples who were all black, but whose internal ethnic and tribal differences were as deadly in their effects as similar differences among Europeans.

If race were conceived of in purely biological terms, it would be a concept that could be applied to only a relative handful of people on a few small isolated islands in the oceans. Throughout Europe, Asia, and especially America, racial intermixtures over the centuries have left hybrid populations in every country. What are called "races" in this context are simply groups of people with substantially differing proportions of genes from various racial stocks. In the United States, for example, more than three-quarters of the black population have at least one white ancestor,[3] while tens of millions of whites have at least one black ancestor[4]—and it is not uncommon for either blacks or whites to have a native American Indian ancestor. Discussions of race as a social phenomenon are discussions of relationships between groups perceived as biologically different to a degree that is significant to those involved. It is more accurately ethnicity, but is often thought of and discussed as race. Outsiders may think of Malaysia as a multi-*ethnic* society, but the Malays and Chinese there consider themselves different *races*.[5]

Racial and ethnic differences have made stable government difficult to achieve in many countries, and free stable governments all but impossible. Yugoslavia's emergence as a free and independent nation after World War I led to such bitter and violent internal struggles among the Serbs, Croatians, Macedonians, etc., that parliamentary democracy was soon replaced by military authoritarianism. Racial, ethnic, and tribal conflicts have caused a similar pattern to be repeated in various African and Asian nations that emerged into independence after World War II. Sometimes authoritarian governments have been created specifically to impose a particular racial dominance, as in Rhodesia or South Africa. Other authoritarian governments, created for different purposes, have also been used for repression of racial and ethnic minorities, as in Russia under both the Czars and the Communists. Still other nations have tried to preserve a precarious internal peace by following policies that were not in the nation's best interests otherwise, but were useful in appeasing contending groups. Yugoslavia has invested in developing a southern port, for example, when a northern port would be more economically advantageous, because otherwise those groups concentrated in the south might feel neglected.[6] In Lebanon, the government has not dared to conduct a census for more than 40 years, for fear that news of population composition changes would set off new political demands and upheavals, in a country that has already been repeatedly torn by internal disorders and civil war.[7]

Race and ethnicity involve not only issues of group solidarity, but also assertions of group superiority and inferiority. Back in the days of the Roman Empire, Germans were considered to be "blond barbarians"[8] with a "nauseating stink,"[9] and were not permitted to intermarry with Romans, though they had a place in the society as servants or as soldiers.[10] In more recent centuries, Negroes have been targets of racial inferiority doctrines, along with various Caucasian groups from southern and eastern Europe. At other times, Nordic supremacy doctrines have exalted one segment of Caucasians at the expense of all the rest of the human race—though several centuries before Christ, Mediterraneans (including Aristotle) considered themselves intellectually superior to Nordics. Racial hostility, however, has not been directed only to groups considered inferior. Antagonism to Chinese immigrants in nineteenth century America was often based on the belief that they were *too* hardworking, thrifty, and diligent for American workers or businessmen to be forced to compete with them. Much of the hostility to Jews in the United States and in Europe has had a similar origin. In short, doctrines of racial superiority and inferiority are neither necessary nor sufficient to explain racial and ethnic antagonisms.

Contrary to optimistic hopes that racial and ethnic differences would be eroded by time or eradicated by education, such differences have persisted for centuries longer than the theories which predicted their demise. Until relatively recent years, racial and ethnic distinctions and discriminations were often neglected by scholars, or noted in passing as a regrettable form of "irrationality" that time might dispel. History, however, gives little support to the view that time automatically reduces or eliminates racial aversions, fears, and animosities, or even tames the overt behavior based on such feelings. Not only has race remained salient for thousands of years; group antagonisms have progressively worsened for substantial periods of time, or suddenly erupted to catastrophic levels after long periods of quiescence. Historically, Germany was one of the most favorable places in Europe for Jews—right up to the generation of Hitler and the Nazis.[11] American cities in the late nineteenth century had far less racial segregation in housing than has been common in the twentieth century.[12]

In various countries around the world, the rise of extremist racial or ethnic political movements within the recent past has progressively undermined and co-opted moderates, and swamped all other political issues under over-riding group antagonisms.[13] Apartheid was ridiculed by Jan Smuts' South African government and by the British press in South Africa when it was first proposed in 1948, but the surprising election victory of the Afrikaner extremists marked the beginning of a policy of racial repression unparalleled in the contemporary western world—a policy now supported by much of British opinion in South Africa and by whites who were once moderate on racial issues.[14] The pervasive Jim Crow policies that characterized the American south for generations were likewise ridiculed by many white southern newspapers when first proposed at the end of the nineteenth century,[15] but within a few years these policies were so firmly in place—and so sacrosanct—that few dared to question them, and later generations regarded them as things that had existed from time immemorial.

A similar pattern has appeared in countries where racial or ethnic groups are more balanced in power. The rise of extremism in one group has led to counter-extremism in others, and to escalating levels of confrontation in politics, in civil disorders or even outright civil war. Guyana went from an ethnic coalition government elected in 1953 to a virtually all-black government in 1969, ruling a nation that was half East Indian and only 43 percent black.[16] The rise of counter-extremism among East Indians produced violent clashes in the streets, requiring troops to restore order.[17] Trinidad likewise moved in a few years from multi-racial political parties based on broad interests and philosophies to parties based on race, with people of East Indian and African descent being the chief antagonists[18] and with racial violence erupting.[19] Malaysia also began with multi-racial political parties emphasizing other issues but moved in a few years to race-based parties and violence in the streets between the Chinese and the Malays.[20]

The human race has, throughout history, differed greatly in its component parts. At various periods of history, some groups have been far ahead of others in military power, scientific achievements, or organizational skills. But often those who were far behind in one era became far ahead in another era. The Chinese, for example, had a huge and complex empire thousands of years ago, when Nordic Europe was living a primitive, tribal existence. It has been only in the past two or three centuries that their roles have been reversed. The Egyptians once subjugated and enslaved the Jews, but the balance of power is wholly the other way between contemporary Israel and Egypt. The Arabs conquered parts of Europe in the Middle Ages but have suffered conquest by the Europeans in more recent times.

While a cultural relativist might regard this as evidence that all racial, ethnic, or cultural differences are solely in the eye of the beholder, the tangible consequences of these differences—in military power, economic well-being, mortality rates—form a major part of human life and human history. The naive notion of generalized "superiority" may not stand the test of historical changes in the relative positions of races and nations, but at any given time the differences in particular skills, traits, and orientation are significant and consequential. Germans may produce markedly better lenses than the French, while the French produce markedly better champagne than the Germans, even if it is meaningless to say that one is superior over all.

Virtually every portion of the human species excels at something. From an economic point of view, this means that mutual benefits can result from cooperation among different racial and ethnic groups, whether through domestic markets, international trade, or the migration of peoples. From a political point of view, however, it is very difficult to get acceptance of these intergroup differences and their beneficial economic consequences. The conflict between the economic consequences and the political consequences of these group differences is one that appears again and again in the chapters that follow.

CHAPTER TWO

The Overseas Chinese

C hina was a large and complex civilization thousands of
years before Christ. It was—and remained for centuries
—the most advanced nation in the world in technology,
organization, commerce, and literature.[1] China had cast
iron centuries before any nation in Europe.[2] The oldest book in
existence was published in China in 868 A.D.[3] By the eleventh
century, China had achieved a level of economic development that
no European nation reached before the eighteenth century.[4] As late
as the sixteenth century, China had the highest standard of living
in the world.[5]

Geographically, China was split through the middle by a moun-
tainous region, and rugged hills further fragmented the country,
leading to great regional differences in culture, values and language.[6] While there has long been one *written* Chinese language,
spoken Chinese dialects differ so much as to be mutually incompre-
hensible.[7] China has long been a nation with extreme regionalism,
much like other geographically fragmented areas, such as southern
Italy or much of sub-Saharan Africa. In China, villages were often
in a state of war with each other in the nineteenth century.[8]

China was for centuries an insular nation, whose people sought
little contact with—much less immigration to—the outside world
of "barbarians." Still there were Chinese military conquests in
southeast Asia before the birth of Christ, and Chinese merchants
also established trade in the region during the same era.[9] The
immigration of Chinese into southeast Asia became pronounced

during the Ming Dynasty (1368–1644).[10] The Chinese moved down into Siam (now Thailand), Indo-China (now Vietnam, Cambodia, and Laos), Malaya (now Malaysia), the Dutch East Indies (now Indonesia), and the Philippines. The "overseas Chinese" also spread into Latin America and into the United States and Canada.

SOUTHEAST ASIA

When the Chinese began migrating into various southeast Asian countries about 600 years ago, most of these areas were governed by numerous local native rulers. With the passing centuries, however, European colonial powers began assuming control of much of southeast Asia, agglomerating many small entities into larger colonies or nations. But the end of World War II saw the beginning of the end of European colonialism, and the rise of nationalism in southeast Asia. The status of the Chinese minorities in the region was affected by all these historical changes.

In the early centuries of Chinese migration, there were small Chinese settlements scattered here and there in southeast Asia, but these were not a significant part of the life of these countries. China itself took little interest in the fate of these emigrants[11] who, by leaving the country, committed a crime punishable by beheading.[12] The coming of European colonial governments in the region brought the pacification and consolidation of larger areas (sometimes into new countries), with correspondingly greater security and larger scope for economic activities. This was the period of large-scale Chinese migration into southeast Asia. By 1947, there were about 8.5 million ethnic Chinese out of a total southeast Asian population of 157 million.[13] But the rise of independent, nationalistic states after World War II marked the shutting off of emigration from China.[14] Still, the overseas Chinese continued to grow by natural increase. By 1960 there were 11 million ethnic Chinese in southeast Asian countries with a total population of 215 million,[15] and by 1974 there were about 16 million Chinese out of a total southeast Asian population of 309 million.[16] The historic effect of the overseas Chinese on the region was in some ways more profound than that of the Europeans who held imperial power in southeast Asia.[17]

Some of the Chinese were biologically absorbed, some culturally assimilated, some became naturalized citizens, and some have remained completely Chinese in culture and citizenship, after generations—or even centuries—in southeast Asia. The very definition of a Chinese in these countries has presented serious problems for policy-makers and scholars alike. In Thailand, for example, there are thousands of individuals who are identified as Chinese in some social situations and as Thai in others.[18] There are very different numbers of overseas Chinese, if measured by mother tongue or national citizenship, than if measured (as here) by ethnic identification by the individuals themselves.[19]

Today, most of the overseas Chinese in southeast Asia—85 percent—were born in the respective countries in which they live.[20] While the overseas Chinese are about 5 percent of the population of southeast Asia, their proportions vary greatly from country to country. In 1974, the Chinese ethnic minority in Vietnam was not quite one percent of the total population. The Chinese were just over one percent of the population in the Philippines, about 3 percent in Indonesia, 9 percent in Thailand, and 36 percent on the Malay Peninsula. In Singapore, 72 percent of the residents are Chinese.[21] There are also regional variations within each country, the Chinese tending to be concentrated in the urban centers—constituting a majority of urban residents in Malaysia, for example.[22] In Thailand, more than half the Chinese live in or around the capital city of Bangkok.[23] Before the Communists took over the Indo-China region, half or more of the Chinese population of South Vietnam, Laos and Cambodia lived in or around their respective capital cities of Saigon, Vientiane, and Phnom Penh.[24] In the Philippines, more than half the Chinese have been concentrated in the capital city, Manila.[25] In short, throughout southeast Asia, the Chinese have represented a modern, urban, commercial element in traditional, rural, peasant societies.

Historically, most of the Chinese who settled in southeast Asia came from the southeastern provinces of China nearest these countries.[26] Their social origins were usually humble, and sometimes the group included outcasts, vagabonds, and criminals.[27] They were mostly men, and in most southeast Asian countries those who settled permanently intermarried with the local women,[28] while struggling to preserve the Chinese culture for their offspring— usually successfully in the first generation, and less so in later generations.[29] Others had wives back in China and the men either went back to China to rejoin them in later years or else sent for them to follow them to their new homes after establishing themselves financially.

The overseas Chinese usually began his new life in a southeast Asian country as a penniless laborer who worked and saved relentlessly until he had enough money to begin some sort of business.[30] While the Chinese immigrants were willing to work up to eighteen hours a day for as long as it took to reach their financial goals, the native peasants in southeast Asian countries usually devoted half the year to leisure.[31] While the native peasants were willing to go into debt even for luxury items,[32] the Chinese immigrants lived austerely on unappetizing food and packed into overcrowded housing.[33] Where there were Chinese women, they too worked with determined intensity, enduring great hardships. It was not uncommon for a Chinese woman to work in the fields for long hours under a hot sun, bent over, often knee-deep in water, and even carrying a baby on her back as well.[34]

The Chinese brought new economic vitality to the tradition-bound peasant folk cultures of southeast Asia. Working harder and saving more than the native peoples, the Chinese created new functions, crops, businesses, and industries. The Chinese began planting rubber trees and mining tin in Malaya in the nineteenth century.[35] They also established wholesale and retail distribution systems throughout the region.[36] The Chinese gained a reputation for their industriousness, frugality, acumen and reliability in business.[37] Their ability in trades and small business made them feared as competitors.[38] Eventually, they came to dominate commercial activity, and especially retail trade, throughout the region.[39] Despite being only about 5 percent of the population of southeast Asia —the overseas Chinese came to own most of the rice mills in Indo-China,[40] 75 percent of the rice mills in the Philippines,[41] and between 80 and 90 percent of the rice mills in Siam.[42] The Chinese conducted more than 70 percent of all retail trade in Thailand, Vietnam, Indonesia, and Cambodia; about 75 percent in the Philippines and 85 percent in Malaysia.[43] The Chinese have also been financiers, middlemen, and money lenders throughout southeast Asia. By 1974 the Chinese in South Vietnam owned 60 percent of all investment in paper manufacturing and 80 percent of all investment in the manufacture of textiles, iron and steel, and chemical and allied products.[44] In Thailand in 1972, the Chinese owned 80 percent of all investment in medicine, transportation, and service, and 90 percent of all investment in manufacturing, and wholesale and retail trade, as well as 95 percent of all investment in the import and export sector.[45]

Economically, the Chinese have brought with them skills and entrepreneurship lacking in the native cultures, raising the living standards of both the native peoples and themselves. Politically, however, they have been targets of abuse, discrimination, and often mob violence and even wholesale massacres at various periods of history. Even where they have become partly assimilated with the local peoples, hatred of the Chinese has been endemic throughout the region. The Philippines is a typical example:

> . . the Filipino politician who finds himself impelled to declare that 'something must be done about the Chinese' is very likely to proclaim by his eyes and by the bone structure of his face that one or more of his ancestors was Chinese. The same anomaly is found in Siam. . . . Pressed as to his case against the Chinese, the Filipino politician would say that the Chinese were too numerous, that they had more than half of the retail business in their hands, that they charged too high prices, cheated in weights and measures, and made high profits. Should it be objected that if this were so all the Filipino had to do was to open up a *tienda* on his own and put the Chinese out of business in the village, the politican would probably shift his ground. He would now say that the Chinese standard of living is deplorably low; the owner of a Chinese *tienda* is willing to live in a small corner of his store, he eats almost nothing and works day and night; so does his family and his assistant as well if he has one. The Chinese in Manila, he says, persistently disregard the eight-hour law. In fine, the charge now is that the Chinese runs his business with too little, not with too great, overhead expenses and profits. If this is true, then the Chinese give excellent service to the community as distributors. The Filipino can buy cheaply because the Chinese live so meagrely.[46]

When the Chinese were expelled from Manila in the seventeenth century, prices went *up,* not down, and there were shortages of basic necessities, even with rising prices.[47] Eventually, the Chinese had to be allowed back, but complaints that they were impoverishing the natives have never ceased in the centuries since then, either in the Philippines or in the rest of southeast Asia. It has not been unusual for economic processes to render very different verdicts from political processes, either for the Chinese or for numerous other racial and ethnic groups around the world. Often the private attitudes and behavior of the local people betrayed a very different reality from that expressed publicly and politically. For example, the very peasant who blamed the Chinese for his own misfortunes would nevertheless look with favor on the prospect of marrying off his prettiest daughter to a Chinese businessman.[48]

The overseas Chinese in southeast Asia have for centuries been analogized to the Jews in Europe.[49] However, the Chinese controlled far more of the southeast Asian economies than the Jews ever controlled in the more advanced European economies. Perhaps the Jews might be called the Chinese of Europe.

Despite many similarities, these two groups differed in that the Chinese had a homeland to which they eventually returned in many cases. Therefore, the overseas Chinese population of southeast Asia was an ever-changing one with new people coming in at the bottom and old sojourners at the top going back to China. At any given time, the Chinese were represented at all economic levels.[50] In Bangkok, for example, three-quarters of the wealthy and successful leaders of the Chinese community came from China—usually from the lower class, and almost all had made their fortune in Thailand.[51] In Indonesia, the Chinese immigrant usually arrived with "nothing but a bundle of clothes, a mat, and a pillow."[52] Among the Chinese in Malaya, "a few poor coolies founded millionaire families owning mines, plantations, big businesses and banks."[53] In short, the Chinese have not been simply a privileged group sitting permanently at the top of the economic pyramid. They have included many who have had to rise from poverty to affluence, generation after generation.

Most Chinese in southeast Asia have not been rich, but the Chinese have been disproportionately represented among the more prosperous people of the region. In 1936, for example, the total income of the Chinese taxpayers in Indonesia was 64 percent higher than that of all Indonesian taxpayers.[54] In 1970, the average Chinese in Malaysia earned double the income of the average Malay.[55]

The contrast in behavior patterns between the overseas Chinese and the indigenous peoples of southeast Asia has extended beyond commerce and industry. For example, in Malaysia, where there are about equal numbers of Malay and Chinese college students, there are more than three times as many Malays as Chinese in the liberal arts, but the Chinese outnumber the Malays in the more difficult and demanding fields such as medicine (by more than 2 to 1), science (by 8 to 1), and engineering (by 15 to 1).[56] In Thailand's two most prestigious universities, 79 percent of the students are of Chinese ancestry, though only 9 percent of the country's population is ethnically Chinese.[57] Despite anti-Chinese policies in the Malaysian military, it is estimated that one half the pilots in the Malaysian air force are Chinese,[58] though only about one third of the population of Malaysia is Chinese.[59] The Malays and the Chinese differ also in urbanization—the Malays being predominantly rural and the Chinese predominantly urban.[60]

Dominant as the Chinese have been in the economies of southeast Asia, they have studiously avoided political careers or political movements[61]—as did the Chinese in the United States during their rise from poverty to affluence.[62] This was a deliberate refusal of the Chinese to get involved politically,[63] rather than a mere failure to achieve political office. To the overseas Chinese, economic advancement and political visibility were perceived as being mutually incompatible.[64] In some places, the Chinese were forbidden to hold political office,[65] but even where this was not so, the overseas Chinese showed little interest in the politics of the countries in which they lived, and more concern with political events in China, to which they planned to return.[66]

The virtually total absence of Chinese political power in southeast Asia exposed them to all sorts of discrimination as a hated minority throughout the region. The Chinese were sometimes singled out for special taxes,[67] often confined by law to living in particular areas or specific parts of cities,[68] and banned from a variety of economic activities.[69] Generally, the Chinese suffered stoically under these discriminations with "noncommittal blankness."[70] A nineteenth century Chinese "of enormous wealth" was observed with his head bowed in silence as adverse political decisions were read in Siam, but looking "as if a hundred thunder storms were concentrated in that proud, scornful, yet resigned expression. . . ."[71] The Chinese were widely known for their peacefulness, and for being tractable subjects for political rulers.[72] Their political efforts were usually confined to bribing or otherwise corrupting political leaders and petty officials to help them evade the numerous laws, regulations, and taxes that vexed them.[73]

Occasionally, when the oppression became intolerable, the overseas Chinese had uprisings, but these were brutally crushed.[74] In one such uprising in the Philippines in 1603, about 23,000 Chinese were slaughtered.[75] Usually, however, mass violence was initiated by native peoples against the Chinese.[76] Their governments and political movements also carried out mass violence and looting of Chinese communities.[77] In the wake of national independence from European colonial powers after World War II, the nationalist emotions quickly became anti-Chinese emotions. In Indonesia in 1947 there was widespread violence, destruction, looting, rape, and murder against the Chinese.[78] Chinese have also been massacred as far away as Mexico.[79]

Everywhere the basic problem is the same: The "vivid contrast between their own poverty and Chinese commercial affluence" which angered the farmers of Malaysia[80] has outraged similar peasant peoples around the world. The behavioral contrasts behind the economic contrast are seldom perceived or accepted as fundamental causes. Given the virtually inexhaustible sins of any large group of human beings, there are many specific grievances against the Chinese, and these grievances are regarded as the causes for the economic differences, though the Chinese could no doubt present an equally impressive list of the sins of southeast Asians or of European colonial powers in the region.

The contrast between the economic value of the Chinese to various countries and the political resentment they engender among the poor and backward native populace lies behind historical vacillations in government policies toward them—and toward the Jews in Europe, the Armenians in Asia Minor, and other such groups around the world. At various times and places, governments have welcomed the influx of the Chinese into southeast Asia and Latin America, and at other times restricted their immigration or expelled them outright.[81] The skills, entrepreneurship and capacity for hard work of the Chinese are particularly valuable in tropical peasant societies where such traits tend to be rare. In calm times, far-seeing rulers have understood this and encouraged the entry of the Chinese, but once popular animosity toward them has built up, they are a convenient scapegoat for dissatisfaction, a temptation to every demagogue, and a political liability to any government that would defend their rights. At such times, governments have typically either abandoned them to the mobs or have themselves initiated anti-Chinese activity.

With the achievement of independence from European colonial powers after World War II, the nations of southeast Asia launched widespread campaigns of official discrimination against the Chinese, though phrased as pro-native rather than anti-Chinese. Quota systems were established in government employment and in admissions to institutions of higher education in Malaysia,[82] and a "target" of 30 percent Malaysian ownership established in business and industry.[83] In Indonesia, a 1959 law forbade the Chinese to engage in retailing in the villages,[84] and there was "preferential" allocation of import licenses and foreign exchange to businesses owned by indigenous Indonesians. Chinese-owned rice mills were confiscated, and severe restrictions placed on where Chinese could work or live.[85] In Thailand, employment quotas were established for indigenous Thais.[86] In the Philippines, it was decreed that no new Chinese import business could be established, and Chinese retail establishments were closed down by law.[87] Among the economic consequences of these measures were acute grain shortages,[88] a flight of Chinese capital,[89] and widespread evasions[90] which prevented these measures from having as devastating an effect on the economies of southeast Asia as they would have had if the Chinese contribution were as effectively restricted as intended.

The Chinese—politically weak, foreign, but prosperous, visible and unpopular[91]—found themselves under political attack throughout southeast Asia. Their private schools became increasingly regulated by governments that prescribed languages and curricula and proscribed books and educational philosophies that displeased the ruling politicians. In some cases, locally born Chinese were forced to "return" to a China or Taiwan they had never seen. But despite recurring anti-Chinese policies and pressures, the overseas Chinese have continued to prosper, in part because of their own ingenuity at evading laws and regulations, but more fundamentally because neither native businessmen nor government proved able to replace them in the economy.[92]

Thailand

For 700 years the Chinese have been part of the history of Siam,[93] which since 1950 has been known as Thailand. As of 1960, there were more than 400,000 Chinese nationals living in Thailand,[94] but the total number of *ethnic* Chinese in Thailand is more than 2 million.[95] In the early centuries of Chinese immigration to Siam, they were well-received by the Siamese,[96] and were even accepted to some high positions in the Siamese government.[97] Indeed, there were eighteenth century kings who were part Chinese.[98] Moreover, the prestige of Chinese civilization was high in Siam.[99]

Until well into the twentieth century, Chinese immigrants to Siam were mostly males who married Siamese women, with the children being brought up as Siamese.[100] The Chinese and their offspring supplied the kind of energy and initiative that were rare among the indigenous Siamese,[101] though in external culture the Chinese became Siamese.[102] A British visitor who arrived in Bangkok before daybreak on May 10, 1833 found that "vast numbers of Chinese blacksmiths were busily employed forging iron works."[103] The Chinese in various occupations were noted as the first to rise in the morning in Bangkok.[104] Their occupations ranged from coolie laborers and rickshaw pullers (a job no Siamese would take[105]) to butchers, bakers, scavengers, sweepers, peddlers and merchants. The Chinese came to dominate the mechanical occupations in Siam,[106] and in the twentieth century the Chinese constituted almost all the labor in the rice mills of Siam.[107] Most of the native Siamese worked in agriculture[108] but most of the non-agricultural work in the country was done by the Chinese, who were willing to endure the long hours and hard work in industrial and commercial occupations.[109] Even in agriculture, however, it was the Chinese who introduced into Siam such crops as sugar cane, pepper, and many fruits and vegetables.[110]

In Siam, as elsewhere throughout southeast Asia and around the world, wherever the Chinese went there were secret societies or *tongs*. [111] Historically, these had originated in China as religious and patriotic groups with popular support[112] but over the centuries they degenerated into extortionists and criminals.[113] Their illegal and violent activities brought discredit and suspicion on the whole Chinese community, which was typically quiet and hard-working. In Siam, the Chinese secret societies were responsible for riots in 1889 and for street fighting with firearms in 1895.[114]

By the 1840s there were 15,000 Chinese immigrants arriving annually in Siam.[115] In the early nineteenth century, it was estimated that half the population of the capital was Chinese.[116] About 40 percent of the Chinese immigrants settled permanently in Siam, and of those about half married Siamese women.[117]

In Siam as elsewhere, the Chinese deliberately avoided political activity.[118] Discrimination usually elicited little protest from the Chinese but only "bland acquiescence."[119] On the few occasions where they did attempt to revolt, they were dealt with mercilessly in Siam, as elsewhere in southeast Asia. A Chinese insurrection in 1847, for example, was put down by Siamese troops who then engaged in "a general massacre of unresisting men, women and children."[120] Politically, the Chinese were thoroughly subservient to the Siamese overlords.[121] Those Chinese who did not renounce their Chinese citizenship were subjected to a special tax, and an observer reported that "there is nothing that a Siamese policeman so much enjoys as leading some unfortunate Chinaman to pay the tax."[122] Yet the economic success of the Chinese produced admiration and emulation as well. Some Siamese even affected Chinese hairstyles in order to pass for Chinese.[123]

By and large, the Chinese and Siamese co-existed with relatively little friction[124] on into the early twentieth century. The rise of nationalism in both China and Siam quickly changed that, however. China passed a nationality law in 1909, in which people of the Chinese race were granted citizenship in China, regardless of where they lived. The 1911 revolution in China reinforced these nationalistic trends and marked the beginning of active propaganda by China among the overseas Chinese—a policy continued over the years by both the Kuomintang and Communist governments. At about the same time, large numbers of Chinese women began migrating into Siam for the first time. "In 1910 a Chinese woman was a rare sight in the streets of Bangkok; twenty years later there were hundreds of them to be seen."[125] They were more in demand by Chinese men than were Siamese or racially mixed women, as indicated by the bride prices paid.[126] The arrival of Chinese women in Siam, as elsewhere in southeast Asia, marked a reduction in the rate of biological and cultural absorption of the Chinese into the host society.

The Siamese also had a growing nationalism. In 1919, the Siamese government imposed regulations on the private Chinese schools that operated in that country, as in the rest of southeast Asia, to perpetuate a separate Chinese culture.[127] Over the years this regulation became ever tighter to cope with continuing Chinese evasions. In 1934, fifty Chinese books were banned in Siam.[128] In 1940, most Chinese newspapers were closed by the government amid raids on Chinese schools, homes, and businesses and the jailing of Chinese for illegally continuing to send money to China.[129] Petty harassments included taxing sign boards written in Chinese, and more serious discriminatory efforts included laws and policies designed to force the Chinese out of whole industries.[130] There was discriminatory taxation of aliens (mostly Chinese) and at the same time it was made more difficult to become a naturalized citizen.[131] In 1942, those Chinese who were not citizens of Siam were legally excluded from living in certain cities.[132] Occupations began to be legally reserved for citizens of Siam.[133] Ironically, many of the Siamese officials who promoted this nationalistic discrimination were themselves part Chinese[134]—products of an earlier and more tolerant era. This was only one of many historic instances of sustained retrogression in racial and ethnic relations, in various countries around the world.

The very attempts at preventing the development of Chinese separatism had the effect of fostering a heightened sense of ethnic identity in the beleaguered group,[135] and the economic advantages of the Chinese persisted as well. They continued to own from 80 to 90 percent of the rice mills—the largest enterprises in the country. Moreover, the Chinese dominated every phase of rice production except the actual farming. Siamese farmers borrowed from the Chinese in order to live between planting time and harvest time, and after the harvest the Chinese bought the rice, transported it, milled it, and did three-quarters of all the exporting of rice from Siam.[136]

Although many of those in dominant economic positions in Siam were Chinese, this did not mean that most Chinese in Siam were affluent. In the countryside, the Chinese typically lived in a palm leaf hut with the earth for a floor, lighted at night by a kerosene or coconut oil lamp, and with his animals in an adjoining room. In town, the Chinese businessman's home was likely to be part of the same structure as his shop and his toilet facilities consisted of a bucket that was emptied into a canal twice a day.[137] But what the Siamese masses saw was the over-representation of the Chinese among those few who were affluent. Moreover, this was not attributed to the historic role of the Chinese in the economic development of the country but to exploitation: The Siamese generally blamed the poverty of the peasants on the Chinese money-lender.[138]

The political expression of these popular views was a series of programs designed to force the Chinese out of various economic positions, replacing them with members of the indigenous population. The Siamese government encouraged alternate sources of credit and marketing for Siamese peasants, and itself built and operated factories, and created corporations with a monopoly of the sale of rice, liquor, and other commodities.[139] It excluded the Chinese from a number of occupations. But despite many discriminatory laws and policies, the Chinese have continued their dominant economic role in Thailand. As of 1972, they owned between 50 and 95 percent of the capital in Thailand's banking and finance industry, medicine, transportation, wholesale and retail trade, restaurants, and the import and export business.[140] Although the goal of government policy was to "transfer the control of business to nationals by ousting the Chinese," they encountered the same underlying reality as other governments pursuing the same policy elsewhere in southeast Asia—namely, that a native population from a peasant background provided relatively few people with the inclination, the money, or the experience to operate businesses,[141] or even to perform skilled industrial labor. A law in 1935–36 requiring rice mills to employ a minimum of 50 percent Siamese workers proved impossible to carry out, due to a lack of such labor.[142] Even some of the government-owned enterprises, set up to reduce the role of the Chinese in the economy, ended up hiring Chinese managers.[143]

Malaysia

The independent nation of Malaysia was created in 1963, combining Malaya, Singapore, and other territories in the region. As of 1965, however, Singapore became an independent city-state. The history of Malaysia is thus essentially the history of Malaya, Singapore and parts of the island of Borneo, the rest of which belongs to Indonesia.

In Malaya, as in other parts of southeast Asia, there were relatively few Chinese before the era of European colonialism. There was a more or less permanent settlement of Chinese in fourteenth century Malaya,[144] but the numbers never reached the proportions achieved later in history, when the growing Chinese population for a time even outnumbered the Malays.

When the Dutch captured Malacca in 1641, they found three to four hundred Chinese shopkeepers, craftsmen and farmers.[145] By 1827, there were about 4,000 Chinese out of a total population of about 29,000 in the city.[146] In 1795, the British captured Malacca as part of a growing British empire in the region. The British also acquired, by lease from a sultan, the virtually uninhabited island of Penang, off the west coast of the Malay peninsula.[147] Malays and Chinese subsequently settled on the island, the Malays cutting down the trees and all the rest of the work of preparing the land for cultivation being done by the Chinese.[148] A report on the Penang settlement written by the top British official there in 1794 said:

> The Chinese constitute the most valuable part of our inhabitants; they are men, women, and children, about 3,000, they possess the different trades of carpenters, masons, and smiths, are traders, shopkeepers, and planters, they employ small vessels and prows and send adventurers to the surrounding countries. They are the only people of the east from whom a revenue may be raised without expense and extraordinary efforts of government. They are a valuable acquisition, but speaking a language which no other people understand, they are able to form parties and combinations in the most secret manner against any regulations of government which they disapprove, and were they brave as intelligent they would be dangerous subjects, but their want of courage makes them bear many impositions before they rebel. They are indefatigable in the pursuit of money. . . .[149]

The British maintenance of law and order in Malacca, Penang, and Singapore, while law and order were breaking down in China, during and after the Taiping Rebellion in the middle of the nineteenth century, attracted substantial Chinese immigration.[150] The Chinese lived mostly to themselves, governed through heads of Chinese communities appointed by the civil authorities.[151] Although the Chinese men in Malacca married local women, the children were almost all raised in the Chinese culture.[152] The Chinese enclave also contained tongs, or secret societies. The intrigues and violence of the tongs erupted in riots from 1846 to 1885.[153]

The British colony at Singapore, on the tip of the Malay Peninsula, was founded in 1819. At that time the only inhabitants were 120 Malays and 30 Chinese.[154] Under British rule, the population grew rapidly to 4,727 in 1821, of whom 1,159 were Chinese. Two years later, the population was more than 10,000 of whom more than 3,000 were Chinese. Here, too, the top official of the colony reported that the most valuable of its inhabitants were "beyond doubt the Chinese," even though he had to separate those Chinese from different provinces in China, in the interest of tranquility.[155] The Chinese population of Singapore rose both absolutely and relative to the total population there. The Chinese were about half the population of Singapore by 1840, three-fifths by 1881, and nearly three-quarters by 1931.[156] Later, after Malaysian independence, Singapore was separated from the rest of the country because its heavily Chinese population would have given the Chinese a majority in the country. It was one of the rare cases of a nation deliberately parting with some of its own territory and people.

The Chinese in early Singapore were plagued by the tongs, especially because many of these Chinese were Christians outside the orbit of the secret societies. More than 500 Chinese in Singapore were killed by the tongs in a week of riots in 1851. Four hundred were killed in another set of riots in 1854.[157] Regional differences exacerbated religious and other differences reflected in these clashes among the Chinese in Singapore.

The Chinese began planting rubber and mining tin in Malaya in the nineteenth century. Both became major industries and major exports of the country. The early tin miners were mostly Malays, but the discovery of rich deposits in the middle of the nineteenth century brought a large influx of Chinese miners.[158] There were about 9,000 Chinese miners in 1877 and 50,000 by 1882.[159] By 1931, there were more than 70,000 Chinese mining tin and more than 160,000 Chinese growing rubber.[160] European capital and technology competed with the Chinese in Malaya tin-mining, and eventually became predominant. As of 1920, the Chinese-owned mines produced nearly two-thirds of the tin in Malaya, but by 1938 the European mines produced two-thirds.[161] The Malays themselves played a negligible role as investors, owners, or managers. By 1931, Europeans and Americans owned 84 percent of the rubber holdings in Malaya, the Chinese 13 percent and the Malays 2 percent.[162]

Malays remained largely peasant proprietors, and the policy of the Malay government reserved the best rice land for them. The Malays also engaged in fresh water fishing, but the Chinese dominated the preparation of cured and dried fish, which required capital, entrepreneurship, and business connections abroad.[163]

Free education was established for all Malay boys and girls, but not for the Chinese. This education (in English) emphasized literary rather than scientific, commercial, or technical training. It turned out more potential clerks than employers could hire.[164] The Chinese set up their own private schools, not nearly as well financed as the government schools, taught in Chinese and featuring much nationalistic Chinese propaganda—both Kuomintang and Communist.[165] The general trend of Malay education is apparent even today, when they predominate over the Chinese in the liberal arts but are vastly outnumbered by the Chinese in scientific and technical fields.[166]

Politically, the Malays have remained ascendant over the Chinese. Even under the British rule, which lasted until 1963, the Malays were given preferential treatment in government employment.[167] When Japan conquered Malaya in World War II, the Japanese army of occupation singled out the Chinese for especially brutal treatment, including a public massacre of 5,000 in 1942.[168] The Chinese remained loyal to the British, often giving aid to British troops at the risk of their lives,[169] while many Malays collaborated with the Japanese. These wartime experiences drove the Malay and Chinese communities further apart, and violence broke out between the two groups after the war was over.[170]

Postwar Malaya was very much split politically and ethnically. In 1948, the Chinese were 45 percent of the population, the Malays 43 percent, and the Indians 10 percent. All three groups were separate and hostile to the others.[171] In addition, anti-Japanese guerillas from World War II—virtually all Chinese—became the basis for a Communist-led guerilla movement aimed at driving the British out of Malaya. Ironically, the greatest obstacle to British withdrawal was the divisiveness among the population, which jeopardized the survivability of an independent state. Before the war, demands for independence were negligible, precisely because the various groups in Malaya did not trust each other enough to want the British to leave,[172] though the British had set up machinery for moving toward independence as early as 1917.[173] After years of fighting, the guerillas were defeated in 1960, and Malaya became an independent Malaysia in 1963, with Singapore and its Chinese majority becoming a separate state two years later. In Malaysia as presently constituted, the Malays are 53 percent of the population, the Chinese 35 percent and the Indians 10 percent. This is not very different from the ethnic composition of the same geographical area in 1921.[174] Still the Chinese outnumber the Malays among the urban population and in two of the country's eleven states.[175] There are few inter-racial neighborhoods in Malaysia and little intermarriage.[176]

Although Malays are barely half of the population, the Malaysian constitution reserves four-fifths of the civil service jobs for Malays, as well as three-fourths of the university scholarships.[177] Malays are also 84 percent of the registered voters,[178] and the districts are so weighted that a rural Malay is politically equivalent to two urban Chinese.[179] Economically, however, the Chinese in mid-century Malaya still earned more than double the income of Malays in 1958[180] and in 1970 exactly double.[181] Chinese income remained double the income of Malays in 1976, despite a massive government program imposing preferential treatment of Malays in the private economy.[182]

Predominantly Chinese Singapore has likewise had a per capita income nearly double that of the country from which it was separated, as well as a higher growth rate.[183] As for the ownership of corporations in Malaysia—including government corporations—that is now 63 percent Western, 27 percent Chinese and 2 percent Malay.[184]

Indonesia

The nation of Indonesia developed out of various territories consolidated under colonial rule as the Dutch East Indies. Indonesia consists of more than 3,000 islands—including Java, Sumatra, and most of Borneo—strung across the equator and separating the Pacific Ocean from the Indian Ocean. As far back as the ninth century, Chinese traders were known to have visited Java.[185] By 1733 there were 80,000 Chinese on Java, in the city of Batavia alone.[186] The ruling Dutch East India Company allowed the Chinese to live in their own communities, and dealt with them through Chinese headmen appointed by the colonial power.[187]

The Chinese not only lived separately from the indigenous people but were known for being hardworking and more frugal.[188] They were also more entrepreneurial. It was the Chinese who introduced sugar-processing mills on Java, though sugar cane had been grown by the natives before.[189] A seventeenth century Catholic priest observed:

> Since the Chinese are industrious and clever, they are of the greatest value at Batavia and without their help it would be difficult to live at all comfortably. They cultivate the land; there are scarcely any artisans except Chinese; in a word they are nearly everything.[190]

Along with the industrious and entrepreneurial Chinese came the tongs or secret societies that followed them everywhere. As elsewhere, these criminal elements were not only a direct burden to the Chinese community but also a source of bitter friction with the surrounding society. In 1740, the Dutch authorities in the East Indies decreed that any Chinese who could not establish that he was making an honest living would be sent to Ceylon—as a slave.[191] The alarm that this policy spread among the Chinese led to an uprising, in which thousands of Chinese were killed. This was a "wanton slaughter after all effective resistance had ceased."[192]

By the beginning of the nineteenth century, the Chinese dominated both the domestic and import-export markets of Java,[193] and were amassing well-concealed riches in Borneo.[194] They became middlemen, not only in the usual sense but also as intermediaries between the European colonial powers and the native peoples. The natives bought from the Europeans through the Chinese and sold to the Europeans through the Chinese.[195] Large-scale businesses were usually in the hands of the Europeans,[196] but the Chinese were prominent as money-lenders and tax farmers—people directly in contact with the poor and therefore widely detested. As elsewhere in southeast Asia, the peasant farmer who could not repay his debts to the Chinese money-lender became virtually a slave to his creditor.[197] While the natives complained of exploitation, the Europeans had the opposite complaint—that the Chinese were "ruining" their market by offering similar articles at much lower prices.[198]

Despite their economic prosperity, the Chinese did not enjoy a free or equal status in the Dutch East Indies. It was the early twentieth century before the Chinese could live outside designated quarters or even travel freely in the country. Nor were these merely colonial oppressions. The Chinese had been even more severely restricted by native rulers centuries earlier, before the Dutch colonized the area.[199] In the twentieth century, the Chinese gradually advanced toward complete equality with the Europeans,[200] but were still subjected to heavier taxation—without political representation.[201] The Chinese, however, remained noted for being "the perfect type of quiet citizen," distinguished primarily by his industry, frugality, and reliability.[202]

As elsewhere in southeast Asia, the Chinese were found at every economic level of Indonesian society. They were coolie laborers on plantations, farmers, miners, retailers, and bankers. Before about 1870, Chinese capital was the principal capital available in the East Indies, but afterwards large-scale European capital poured in. By 1921, the Dutch had 73 percent of the capital in the country, the Chinese 11 percent and the British 9 percent.[203] European businesses were large impersonal enterprises supported by many anonymous stockholders, and able to grow larger with the passing decades. The Chinese enterprise was typically a one-man operation that usually ended when its founder died.[204] But although European incomes in the East Indies were substantially higher than those of the Chinese, the Chinese earned more than the Indonesians,[205] and this was politically important in terms of jealousy and hatred. As elsewhere in southeast Asia, the presence of the colonial power protected the Chinese, but the early World War II victories of the Japanese jeopardized them:

> . . . when the Japanese landed in Java Chinese residents were the main victims of robbery by the natives. In the majority of the cases the trouble started with the robbing of one or two houses by a few bandits. When no police appeared and no resistance was encountered, the whole of the inhabitants of the town or village, who in the past had never committed robbery or any other criminal act, participated in the looting. Moreover, now that civilized controls were removed, a number of excesses occurred and there was murder and rape.[206]

During the postwar struggle of the Indonesians for independence from the Dutch, the Chinese were caught in the middle and viewed with suspicion by both sides. Six hundred Chinese were slaughtered in one settlement and their villages set on fire, though this involved the burning alive of women and children, among other atrocities. One report said:

. . . the suburbs of Tamerang have been turned into a hell for the
Chinese who for many years had lived so amicably with the Indonesians
and adjusted themselves to their environment so well that foreigners
could hardly distinguish them from real Indonesians. As the Chinese of
this area have practically become assimilated, it is incredible that they
were so treated.[207]

Smaller massacres also occurred in various other parts of Indonesia
in 1946 and 1947.[208]

In Indonesia, as it emerged into independent nationhood after
World War II, there were more than 2 million Chinese, nearly
three-quarters of whom had been born there.[209] By the 1960s,
there were at least 2.5 million Chinese in Indonesia,[210] out of a total
population of about 96 million.[211] How many of the ethnic Chinese
were *citizens* of Indonesia is less clear. It has been estimated that
between 40 and 45 percent of the Chinese are Indonesian citizens.[212] However, Indonesian citizenship has not protected people
of Chinese ancestry from discriminatory laws and policies followed
by the Indonesian government. These included the banning of
Chinese newspapers and magazines, pressures against Chinese
schools that reduced their number from over a thousand to a few
hundred, import restrictions, foreign exchange restrictions,[213] and
other restrictions that were complicated and extensive.[214] There
was a confiscation of Chinese-owned rice mills and an expulsion of
Chinese retailers from the rural areas.[215]

The initial anti-Chinese thrust of the Indonesian government
under President Sukarno immediately after World War II has been
moderated under President Suharto. Some previously nationalized
Chinese enterprises were returned to their owners after 1967.[216]
Still, preferential treatment for indigenous Indonesians continues,
along with a popular undercurrent of anti-Chinese feeling. Anti-
Chinese riots continue to break out from time to time in Indonesia.[217] Such riots rocked Java in November 1980, leaving
eight dead, dozens injured and millions of dollars in property damage.[218] While President Suharto opposed the rioting, saying that it
"smacked of racialism," he also warned the Chinese not to "demonstrate an attitude and lifestyle that may offend the surrounding
larger community."[219] How the Chinese were to prosper, without
offending the less prosperous Indonesians, was not explained.

The Philippines

The Philippines were conquered by Spain in the sixteenth century, and then by the United States at the beginning of the twentieth century. There were Chinese in the Philippines centuries before the Spaniards arrived, and in 1590 there were from 3,000 to 4,000 living in the Chinese quarter of Manila, and from 6,000 to 7,000 Chinese in the city and suburbs.[220] They were initially welcomed by the Spanish authorities[221] and became an important part of the economic life of the islands. The Chinese were the principal artisans and laborers—the carpenters, tailors, cobblers and other workers who supplied the day-to-day needs of the Spanish community.[222]

A contemporary account said that "from China come all who supply every sort of service, all dextrous, prompt, and cheap."[223] Nevertheless, the Spanish authorities restricted the Chinese in where they could live or travel, and in the prices charged for their goods.[224] A Chinese uprising in 1603 led to a massacre of more than 20,000 Chinese by the Spaniards.[225] Afterwards, the loss was felt in economic activities formerly carried on by the Chinese, for the Filipinos were unable to replace them, even in agriculture.[226] Another uprising occurred in 1639, with most of the Chinese population of Luzon being exterminated, due to lack of firearms. Again, more than 20,000 Chinese were killed, compared to 300 Filipinos and less than 50 Spaniards.[227] Smaller scale massacres of Chinese occurred from time to time on into the early nineteenth century.[228]

The Chinese in the Philippines were predominantly male and intermarried with the native women, producing a mixed offspring described as "one of the most capable, prosperous and powerful elements of the Filipino people." By the 1940s there were about three-quarters of a million Chinese-Filipinos. Some of those who entered politics were among the most strongly anti-Chinese elements in the Philippines.[229]

Among the sources of intergroup friction was that Filipinos were continually in debt to Chinese.[230] The Chinese, on the other hand, were so frugal that a saying among Filipinos was that the Chinese worker, making 12 dollars a month, saved from 16 to 18 dollars out of his pay![231] The Chinese domination of skilled occupations lasted for centuries. Even as late as the early twentieth century,

American businessmen in the Philippines were pressing for allowing immigration from China, because of insufficient skilled labor among the Filipinos.[232]

Under the American colonial rule in the Philippines, Chinese investments were second only to U.S. investments. The Chinese also conducted about three-quarters of all the retail trade and owned about three-quarters of all the rice mills in the islands.[233] All this occurred despite laws, dating back to Spanish colonial rule, which kept 90 percent of the land in the hands of Filipinos.[234]

Filipino resentment of the Chinese was expressed in many ways, from special discriminatory exactions to sporadic mob violence.[235] When the Philippines became an autonomous Commonwealth in 1935, discriminatory policies against the Chinese increased. The government promoted and subsidized businesses to compete with the Chinese, and restricted the latter's occupations.[236] Still, as of 1947, about a third of the trade in the Philippines was in the hands of Americans, another third in the hands of the Chinese, and less than a fourth in the hands of Filipinos.[237] The rise of Chinese Communist guerillas in the Philippines during and after World War II further inflamed racial animosities. But eventually, as of the end of the 1950s, the Chinese were apparently almost legislated out of the retail trade, owning only 13 percent of the businesses, with 37 percent of the capital.[238] However, the official figures are open to question, since Chinese businessmen in the Philippines have been known to operate with some Filipino as owner in name only, or to have businesses in the name of a Filipino wife, or to become a naturalized citizen of the Philippines, though naturalization for a Chinese was very expensive and difficult even when he had been born in the Philippines.[239]

Indo-China

The countries more recently known as Vietnam, Cambodia and Laos were once parts of a regional agglomeration known as Indo-China. At various periods of history this region has been divided into other political units (Tongking, Annam, Cochinchina, etc.) and it has also encompassed many peoples and cultures, including the Chinese. Indo-China has been subject to diverse cultural influences from the great civilizations of India and China (whence its name), and from Malay and Indonesian peoples, as well as from the French who ruled it from about the middle of the nineteenth century to the middle of the twentieth century. For nearly a thousand years, ending in the tenth century, A.D., parts of Vietnam were subjugated under the empire of China.

Chinese communities existed in the region long before it became part of the French colonial empire. A Chinese community established near Saigon was the scene of a native massacre of more than 10,000 Chinese in the eighteenth century, with burning and looting of Chinese shops. In Annam (in central Vietnam) and in Cambodia, the Chinese lived in separate communities, internally divided by region of origin in China. Each community was represented by a Chinese captain selected by the native authorities and held responsible for law and order and tax collection.[240]

The French colonial powers tried to restrict Chinese immigration into Indo-China in the late nineteenth century, and to regulate their movements and activities while in the country, through laws and regulations "which looked splendid in Paris but worked badly in Saigon."[241] When these repressive policies caused the Chinese to begin leaving Haiphong, "the European found himself helpless without the assistance of Chinese in his plantations and mines, his boats and wagons, his ships and houses."[242] Eventually, it was necessary to ease restrictions on the Chinese. Still, both the French and the Indo-Chinese natives continued to complain of "the Chinese stranglehold on Indochina," "the Chinese cyst," and similar pejorative phrases.[243] The Chinese businessman was too much competition for "the Annamites and Cambodians who almost entirely lacked his qualities of economy and perseverance." At the same time, he generally bested the Europeans in economic competition, being more familiar with the native languages and cultures and requiring less to live on.[244] Moreover, the much-hated Chinese money-lender did not require as much security as the banks.[245] What others called "exploitation," an economist might consider a risk premium.

The feeling that the Chinese had excessive economic rewards persisted after independence, in both Communist and non-Communist regions of Indo-China. So did efforts to prevent this, followed by an exodus of Chinese, the loss of Chinese skills and consequent economic losses suffered by the other peoples of the region. The Communist takeover of North Vietnam in 1954 led nearly a million Chinese there to flee to the South.[246] The South Vietnamese government in 1956 issued sweeping restrictions on the kinds of occupations in which non-naturalized Chinese could engage, and clamped government controls on private Chinese schools.[247] Laos and Cambodia likewise restricted many occupations to their respective citizens.[248] Nevertheless, by naturalization or by one evasion or another, the Chinese continued as a major economic force in the region. As of 1974, Chinese investments in South Vietnam were half of all investments in restaurants, 60 percent of all investments in paper and in fisheries, and 80 percent of all investments in iron and steel, textiles, and the chemical industry.[249] The two million Chinese in South Vietnam were just one percent of the country's population.[250] In Laos, where the Chinese were 2 percent of the population, they controlled an estimated 70 percent of small scale industry, before the Communist takeover—after which many of those enterprises closed down.[251] In Cambodia, where the Chinese were 5 percent of the population, they owned about 70 percent of the industrial investment before the Communists took over.[252]

With the Communist takeovers of Vietnam, Laos, and Cambodia in the 1970s, a new phase of anti-Chinese policy began. About a million refugees fled from Vietnam between 1975 and 1979.[253] An estimated 70 percent were ethnically Chinese.[254] They fled both legally and illegally, by land and by sea, some in seaworthy vessels but many more on boats too small or too leaky to be safe on the open seas. It is estimated that as many drowned at sea as ever reached land—and the latter amounted to many hundreds of thousands. These were the "boat people"—refugees who found little refuge anywhere. Many boat people were victimized on the high seas by the crews of other vessels from various parts of southeast Asia, who boarded the refugee boats to rob, assault, rape, and kill the hated and helpless Chinese. Such incidents became so common that refugee officials recording these episodes developed the shorthand code "RPM" for rape, pillage, and murder. Nearly one-third of the boats leaving South Vietnam were struck by raiders on the high seas, and about one-third of these suffered all three acts summarized as RPM.[255]

Those who reached land were interned in overcrowded refugee camps in Malaysia, Thailand, Hong Kong, Indonesia and other parts of southeast Asia. Communist China took in more than 200,000 refugees, almost all from North Vietnam.[256] As the massive influx of refugees continued, many countries forbade any more to land. Hong Kong forcibly prevented a shipload of Vietnamese refugees from landing. Malaysia sent 55,000 refugees back to sea —many to certain death on flimsy and leaky boats. One Malaysian high official openly threatened to have boat people shot on sight if any more landed in his country—though adverse world opinion forced a recantation on this. While some southeast Asian nations argued that they simply could not support such large numbers of refugees, the Malaysian government candidly conceded that it feared that more Chinese would upset the country's ethnic balance.[257]

A fortunate minority of the refugees—about 200,000—were resettled in other countries, two-thirds of these in the United States. In America, the Vietnamese refugees exhibited many of the traits that have long marked the overseas Chinese in southeast Asia. Despite their newness in a strange land, they entered the labor force about as often as Americans in general, and had a lower rate of unemployment.[258] In the schools, their children suffered from lack of knowledge of English and other cultural differences, but they scored higher on mathematical tests than American children and spent more time on their homework.[259] Many adults began opening small businesses. Perhaps it marks the beginning of another chapter in the story of the overseas Chinese, overcoming adversity and hostility to survive and prosper once again.

THE UNITED STATES

Chinese immigration to the United States began in the middle of the nineteenth century, sparked by the discovery of gold in California in 1849. Unlike southeast Asia, the United States already had entrepreneurs, investors, retailers, bankers, and other important economic roles filled by the Chinese in the far east. Moreover, many Americans were unwilling to accept the Chinese in any but menial positions.

The initial Chinese immigration to the United States began much as it did in southeast Asia, with masses of poor young men, lacking skills or education but willing to work long and hard to establish themselves or to save enough to return to China in prosperity. Many crossed the Pacific in steerage, packed together shoulder-to-shoulder and head-to-toe in poorly ventilated holds. Sometimes *standees* were carried, and they took turns sleeping on the bunks during a voyage that could last three months on wind-driven ships, depending on the weather. With water scarce and food of poor quality, many died before reaching America.[260] Those who reached the United States found "the institutional network with its threads reaching back home was there to greet them the moment they got off the boat."[261] As in southeast Asia, the Chinese community in America was a separate, self-enclosed enclave. It handled most of its own problems and disputes without recourse to the courts, political system, police force, or other institutions of the surrounding society. The Chinese Consolidated Benevolent Association—better known as the Six Companies—presented a united front to the outside world and controlled individual Chinese internally. For example, "no Chinese could buy passage back to China unless he had paid his debts in the United States and got the requisite clearance from the Six Companies."[262]

By 1880, there were more than 100,000 Chinese in the United States,[263] more than four-fifths on the Pacific coast,[264] and 95 percent of them were males.[265] Ironically, few Chinese ever mined the gold that first attracted them to America. The Chinese were the first of many foreigners to be excluded from the mining camps as miners, though they were tolerated there as cooks and washers of clothes.[266] Vigilantes enforced these exclusions, and violence and the threat of violence drove the Chinese from one community after another in the Pacific and Mountain States, and in Alaska as well.[267]

Beginning in the 1860s, thousands of Chinese began working for the Central Pacific Railroad,[268] building railroad tracks from the west coast across the mountains into Utah, where they met the Union Pacific tracks being built in the opposite direction to form the first railroad linkage across America. The work going across the mountains was so difficult that whites seldom lasted on the job, but the smaller Chinese—who had been expected to "fall in their tracks"[269]—stayed on and completed the work:

> Yellow-skinned, blue-clad, flat-hatted, scrawny but tireless, they pick-and-shoveled the Central Pacific over the Sierras to meet the Union Pacific, one of the great railroad building feats of all time.[270]

Long and hard work became the hallmark of the Chinese in many occupations in America, as in southeast Asia. Chinese agricultural laborers established such a reputation for hard work that they rose from one-tenth of the agricultural laborers in California in 1870 to one-half by 1884.[271] Chinese workers planted the great vineyards that produced the California wine industry. They were 80 to 85 percent of all vineyard workers in the 1880s but were driven out by discriminatory taxes, pressure and violence.[272] Half the shrimp fishing in California in the 1860s was done by Chinese fishermen, but decades of discriminatory legislation eventually drove them from that occupation.[273] In the 1870s, the great majority of cannery workers in California and Oregon were Chinese.[274] In 1866, most of the cigar makers and half the cigar factory owners in San Francisco were Chinese.[275] Half the boots and shoes in San Francisco in 1873 were made by the Chinese.[276] The Chinese were also 80 percent of the shirtmakers in San Francisco in 1880.[277] Chinese workers drained the swamps and marshlands to make possible the development of California's great central valley and the building of the city of San Francisco.[278]

The Chinese saved out of their low wages and sent substantial remittances back to China—an estimated $11 million in 1876 alone, for example.[279] The great bulk of the nineteenth century Chinese immigrants came from one localized region of China— Toishan, one of 98 districts in Kwantung Province in southern China[280]—and this became one of the most prosperous parts of China, as a result of money sent from America by hard working Chinese laborers.[281]

In America as in southeast Asia, the Chinese became hated for their virtues. American workers could not compete with the Chinese, either in endurance or frugality. Labor unions and political radicals like Jack London spearheaded the anti-Chinese movement, which spread through the press, the state legislature, and eventually the halls of Congress. Special taxes and job restrictions hounded the Chinese out of whole industries and occupations,[282] mob violence drove them from many communities. Eventually, Congress passed the Chinese Exclusion Act of 1882 which brought the influx of Chinese to the United States to an almost complete halt. As many Chinese continued to return to China after a sojourn in the United States, the total Chinese population in the country steadily declined from a nineteenth century peak of more than 100,000 in 1890 to about 60,000 in 1920.[283]

Those Chinese who would not or could not return to China faced a grim existence in the United States. The Chinese Exclusion Act of 1882 not only drastically curtailed immigration from China but also made Chinese immigrants ineligible for American citizenship. This in turn facilitated many other forms of legal discrimination by state and local governments against "aliens ineligible for citizenship"—technically non-racist and therefore getting around the Fourteenth Amendment requirement of equality under the law. Chinese were thus forbidden to own land in California, or to engage in many occupations. In addition, some employers feared violence if they employed Chinese workers, and so refused to hire them. The net result was that the Chinese had very few ways to earn a living. The Chinese hand laundry became an American institution largely because of the lack of alternatives. By 1920, more than one-fourth of all Chinese men in the United States were laundry workers[284]—usually in tiny one-man operations. Another 10 percent were restaurant workers, usually in Chinatowns. Others were personal servants—houseboys, cooks, etc.—or worked in agriculture. Less than one percent had professional occupations.[285]

The social existence of the Chinese was as grim as their economic existence. The huge sex imbalance characteristic of early Chinese immigration was perpetuated by immigration restrictions—and unlike the situation in southeast Asia, Chinese men in the United States were seldom married to local women. There were 25 Chinese males for every Chinese female in 1890, and there was a seven-to-one ratio as late as 1920.[286] Even these figures understate the imbalance, for many of the Chinese females were babies or children. The Chinese men stranded in America often found themselves suffering poverty, lack of female companionship, and had no hope for establishing a family, the central feature of Chinese life. Some slept ten or twelve to a room in Chinatown tenements.[287] Drugs and prostitution became prominent features of American Chinatowns.[288] So did high rates of suicide.[289] The phrase "not a Chinaman's chance" came into being during this era.[290]

As in southeast Asia, the Chinese in the United States made little or no political effort to redress their grievances. Laws were evaded where possible, a few women were smuggled in, usually as prostitutes, and the Chinese continued hard working, frugal, and too self-sufficient to resort to charity, even after such calamities as the San Francisco earthquake or the Great Depression of the 1930s.[291] Demography eventually turned the tide. A very few

Chinese did marry—about half to American women in the early twentieth century[292]—and so native-born Chinese-Americans began to appear, immune to the many legal restrictions against "aliens ineligible for citizenship," though still subject to other forms of discrimination, including segregated schools.[293] In 1870, only one percent of the Chinese in the United States were American born, but by 1900 the percentage was up to 10 percent and by 1940, half of all the Chinese in the United States were American-born citizens.[294]

The younger generation of Chinese-Americans carried into the schools the same sense of purpose and perseverance that characterized the Chinese in many activities in countries around the world. As school children, they were better behaved and more hard working than white students.[295] Later, in colleges and universities, the Chinese specialized in the more difficult and demanding—and lucrative—fields, such as medicine, the natural sciences, and engineering. As of 1940, the proportion of Chinese who worked in professional level occupations was less than half that among whites, but by 1960 the Chinese had passed whites and by 1970 they had widened the gap—now having higher proportions in such occupations than any other American ethnic group.[296] Among Chinese males, 30 percent worked in professional and technical fields—double the proportion among white males. Moreover, a higher percentage of Chinese men were engineers and college teachers of physics, mathematics, and chemistry.[297] The income of Chinese Americans passed the national average in 1959, and that gap has also widened.[298]

In the wake of these economic achievements came more social recognition. Today, most Chinese do not live in Chinatowns, but largely in white neighborhoods.[299] Those who coined the phrase "not a Chinaman's chance" knew little of the resolution and perseverance of these people.

CHAPTER THREE

Emigrants from Europe

In "the age of white expansion" from 1450 to 1950, some seventy million are estimated to have left the European homeland for transoceanic areas (and Siberia) where they mingled with, pushed out, or destroyed the indigenous peoples.[1]

Of the 70 million people who emigrated from Europe over the centuries, nearly 50 million immigrated to the United States[2]—and 35 million of these came in just one century, from 1830 to 1930.[3] Much European immigration, however, was to other parts of the western hemisphere —notably Brazil and Argentina—or to Australia, and there was (and is) substantial emigration within Europe itself. Four million immigrants settled in Brazil between 1884 and 1939.[4] Argentina received six million immigrants between 1853 and 1932.[5] Immigration also contributed greatly to the rapid growth of Canada's population in the late nineteenth and early twentieth centuries— sometimes as many as a quarter of a million immigrants a year.[6] Australia in some years had more British immigrants than Canada, or even the United States.[7]

Although the total immigration to the United States dwarfs that to other countries, immigrants have been a larger proportion of the populations of some other countries, and ethnic diversity more pronounced. Immigrants have also contributed more to the development of some other nations. For example, early nineteenth century Brazil, under Portuguese colonial rule, was a very undeveloped country, before large-scale immigration began. Almost everything beyond the barest necessities had to be imported—bricks, windows and doors from Europe, furniture and shoes from the United States. Even such food items as salt, sugar, flour or rice were imported.[8]

Nearly four-fifths of the industrial activity in the Brazilian states of Rio Grande do Sul and Santa Catarina were developed by later immigrants and their descendants. These immigrants, unencumbered by the Portuguese settlers' disdain for manual labor, provided the artisans, small farmers, and technicians who were much needed in Brazil.[9] Many were German and Italian. German immigrants established the first textile mill in Brazil in 1874,[10] as well as introducing new crops in agriculture,[11] and manning numerous crafts.[12] Italian immigrants developed rice and wine production,[13] and Japanese immigrants silk production and tea production.[14] Much of the twentieth century industrial development of Brazil was likewise the work of immigrants. All industrial machinery in Brazil was imported when the Germans built the first starch mill in Santa Catarina in the 1920s, but by the mid-1930s, a second starch mill was equipped with machines made in Brazil by German immigrant engineers. Similarly, as late as 1941 a large tea processing plant was founded using machines imported from Japan, though later on Japanese immigrants began to produce this kind of machinery in Brazil itself.[15]

Although Brazil was founded as a Portuguese colony, and most Brazilians today are of Portuguese ancestry, much of the industrial development of the country was due to immigrants from other parts of Europe (or Japan), and their descendants are still over-represented among owners of industrial enterprises in Brazil. In the state of São Paulo, nearly three-fourths of the industrial enterprises were in the hands of Brazilians of non-Portuguese origins.[16] By 1950, more than four-fifths of the industrial enterprises in the metropolitan area of São Paulo were in the hands of non-Portuguese Brazilians.[17] Most of these non-Portuguese entrepreneurs were from Europe. Nearly half were of German ancestry.[18]

In Argentina as well, there was almost no agriculture before the large scale immigration from non-Hispanic Europe (notably Italy) that began in the second half of the nineteenth century.[19] Nor was there industry or education,[20] or even a willingness to engage in steady work, except for cattle herding.[21] Even in the early twentieth century, it was said that "if you want a shoe soled, a lock or kettle mended, a bookcase made, a book bound or a pamphlet printed, a roll of film developed or a camera repaired, you will go to an immigrant or the son of an immigrant."[22] Argentine railroads were "wholly English, organized in England by Englishmen with English money and using English locomotives."[23] Even the engineers who drove the trains were from Britain.[24]

There is also a long history of emigration within Europe, usually from the poorer to the more economically developed countries. West Germany, for example, had more than 100,000 workers from Spain in 1975, more than 200,000 from Greece, more than 300,000 from Italy, and more than half a million from Turkey. Altogether, Germany had about four million foreign workers and France a similar number.[25] Italy is the leading "exporter" of immigrants—about 40 percent of the total European flow[26]—and has a long history of both temporary and permanent immigration to other parts of Europe, as well as to North and South America.[27]

GERMANS

Historically, German immigrants have settled principally in the United States; but there has also been a substantial immigration of Germans to South America—notably Brazil and Argentina—and to Australia. In the period immediately following the Napoleonic Wars, about one half of all Germans who went overseas between 1816 and 1830 went to South America.[28] But beginning in the decade of the 1830s, most went to the United States—about 90 percent of the overseas German immigrants during the rest of the nineteenth century and almost up to the eve of World War I.[29] As an indication of the relative magnitudes involved, Brazil's notable German minority reflects an immigration of less than 200,000 Germans over a period of more than 50 years.[30] More Germans than that have immigrated to the United States in a single year.[31] In Argentina as well, the total number of Germans immigrating over a period of nearly a century added up to less than 200,000 gross and less than 100,000 net, after subtracting Germans who departed.[32] German immigration to Australia began during the mid-nineteenth century gold rushes, but the total numbers of immigrants were even smaller than in Argentina and Brazil. At their peak in 1891, German-born immigrants were the largest non-

British minority in Australia, but there were only 46,000 of them.[33]

The United States

In eighteenth century America, it was possible to "talk German from Pennsylvania to Georgia,"[34] for the Germans preserved their language and culture in socially enclosed enclaves strung along hundreds of miles through the Cumberland Valley, the Shenandoah Valley, and the Carolina Piedmont. Much of this region the Germans shared with the Scotch-Irish but there was little social mixing or intermarriage between these two very different groups.

The Scotch-Irish were the frontiersmen par excellence—sharpshooting Indian fighters and builders of log cabins. Hard-drinking brawlers, they worked sporadically, and moved on restlessly to lead the expansion of the frontier.[35] Their descendants became the poverty-stricken "hillbillies" of the region. The Germans, by contrast, typically followed in the wake of the Scotch-Irish, buying up their lands and by unrelenting hard work turned them into some of the most successful farms in America.

German farmers established a reputation for being the hardest working and most careful and thorough farmers in the country. Where others cut down trees and left the stumps in the ground, the Germans laboriously pulled the whole stumps and roots out of the ground in order to farm all the land.[36] Where others let their farm animals roam at large, the Germans built huge barns for them, like those in their homeland. German farms were visibly notable for their abundance and neatness, and the Germans themselves for their thriftiness and plain living.[37] A contemporary observer found the Germans living "much better" than other Americans and "less addicted to the use of spiritous liquors."[38]

German craftsmen likewise quickly established a reputation for skill and quality. Their glass blowers produced the exquisite Steuben glass, their wagon-makers the Conestoga wagons that settled the west, and their gunsmiths created the Pennsylvania rifle later made famous by Daniel Boone as the "Kentucky" rifle. The Germans in colonial America also pioneered in printing (including the first bible printed in America), and in building iron furnaces and paper mills.[39] Germans were preferred to other nationalities as workmen in various skilled trades.[40]

The nineteenth century German immigrants were not as agricultural as their eighteenth century predecessors. Industrial and commercial occupations were more common than agricultural ones among the late nineteenth century German emigrants.[41] More than half the cabinet makers in New York were German.[42] One half or more of all Germans employed in mid-century Milwaukee, St. Louis, Detroit, New York and Boston were skilled manual workers. Some were also non-manual workers or businessmen, but few were unskilled laborers. The proportion of Germans who were unskilled laborers in the same cities was less than half the proportion found among the Irish.[43] In Philadelphia, more than half the Irish were unskilled laborers, while only 14 percent of the Germans in the same city worked at such jobs.[44]

Like their eighteenth century predecessors, the nineteenth century German immigrants lived largely to themselves—in German-speaking communities, with numerous German language newspapers and periodicals, and with their own special foods, drinks, and social organizations.[45] In mid-nineteenth century New York City, the German population of 100,000 had 20 churches, 50 schools, 10 bookstores, 5 printing shops and a German theatre.[46] In various parts of the country there were such German newspapers as the *Tennessee Staatszeitung, Der Alabama Pionier,* the *Richmond Anzeiger,* and the *Arkansas Freie Presse.*[47] During the Civil War, there were all-German units in the Union Army, with their commands being given in German.[48]

With the passing of the generations, Germans slowly began to absorb some of the language and culture of the United States. They also profoundly affected the culture of other Americans. It was the Germans who introduced the kindergarten, the gymnasium, and the Christmas tree in America, as well as promoting all kinds of music—from marching bands to symphony orchestras and choral groups. Perhaps more important than all of these, they changed American attitudes toward enjoyment. The Anglo-Saxon culture of colonial America and in the early United States viewed recreational activities suspiciously at best, and as sacrilegious if engaged in on Sunday. The Germans, however, brought with them a whole array of innocent family amusements, from picnics to parades, concerts, games, gymnastic exhibitions, literary societies and folk dances. At first, more puritanical Americans were scandalized by the Germans, especially when they conducted these activities on Sunday. Yet the example of these sober, well-behaved people enjoying themselves with no harm to others slowly but surely won over the rest of the population to a pattern that is now part of the American way of life.[49]

The Germans made important economic as well as cultural contributions. The beer industry, which began in Milwaukee in the 1840s to serve a largely German clientele, spread out to become part of American industry in general as the taste for their product became nationwide. Germans created the American piano manufacturing industry, and the firms they established remain among the leading ones today—Steinway, Schnabel and Knabe. Germans also created the leading American organ—the Wurlitzer. The largest American optical company was one created in the nineteenth century by two German immigrants named Bausch and Lomb. The first suspension bridges were built in America by a German immigrant named John A. Roebling, who also designed wire cables that made such bridges possible. In the early twentieth century, 90 percent of the lithography firms in the United States were owned by individuals of German ancestry.[50] Firms established by Germans have been among the giants in such diverse fields as automobiles (Studebaker, Chrysler), forest products (Weyerhauser), candy (Hershey) and prepared foods (Heinz). It was a German immigrant, Charles P. Steinmetz—who was also a crippled dwarf—whose genius created the technology on which the General Electric Corporation was built.

Most German Americans were not, of course, at these Olympian levels. What they had, more than specific skills, were a set of attitudes —toward work, thrift, and education—that sustained and advanced them economically, both when they lived in isolated enclaves and after they entered the mainstream of American society.

Brazil

Early German immigrants to Brazil, like early German immigrants to the United States, became small independent family farmers[51] and lived in self-contained, German-speaking enclaves.[52] German farmers introduced crops such as tobacco, potatoes, rye, and wheat to Brazil.[53] As in the United States, these German farmers prospered, creating a rural middle class.[54]

The German Brazilians had many community organizations, unlike Brazilians of Portuguese ancestry, but very much like Germans in the United States. The German Brazilians had theatrical clubs, cooperatives, dance circles, rifle clubs, and choral societies. The early German immigrants also established their own schools, at a time when the Brazilian government was slow to set up public schools.[55] Early German Lutheran churches conducted their services in the German language, though later generations spoke Portuguese, the prevailing language of Brazil.[56] German Catholics readily fitted into the Catholic church in Brazil.[57] Germans were only about 4 percent of the more than four million immigrants to Brazil in the period from 1884 to 1939,[58] but their economic contributions were out of all proportion to their numbers. In addition to introducing diversified agriculture into Brazil,[59] changing the country's eating habits thereby,[60] the Germans also introduced the dairy industry[61] and established the first textile mill in the Brazilian State of Rio Grande do Sul.[62] This German industrial headstart in Brazil was reflected in their continued over-representation among owners of industrial enterprises in twentieth century Brazil. Over half of the leather products factories in Rio Grande do Sul were owned by Germans and German Brazilians in 1920.[63] Although Germans were only 12 percent of the population of Pôrto Alegre in 1930, they owned nearly one third of the industries there.[64] In the middle of the twentieth century, nearly half of the industrial enterprises in the southern Brazilian states were owned by Germans, compared to only one fifth owned by Brazilians of Portuguese ancestry, who make up a majority of the country's population.[65]

Australia

In 1861, the Germans were the third largest group in Australia, behind people of British and of Chinese ancestry.[66] In absolute numbers, there were still only 27,000 Germans. By 1891, the Germans had increased in numbers to 46,000—about one and a half percent of the growing Australian population,[67] but more than half of the total European-born immigrants.[68]

In Australia, as in the United States and Brazil, the Germans settled largely in separate enclaves.[69] Here the Lutheran religion prevailed, as did the German language, German schools, a German-language press, and German customs.[70] These German cultural enclaves in Australia, as in the United States, were dealt a blow by World War I, when anti-German feeling led to reduced use of the German language and the abandonment of German place names.[71] The Germans had little effect on the general social and cultural life of Australia, however, because the German Australians lived so much to themselves.[72]

The isolation of Germans in Australia did not remain permanently, however. Eventually, intermarriage, naturalization, and the substitution of the English language for German, led to a fuller absorption of Germans into the general population.

Intermarriage was far less common among Germans in Australia during the nineteenth century than it became in the twentieth century. During the quarter century beginning in 1842, more than three-fourths of all German men who married had German brides. During the same period, more than 90 percent of German brides had German grooms.[73] But in the twentieth century, intermarriage became the rule rather than the exception. From 1908 to 1940, upwards of three-fifths of the German brides in Australia had non-German grooms. For German men, the intermarriage rate was even higher: More than four-fifths married non-German women.[74] The pattern of naturalization likewise indicated a growing assimilation of Germans in Australia. In the nineteenth century, only about one-third of those Germans who settled permanently in Australia became citizens. But in 1921, the census indicated that four-fifths of German-born Australians had become citizens.[75]

Early in their history in Australia, the Germans established the same kind of reputation they enjoyed in the United States, Brazil, and elsewhere as sober, industrious, frugal, honest, and law-abiding people.[76] As in the United States, the early settlers were largely farmers—and successful farmers.[77]

Germans in Australia made important contributions in science, the arts, and the economy, as in the United States and Brazil. In the nineteenth century, Germans in Australia contributed to scholarly research in zoology, botany and geology.[78] The first piano factory in Australia was established by Germans,[79] just as they founded the American piano industry. Germans also pioneered in growing wheat under adverse conditions in Australia.[80] German skilled workers manned the Australian wine industry, financed by British capital.[81]

In short, Germans in Australia showed the same pattern of prominence in family farming, science and technology as in Germany and in other overseas nations. They carried their own social patterns with them, and were not simply shaped by the "society" immediately around them.

THE IRISH

The Irish became an ethnic minority in England and the United States through immigration, and a minority in part of their own country through the settlement of Englishmen and Scots in Ulster County. A long history of disunited, warring factions among the Irish made Ireland "easy to invade, and difficult to conquer."[82] There was no central power whose defeat would signal the capitulation of the nation. Rather, the British invasion of 1169 marked only the beginning of centuries of skirmishes and battles over shifting boundaries between British-held territory and lands under the control of various Irish forces. As late as the fifteenth century, the British controlled only some walled towns and a coastal strip around Dublin.[83] Eventually, however, the British prevailed throughout Ireland, though bloody uprisings occurred sporadically and were mercilessly crushed.

Vast grants of lands and power to individual Britons in Ireland made the Irish not only subjugated to England and its laws and interests, but also at the mercy of the caprice of local powers under no real constraint from laws. In Arthur Young's celebrated travels through Ireland in the eighteenth century, he noted that a landlord would punish disrespect, or even "sauciness" with his cane or his horsewhip—and the Irish recipient of this punishment "could have his bones broken, if he offered to lift his hand in his own defence." Some landlords had their own private prisons for punishing Irish workers, and though this practice was illegal, indictments against landlords who did this invariably failed to be sustained by grand juries.[84] Young also noted:

> It must strike the most careless traveller to see whole strings of cars whipt into a ditch by a gentleman's footman, to make way for his carriage; if they are overturned or broken in pieces, no matter—it is

taken in patience; were they to complain, they would perhaps be horse-whipped.[85]

The period of the greatest oppressions in Ireland dated from Cromwell's punitive expedition in 1649 to avenge Protestants slaughtered in a Catholic uprising in 1641. The warfare itself and the famine and disease accompanying it killed more than half a million people—about 40 percent of the total population of Ireland at that time.[86] Cromwell was merciless, not only in battle, but also in wholesale slaughter of surrendered soldiers and Irish Catholic civilians, including priests, who were "his especial quarry."[87] Moreover, he had orphans, paupers and others shipped off to the West Indies "as hands, servants or for whatever other uses the owners saw fit, or unfit—altogether some six thousand of these poor derelicts."[88]

Many Irish landowners were dispossessed of the best land, which was turned over to English and Scottish Protestant settlers. Cromwell herded many of the Irish gentry to the province of Connaught, on pain of death, with the blunt ultimatum: "To hell or Connaught!"[89] In 1641, the indigenous Irish Catholics held an estimated three-fifths of the land in Ireland but by 1665 this was down to one-fifth, mostly in Connaught.[90] By 1790, Irish Catholics owned only 14 percent of the land in their own country.[91]

After Cromwell's victory came the so-called Penal Laws, designed to stamp out the Catholic religion and prevent the indigenous Irish from rising economically or politically. The activities of the Catholic church were severely limited, just short of outright banning, and Catholics were legally liable to pay tithes for the support of the established Protestant church. Only Protestant education was permitted, and sending children abroad to be educated required a special license, without which severe penalties were imposed.[92] A Catholic could neither vote, nor hold political office nor a military commission.[93] He could not purchase an estate and was prohibited from displaying luxuries considered inappropriate to his status by Protestants. He could not, for example, own a horse worth more than five pounds sterling.[94] He could not legally marry a Protestant,[95] though there was little likelihood of that in any case.

Not all these—and other—minute laws and regulations were carried out to the fullest in practice. Nor were they all part of a coherent plan. Rather, they emerged *ad hoc,* piecemeal and often with no visible connection or consistency with one another.[96] Their only guiding principle was keeping Catholics down, and trying to force them to convert to Protestantism. But while not all the laws were executed to the fullest, other oppressions were freely used against the Irish without any legal sanction.

As in other parts of the world, extremism in Ireland led to counter-extremism. The Irish masses developed underground terrorist groups, the best known of which in the eighteenth century were the Levellers or Whiteboys—so named because of the white shirts they wore to locate each other in nocturnal meetings. According to Arthur Young's contemporary description:

> It was a common practice with them to go in parties about the country, swearing many to be true to them, and forcing them by menaces, which they often carried into execution. At last they set up to be general redressers of grievances, punished all obnoxious persons, and having taken the administration of justice into their own hands, were not very exact in the distribution of it. Forced masters to release their apprentices, carried off the daughters of rich farmers, ravished them into marriages . . . They levied sums of money on the middling and lower farmers, in order to support their cause . . . and many of them subsisted for some years without work, supported by these contributions. . . . The barbarities they committed were shocking. One of their usual punishments (and by no means the most severe) was taking people out of their beds, carrying them naked in winter, on horseback, for some distance, and burying them up to their chin in a hole filled with briars, not forgetting to cut off one of their ears.[97]

Efforts to catch and convict the Whiteboys proved futile for many years, both because of their support among the Irish masses and because anyone who testified against them was marked for death. Extraordinary protection was given to those few witnesses who came forth, and after trial they had to choose exile or the risk of death. Eventually, however, the movement was suppressed and many of its leaders hanged.[98]

Another Irish movement, wholly non-violent, proved more successful. As the Penal Laws were relaxed enough to permit some political activity, Daniel O'Connell organized the Irish to press for their complete repeal. This finally happened in 1829, an historic event known as Catholic Emancipation.[99] Economically, the Irish remained very poor, however. Writing in the 1830s, Gustave de Beaumont said:

> I have seen the Indian in his forests and the negro in his chains, and thought, as I contemplated their pitiable condition, that I saw the very extreme of human wretchedness; but I did not then know the condition of unfortunate Ireland.[100]

This was not mere exaggeration for effect. The average slave in the United States had a life expectancy of 36 years; the average Irish peasant, 19.[101] The Irish peasants ate mostly potatoes, and occasionally fish; and many families never saw meat "from one year to the next."[102] Slaves in the United States ate a wide variety of coarse foods, including low grades of meat and poultry. The Irish lived in mud huts with thatched roofs and usually no ventilation, except the doorway;[103] slaves lived in log cabins with windows. In the United States, slaves built roaring wood fires in their cabins[104] but in deforested Ireland, the Irish poor burned turfs from the bogs.[105] It was considered an unusually cruel slaveowner who did not provide mattresses for slaves,[106] but beds were rare among the Irish poor, who slept in piles of straw.[107] When the slaves were freed, they were destitute by American standards, "but not as poor as the Irish peasants," according to W.E.B. DuBois.[108]

In short, Irish poverty was unique, and "neither the model nor the imitation can be found any where else."[109] The Irish peasant wore rags handed down from generation to generation. Often this clothing was not new, even when originally purchased, for there was a flourishing market in second-hand clothing, much of which was imported in bulk from the cast-off clothing dealers in London.[110] According to a contemporary account, the more fortunate of the Irish "eat potatoes three times a day; others, less fortunate, twice; those in a state of indigence only once; there are some still more destitute, who remain one or even two days without the slightest nourishment."[111] Moreover, it was a poverty in stark contrast with the wealth of foreign landowners, with virtually no middle class in between.[112]

The low standards of living in Ireland in the 1830s were merely a prelude to the catastrophes of the 1840s, when the potato blight spread across the country, destroying the principal food of the poor and creating a massive famine. About a million people died of starvation and diseases related to it,[113] and closer to two million emigrated from the mid-1840s to the mid-1850s.[114] Ireland was one of the rare examples of a country declining in population for generations.

The historic injustices done to the Irish by the British—some condemned even by such a British patriot as Winston Churchill[115]—cannot automatically be assumed to be the reason for Irish poverty, without confusing morality with causation. Ireland was poor and fragmented before the British arrived, and long after achieving independence has remained one of the poorer nations of western Europe. Moreover, the Irish as a people have languished in poverty for generations after immigrating to other countries, even when (as in the United States) they ultimately advanced to prosperity.

The soil and climate of Ireland would not explain its poverty. A higher proportion of the land of Ireland than of England was cultivated, and was of greater natural fertility.[116] A group of German farmers who settled in Ireland in the seventeenth century were, by the eighteenth century, better fed, clothed and housed than the Irish peasants. These German farmers were by contemporary account "industrious" and "remarkable for the goodness and cleanliness of their houses."[117] In all these respects, they differed from the indigenous Irish.

Arthur Young's travels through eighteenth century Dublin convinced him that the Irish there had "no idea of English cleanliness, either in apartments, persons, or cookery."[118] In Ireland, in England, and in the United States, the Irish kept pigs, chickens, and other creatures living in their homes, even in urban communities.[119] The eighteenth century Irish were described as lazy at *work* but "spiritedly active at *play.*"[120] Initiative was undermined by laws which made a tenant's improvements the property of the landlord, who could then raise the rent, because the property was more valuable.[121] Neither education nor entrepreneurship was part of the Irish tradition. Pre-invasion Gaelic society was "hostile" to literacy,[122] and medieval Ireland was the only nation in Europe that did not build a single university during the Middle Ages.[123] Self-reliance was also lacking; the Irishman was "habituated to working for others, not striking out on his own."[124] The Irish had "little feel for trade and commerce" and seldom chose such careers for themselves or their children.[125]

Alcohol and alcoholism added to the problems of the Irish for centuries, both in Ireland and overseas. Widespread drunkenness was noted by travellers in sixteenth century Ireland, and as late as 1970 the percentage of personal income spent on alcohol in Ireland was the highest of any country in Europe.[126] In the United States during World War II, the percentage of men rejected for military service for chronic alcoholism was higher among the Irish than among Negroes, Italians, or Jews.[127] Similar patterns existed in World War I. Contemporary studies of Irish Americans show that they "drink more and more frequently than any other ethnic group" in the United States.[128]

Fighting was another feature of life in Ireland that was to mark the Irish wherever they went. "The fighting Irish" was a cliché long before it was adopted by American sports reporters as a nickname for Notre Dame athletic teams. Irish fighting was the impulsive brawl rather than the implacable vendetta of the Italians. This fighting could range from man-to-man combat to the mass melee known as a Donnybrook, named for a town in Ireland.

While the Irish had these various social handicaps, they also developed many skills and traits that would ultimately work to their advantage, at home and abroad. Over the centuries, they slowly abandoned Gaelic, their native tongue, for English—giving them advantages over other immigrants to the United States, Canada, and Great Britain. They developed a variety of grass-roots organizations to cope with their disadvantages and oppressions under the Penal Laws in Ireland, and these provided both group cohesion and organizing skills that would later pay off in many ways, from the struggle for the independence of Ireland to Irish-run political machines that dominated American cities for generations. The verbal facility and human touch of the Irish was a key ingredient in their success in politics as well as in the clergy, writing, and the law. The Irish fascination with words has a long history. There was a "constant jibing and joshing among themselves" and a "genius for the apt nickname."[129] They filled their language with "poetic images and metaphors."[130]

The Irish developed the "moral standards of a people tyrannized by an alien power," regarding the established institutions as illegitimate, evasion as a shield, and open defiance as suicidal.[131] They were constantly tipping their hats to their overlords and "lowered their eyes in the presence of the gentry," but at other times overcompensated with "boasting and bluster."[132] A nineteenth century observer described the Irishman as "full of insolence when he is not cringing."[133] Begging from private individuals and acceptance of public charity were long-standing patterns among the nineteenth century Irish, in their often desperate struggles for survival. Often families went begging through the countrysides,[134] or the women and children might go, when the man was too proud.[135] Later generations of the Irish in Britain and America would also become wards of public charity.

Many of those who left Ireland in the nineteenth century fit the description of Irish immigrants given by a Canadian writer: "Men have come here who were unable to spell, who never knew what it was to have a shoe to their foot in Ireland . . ."[136] Whatever the characteristics of the Irish that formed over the centuries in Ireland, the massive migrations that started with the great famines of the 1840s took them to very different lands and new influences. By 1891, nearly 40 percent of all people born in Ireland lived outside Ireland.[137] Some went to other parts of Great Britain, but of those who left the British Isles in the century after 1825, 90 percent went to the United States.[138] Ireland was one of the few countries in the world with sustained declines in population for decades. In 1841 there were more than 8 million people in Ireland; by 1926, just over 4 million.[139] Even today, there are not as many people living in Ireland as in the 1840s.[140] There are more people of Irish ancestry in the United States than in Ireland.[141]

Britain

Nearby Britain was one of the first destinations of Irish emigrants. As early as 1243 A.D., there was a law in Britain used to expel Irish beggars.[142] By the time of the great famine of the 1840s, there was a long history of Irish immigration to Britain, which absorbed half of the one million Irish emigrants fleeing the famine. In one year 20,000 landed at Manchester, 50,000 at Glasgow, 250,000 at London and 300,000 at Liverpool. Even today, many of the districts in which they settled are still identifiably Irish.[143] The Irish immigrants generally lived in "the decaying districts of the towns and cities" and a contemporary described them as "crowded together with all their native habits of filth and indolence."[144] Nor can these accounts all be dismissed as biased, for the nineteenth century Irish immigrants in Britain were seen in very similar terms by writers ranging from the British conservative Thomas Carlyle to a young German radical in Manchester named Friedrich Engels.[145] According to Carlyle, the Irishman in "his rags and laughing savagery" performed "all work that can be done by mere strength of hand and back—for wages that will purchase him potatoes."[146] Engels likewise characterized the Irish immigrant as having a "crudity" that "places him little above the savage."[147] The Irishman, according to Engels, "deposits all garbage and filth before his house door here, as he was accustomed to do at home, and so accumulates the pools and dirt heaps which disfigure the working people's quarters and poison the air."[148] Drunkenness was his hallmark, and while he could perform "all simple, less exact work," for any "work which requires long training or regular, pertinacious application, the dissolute, unsteady, drunken Irishman is on too low a plane."[149]

In Britain as in the United States, the rural Irish became city-dwellers, undergoing a major social transformation rather than simply making a journey. Most lived in the largest and fastest growing urban industrial communities.[150] During the era of the famine, the poorest immigrants went to Britain rather than across the Atlantic, because of travel cost differences. Families with young children were also more likely to go to Britain rather than subject the children to the long, taxing voyage to the United States.[151] Cost affected where the Irish settled in Britain. From their respective places of origin, they usually left by the nearest port in Ireland for the nearest major port in Britain.[152]

The Irish in London lived mostly in side streets and back alleys, close to the English, in enclaves located within English working-class neighborhoods, but neither geographic nor social assimilation took place.[153] Entering some of the Irish enclaves "required thick boots and a strong stomach." They were crowded with pigs, dogs, and fowl, and strewn with discarded fish and other refuse interspersed with little pools of undrained water.[154] Instead of plumbing and running water, it was common to have a barrel or tank of water sitting in the yard for common use, near privies and trash heaps. A contemporary official report spoke of "a most offensive effluvia" that was especially "perceptible" in warm weather.[155] Diseases such as typhus and cholera flourished in these surroundings.[156]

The Irish entered the British economy when it was the leading industrial economy in the world, producing one-third of the world's manufactured goods, mining half its coal and making half its textiles.[157] The Irish were disproportionately represented among the workmen building the railroads of Britain, though they were never a majority and seldom exceeded 30 percent of the work force.[158] In mid-nineteenth century London, the Irish were concentrated in a few low-skill occupations.[159] Thirty-one percent of the men worked in the "general labor" category, and 43 percent of the women were domestic servants.[160] About 20 percent of the London population had occupations classified as middle class, but only 4 percent of the Irish reached such occupational levels.[161]

As a low-paid group desperate for work, the Irish were feared as competition by English and Scottish workers in the same fields. Many fights broke out among the groups. The greatest hostility came from the Scots who, "with pick-handles at the ready," tramped across the country to beat Irishmen, burn their huts, and terrorize Irish women.[162] Employers learned to separate their workers by nationality.[163] Trifling episodes could set off major riots between them.[164]

While Britain shared about equally with the United States in the famine emigration from Ireland, after the 1870s the great bulk of the Irish immigration went to America—five times as many people to the United States as to Great Britain in 1880 and thirteen times as many in 1890. Irish immigration to Britain also declined absolutely, from about 20,000 in 1877 to about 10,000 in 1883, and never that high again through the remainder of the century.[165] Although a million Irish had arrived in Britain in the two decades after 1840,[166] less than one-tenth that many arrived in the first two decades of the twentieth century.[167]

In short, the passing years saw an increasingly assimilated Irish population in the British isles. They did not disappear in a melting pot, but they became a more familiar element to the British, and vice versa. Still, as late as the 1870s, Irish neighborhoods "were shunned by 'respectable' citizens and the police entered only in numbers."[168] Fighting was endemic, and especially among Irishmen from different counties in Ireland. Some ale-houses became segregated—patronized only by men from one county.[169] Sometimes the fighting was between the Irish and the English, and these too could reach mob riot proportions.[170]

By the end of the nineteenth century, there was an established Irish community of nearly a million people, in a country of 30 million. They built Catholic churches and published their own newspapers, worked as laborers and street vendors, and fought in the British army in the Crimea and southern Africa.[171] Anti-Irish feeling was declining in the population at large, and the loyal fighting of Irish soldiers in the British army during World War I increased their acceptance.[172] World War II had a similar effect.[173]

By the middle of the twentieth century, more than one-fifth of the Irish in Britain worked in skilled occupations.[174] More than thirty of the Labour Party members of Parliament were Irish.[175] Few of the Irish M.P.s agitate politically over the continuing Catholic-Protestant struggles in Northern Ireland.[176] Still they remained over-represented among criminals and prison inmates. In Birmingham, where the Irish are 7 percent of the population, they constitute 60 percent of those arrested for drunkenness.[177] In short, the Irish in Britain are in many ways assimilated, and yet still show historic social patterns that go back for centuries in Ireland.

The United States

More than 4 million people emigrated from Ireland to the United States from 1820 to 1920.[178] Most were the indigenous Irish Catholics, rather than the Scotch-Irish Protestants who made up most of the emigration from Ireland before that time.[179]

As in Britain, the Irish in the United States typically settled in those large port cities most readily accessible—notably Boston and New York, where cargo vessels docked (few came on passenger ships).[180] As in Britain, the Irish in the United States took the lowest skilled, hardest, most menial and dangerous jobs. Many were destitute, having exhausted all their worldly possessions on the voyage.[181] They were concentrated in one occupation—unskilled labor—more so than any other immigrant group,[182] and many never rose any further.[183] They lived packed into decaying, filthy slums, without indoor running water or any effective means of sewage disposal.[184]

Their own ways of living added to their problems. Fighting gave Irish neighborhoods a reputation as dangerous places, from New York to New Orleans to Milwaukee.[185] This fighting extended from individual brawls to organized street gangs and terrorist organizations, such as had existed in Ireland.[186] In some Irish neighborhoods in New York, policemen travelled only in groups of six.[187] Police vans became known as Paddy wagons because the prisoners in them were so often Irish. The lack of cleanliness in Irish neighborhoods—including "pigs rooting in the streets"[188]—promoted the spread of diseases like cholera, which had been virtually unknown in the United States for generations.[189] Alcoholism also rendered the Irish undesirable as neighbors or employees. The number of saloons in Boston rose by almost 50 percent in just three years during the influx of the Irish in the 1840s.[190] When the Irish moved into many neighborhoods, "the exodus of non-Irish residents began."[191] In parts of nineteenth century New York, Negroes were preferred to the Irish as tenants.[192] Employment advertisements, even for lowly jobs, often used the stock phrase, "No Irish need apply."[193] More delicate advertisers would ask for a "Protestant" applicant but others more bluntly said, "any color or country except Irish."[194]

The Irish in the United States worked in many of the same kinds of occupations as in Great Britain. Irishmen built railroads and canals, mined coal, and performed many other pick-and-shovel jobs, as well as factory work. They worked "wherever brawn and not skill was the chief requirement."[195] Irish women worked as domestic servants—99 percent of all domestic servants in New York City in 1855.[196] As late as 1920, four-fifths of all Irish working women were domestic servants.[197] The Irish in mid-nineteenth century Boston were concentrated in domestic and unskilled labor to a greater extent than blacks in Boston at the same time.[198]

Numerous attempts were made to spread the Irish out from their crowded urban slums into the rural countryside, but they remained overwhelmingly urban despite various agricultural colonies established under philanthropic auspices.[199] What did move thousands of the Irish out of the eastern port cities was the building of railroads and canals. Three thousand Irishmen worked on the Erie Canal alone,[200] and it was just one of many canals that linked the waterways of nineteenth century America. The Irish were also part of the great age of railroad building in the nineteenth century. So many were killed in this dangerous occupation that it was said that there was "an Irishman buried under every tie."[201] The Irish erected shanty towns along the routes of the railroads and canals they built, and many of these eventually became permanent settlements that spread the Irish out across the country.

In the United States as in Britain, politics became a major area of Irish success. A key ingredient in their political success were traits long observed in Ireland: "Irish wit and adaptability, a gift for oratory, a certain vivacity, and a warm, human quality that made them the best of good fellows at all times—especially in election campaigns—enabled the Irish to rise rapidly from ward heelers to city bosses, and to municipal, state, and federal officials of high distinction."[202] Graft and violence were often also part of the Irish political machines of the nineteenth and twentieth centuries.[203] The Irish were democrats, with both a small and a large D. They brought with them a hatred of aristocracy, exclusiveness, or pretentions of superiority.[204] A major factor in the success of the political machine was that it had its roots in communities of ordinary working people and was keenly aware of, and responsive to, their felt needs[205]—in contrast to distant middle class reformers to whom the masses were objects of experiment or reformation.

By the late nineteenth century, Irish political machines dominated American cities from New York to San Francisco.[206] Individual Irish political bosses remained in charge of their respective machines for decades.[207] Richard J. Daley, perhaps the last of the classic machine bosses, was mayor of Chicago for more than 20 years, when he died in office in 1976. Political domination meant control of a variety of municipal patronage jobs, from exalted positions like judge to lowly occupations like street cleaner, that were still very attractive to those to whom any steady job was a blessing. By and large, however, Irish political success did not translate into economic advancement for the Irish masses. As late as 1890, 42 percent of all Irish Americans were servants,[208] and many others were unskilled laborers.

The massive inflow of Irish immigrants led to Irish control of the Roman Catholic Church in America. Even after numerous German, Polish, Italian, and other Catholic immigrants arrived, the Irish retained their dominance in the hierarchy. The church in turn played a major role in the assimilation of the Irish, the promotion of education, and the discouragement of violence and drinking among them. It also discouraged the festive Irish wake and the huge funeral processions which those involved could not readily afford —and which undermined the Irish in the eyes of their fellow Americans.

The growing acculturation of the Irish slowly produced tangible economic results, though the Irish remained the slowest rising

European ethnic group in the United States. Still, their head start had them generally ahead of the Jews and Italians at the beginning of the twentieth century. While Irish immigrants continued to start at the bottom in manual labor occupations, the second-generation Irish were increasingly white collar workers or occasionally professionals.[209] The Irish were also prominent in the labor union movement. At the beginning of the twentieth century, 50 out of 110 presidents of the AFL unions were of Irish ancestry.[210] They were seldom businessmen, however—again, a pattern going back to Ireland.[211]

With the passing years the American-born Irish began to outnumber the Irish immigrants. By 1920, native-born Irish Americans outnumbered immigrants from Ireland by more than three to one.[212] Today, Irish Americans of the first and second generation combined are outnumbered by Irish Americans of older vintage by ten to one. Irish Americans today have equalled or exceeded the American national average in income and I.Q., and their family size and voting patterns are very similar to those of other Americans. Historically, it represents one of the great social transformations of a people.

ITALIANS

A leading historian of Italian emigration has said:

> Emigration from Italy belongs among the extraordinary movements of mankind. In its chief lineaments, it has no like. Through the number of men it has involved and the courses it has pursued, through its long continuance on a grand scale and its role in other lands, it stands alone.[213]

Official statistics did not tell the whole story, for large-scale immigration was underway before statistics were collected,[214] and unofficial research indicates that nearly twice as many people emigrated from Italy as were recorded in the official statistics.[215]

Italian immigrants have long included large numbers of temporary migrants or sojourners, rather than committed settlers in a foreign land. About 90 percent of the late nineteenth century and early twentieth century Italian immigrants to other European countries returned to Italy.[216] Even transAtlantic immigrants returned in surprisingly large numbers—about 30 to 40 percent of Italian immigrants to the United States around the turn of the century and well over half in the period from 1907–1915. In turn-of-the-century Brazil, more than 40 percent of the Italian immigrants returned to Italy, and by 1907–1911, the proportion was more than 80 percent. For Argentina and Uruguay, from nearly half to more than half the Italian immigrants returned to their homeland between 1887 and 1911.[217] Altogether, official figures for the four decades ending in 1911 show 14 million emigrants from Italy, only about one third of whom became permanent settlers abroad.[218]

One sign of temporary immigration or sojourning is an unbalanced sex ratio among the emigrants. In the early years of Italian emigration, nearly 90 percent of the emigrants were male.

At first, during the 1870s and 1880s, most of the emigration was from the more economically and culturally advanced north of Italy. But by the turn of the century, more than half of the emigrants were from the southern provinces. Northern and southern Italy differed greatly in natural advantages—the north having more abundant rainfall and a spring runoff from melting Alpine snows to water the crops. But great cultural differences also separate northern and southern Italy, and these differences persist in the later history of northern and southern Italians in other countries.

Italy has been characterized as "a country in which two civilizations simultaneously exist in one national body."[219] Historically, northern Italy has been the heart of the country's cultural, political, and economic development—the home of the Renaissance, the center of industry and commerce, the source of the forces that unified the peninsula into one nation, and the heir of Roman civilization. Southern Italy has historically been more agricultural, poorer, less literate, with more of an insular folk culture. Northern Italy has shared more of the cultural values of the rest of Europe. In southern Italy, neither church nor state has held any strong allegiance from the people, nor has any other institution except the family. The family, however, has commanded intense loyalties and has provided virtually the whole social life of the individual in southern Italy. Children seldom played with anyone except relatives,[220] and the concept of making friends outside the family was foreign to the culture.[221] Southern Italy was a highly rigid society, both as to its class structure and its traditions.

There was little opportunity or need for individual initiative within the communal family group, or within the *contadino* (peasant) community, because all activities and patterns of thought were based upon traditional folkways and customs.[222]

Children in southern Italy were introduced to work early in life —about age twelve for boys, and age ten for girls, who performed many domestic chores.[223] As late as 1911, over half of Italian children between the ages of 10 and 15 were gainfully employed, despite government policies against child labor.[224] While the proper upbringing of children was a major preoccupation of southern Italian families, formal education was not seen as an important part of that upbringing—and, indeed, was seen as a competitive threat to traditional values and family solidarity, as well as an economic loss of the child's labor which few southern Italian families could afford.[225]

The cultural values of both northern and southern Italians followed them across the ocean and around the world. So too did the historic regional differences and antipathies that fragmented Italy —not only in the over-riding north-south dichotomy but also in innumerable provincial and local differences in dialect and culture.

Argentina

Small numbers of Italians were in Argentina in the eighteenth century and perhaps even as early as the sixteenth century.[226] By 1852, an all-Italian regiment fought in the Argentine civil war.[227] By the early twentieth century, Buenos Aires had almost as many Italians as Rome.[228] Italians were the largest minority in the country, with nearly 600,000 people or 14 percent of the total Argentine population.[229] From the middle of the nineteenth century to the middle of the twentieth century, more than three million Italians arrived in Argentina—and nearly half of these departed.[230]

Before Italian immigration became a major factor in Argentina, the country was largely undeveloped economically. The Spanish had done little with the country in the centuries of their control. As late as 1852, Argentina—now an independent nation—was described as being "almost wholly without trade and industry."[231] Its agricultural methods were as primitive as those used in the days of the Pharaoh. Wheat—destined to become Argentina's great export in the twentieth century—was *imported* from across the Atlantic and the Pacific during this period. Most houses had straw roofs. The only thriving activity in the country was cattle raising.[232]

Then came the Italians—mostly from Piedmont and Genoa and other parts of northern Italy.[233] From the mid- to late-nineteenth century, Italians were part of a rapidly growing immigrant population in Argentina that surpassed a million in 1895—more than one fourth of whom were from Italy.[234] The Italian population of Argentina grew rapidly, not only by immigration but also because of a high birth rate—the highest among the immigrants.[235] High birth rates also characterized Italians in Italy and in the United States.[236]

Argentines of Spanish ancestry continued to predominate in cattle raising,[237] but Italians were responsible for much of the agricultural development of the country.[238] In 1865 there were only 373 square miles of land under cultivation in the whole country, but by 1914 this had increased hundreds of times—cultivation rising both absolutely and even relative to the rapidly growing population.[239] In some parts of Argentina in the early twentieth century, the agricultural laboring population was made up almost wholly of Italians.[240] The arrival of Italian immigrants successively created economic progress and new crops in various parts of Argentina.[241] Though the Italians often had little capital at their command,[242] their hard work[243] and frugality enabled them to prosper. A contemporary said of the Italians: "Phenomenal is their fever for work: all wish to get rich, and quickly."[244] As early as 1860, one third of the depositors in the Banco de Buenos Aires were Italian.[245] Often the Italian immigrant began as a *peon* or day laborer, moved up to become a sharecropper, and finally became a landowner.[246] Among those who came as seasonal workers "almost every cent of their wages was saved to take back to Italy."[247]

In the urban areas of Argentina, the Italian immigrants advanced as well. While native Argentines disdained "menial" labor,[248] Italians worked at whatever was available. Italians were "quick and eager workers," laboring "as many hours and days as possible" so that "a hundred Italians might be as productive as two hundred Argentines."[249] Italians were laborers, barbers, blacksmiths, carpenters, tailors, shoemakers, and masons.[250] Italian boat crews worked in the coastal and inland waterways of Argentina.[251] Most of the tradespeople were Italian, as were many of the artisans, craftsmen, importers, architects, engineers, builders, restaurant and hotel owners.[252] Masons were almost all Italians.[253] By 1890, Italians in Buenos Aires owned more than twice as many food and drinking establishments as the native Argentines. They also owned more than three times as many shoe stores and more than ten times as many barbershops.[254] Italians were also more active in the labor movement in Argentina than were the native Argentines.[255] In Argentine politics, however, the Italians have played little role,[256] and political appointees were almost all native Argentine "Creoles"[257]—meaning in this context, people ranging from partly to wholly Spanish in ancestry[258] and Argentinian in birth and culture. These political appointees were notoriously incompetent.[259]

Very little assimilation occurred among the Italians in Argentina before World War I. Italians spoke Italian in their homes, married other Italians, and only a small percent became naturalized citizens. Argentines excluded them from some social groups and also from some occupations.[260]

While the earlier Italian immigrants who developed Argentine agriculture were predominantly from northern Italy,[261] southern Italian immigrants "flocked to the cities" to become artisans, mechanics, bricklayers, masons, and factory workers, often exhibiting "the drive and ambition native *Criollos* lacked." From humble beginnings, many became wealthy in the construction industry and trade.[262] In the Argentinian value system, however, the successful Italians' poverty-stricken origin was something to ridicule.[263]

Brazil

About one third of all the immigrants to Brazil in the period from 1884 to 1939 were from Italy.[264] Before the twentieth century, more Italians went to Brazil than to the United States.[265] Well over a million Italians immigrated to Brazil in the late nineteenth century —nearly half of all immigrants to that country. Most of these came in the last quarter of the century,[266] and especially after the abolition of slavery in 1888. Northern Italians predominated in the immigration to Brazil.[267]

The rise of Brazil to world dominance in the coffee market was largely the work of Italian immigrants.[268] They were a large majority of the coffee plantation workers.[269] Many of these Italian workers came as contract laborers whose passage across the Atlantic was paid by the great Brazilian plantation owners.[270]

The earlier Italian indentured laborers on the coffee plantations were subjected to many abuses—frauds, sexual assaults on women and girls, and floggings of male workers, all reminiscent of the system of slavery that had only recently been abolished in Brazil.[271] Their living quarters often lacked fresh water or sufficient drainage.[272] Many of these early Italians returned to Italy destitute,[273] but some stayed on, saving to become landowners themselves. Eventually, in some parts of Brazil, there were more Italian than Brazilian landowners.[274] The Italians also had the largest numbers of owners and workers in industrial and commercial enterprises of any of the many ethnic groups in Brazil.[275] By the middle of the twentieth century, the Italians owned nearly half the industrial enterprises in the São Paulo metropolitan area,[276] compared to less than one sixth owned by people of Portuguese ancestry.

Italians in Brazil established the wine growing industry and promoted rice cultivation.[277] Italian architects greatly influenced Brazilian urban architectural styles.[278] Despite being a minority, Italians made an historic contribution to the development of the Brazilian economy and culture.

The United States

Italian immigration to the United States began slowly, and until the 1880s consisted largely of northern Italians, as in South America. The northern Italians were chiefly small businessmen of various sorts, and included the owners of most of the fruit stands in New York City.[279] However, their numbers were small—no more than 20,000.[280] Then the massive Italian immigration to America began —four-fifths originating in the backward southern part of Italy— and eventually reached more than 5 million immigrants, more than 4 million of whom arrived in the twentieth century.[281]

In the United States, as in South America and elsewhere, Italians were sharply divided by regional, provincial, and even village origins. Northern Italians repudiated any ties with southern Italians[282] and moved out of neighborhoods when the latter moved in.[283] But even among southern Italians, there were many internal divisions. People from the same province or village often lived clustered together in the same street or neighborhood.[284] In the first generation, marriages of Italians in America were concentrated among individuals of the same provincial background in Italy.[285] Hundreds of mutual aid societies existed among Italians in the same city, for each was exclusively for Italians from a particular part of Italy.[286] The same was true of Italian mutual aid organizations in South America.[287]

The great majority of southern Italian immigrants to the United States were agricultural laborers, peasants, and other workers without any skills of value in the urban, industrial and commercial economy in which they settled in America. Very few of the early Italian immigrants to the United States settled on the land, though that was where most of them had worked in Italy. Unlike South America, the United States had little cheap frontier land left when the Italians arrived, and the immigrants had too little money even to travel out to the farm belts, much less to buy land there. Italian immigrants to the United States therefore entered the urban labor market at the bottom, as rag-pickers, boot-blacks, street cleaners, pick-and-shovel workers on construction sites, railroad building, or other hard and dirty work. At the turn of the century, all the Italian American doctors, lawyers, and school teachers put together added up to less than one hundred people.[288] In 1910, Italian families in the United States earned less than half the income of American families in general.[289]

New York had by far the largest Italian community in the United States, in both the earlier and the later periods of Italian immigration. In 1870, there were less than 3,000 Italians in New York City but by 1910, there were more than a hundred times that number —340,765. Philadelphia and Chicago were next, with less than 50,000 each.[290] Living conditions in the Italian immigrant neighborhoods were among the most appalling among American ethnic groups. Crowding was the norm. In New York, Italians were packed in at a density rate of 1,000 people per acre, and in some Italian sections of the city there were ten people per room.[291] Partly this reflected sheer poverty but partly too it reflected the transient, young male makeup of Italian immigration, for Italians saved substantial portions—sometimes most—of their meager earnings[292] and used these savings either to return to Italy as prosperous individuals, to support families still there, or to bring over wives and children to join them in America. Eighty five million dollars in savings were sent back to Italy in one year.[293]

Early southern Italian immigrants were noted for their willingness to work but lack of initiative, thereby requiring more supervision.[294]

Initiative by those at the bottom was discouraged in the strongly hierarchical society of southern Italy.[295] But the Italians had the advantage of a very low rate of alcoholism—less than one-fifth that of the Irish,[296] making them more dependable workers.

The overwhelming majority of Italian Americans lived in cities[297] and half worked at unskilled manual jobs.[298] A few had manual skills, but white collar workers and professionals were all but non-existent in the early immigrant generations.[299] In the West, northern Italians were prominent in agriculture, including vineyards, wineries, and vegetable growing.[300] In New York, Italian women had by 1910 become the largest part—more than one-third —of the work force in the garment industry.[301] By 1937, Italian men and women constituted 40 percent of the membership of the International Ladies Garment Workers Union.[302]

Southern Italians came to the United States with one of the highest rates of illiteracy of any racial or ethnic group—54 percent[303] and with the greatest resistance and hostility to formal schooling. This was a pattern brought over from southern Italy, where education was of negligible economic value in a highly rigid class structure, and where it could be socially counterproductive by alienating the child from the family. Italian American children left school at the earliest legal age—or earlier. The children—especially those with language problems—were often unhappy, poor students, and disruptive,[304] and the money they could earn was urgently needed. Italians remained one of the least educated American ethnic groups, on past the middle of the twentieth century.[305]

With the passage of time and the emergence of a second generation of Italian Americans, some occupational advancement occurred, though usually through channels not requiring education. In America, as in Italy, southern Italians had little use for education, though committed to hard work and to acquiring work skills. Whether in construction work or the garment factories, Italians slowly moved up to more skilled work over time. By the turn of the century, 36 percent of the Italian workers were skilled, compared to 19 percent twenty years earlier.[306] Another sign of growing adjustment to the American economy was that the range of industries and jobs expanded with time, indicating an ability to work in new settings that might have been uncomfortable for older generations. Still, the progress of Italian Americans was largely in blue collar jobs or in small business. Education—and particularly higher education—played little role in this progress at first. As late as 1969, only 6 percent of Italian Americans over 35 years of age had completed college—lower than for any other Americans of European ancestry.[307] Younger Italians, however, completed high school at rates comparable to the general population.

Over the years, Italian American incomes rose from less than half the national average in 1910 to just above the national average by 1968.[308] While the southern Italians who came to America did not have the education or the urban background that enabled northern Italians to play a more prominent role in Brazil or Argentina, they did bring a similar commitment to work and thrift that eventually overcame their other handicaps.

Australia

As early as the mid-nineteenth century, there were known to be some Italians in the gold fields of Australia, but the total number of Italians in the country was very small until after World War I. The census of 1881 showed less than 2,000 Italians in Australia, and while there was a steady growth in numbers over the years, there were still less than 6,000 in 1901.[309] By the 1930s, however, there were more than 25,000 persons of Italian birth in Australia,[310] not counting persons of Italian ancestry born in Australia.

As in other countries, the Italian immigrants brought little capital with them and began as laborers. Like Italian immigrants in the western hemisphere, they became noted for their industriousness and thrift,[311] and for their ability to endure poor living conditions.[312] Australians said that Italians could "live on the smell of an oil rag."[313] As the Italians in Australia slowly rose economically in the nineteenth century, many of those who settled on the land went into the production of wine and those in the cities became shopkeepers—selling principally fruit, fish and wine.[314] Italian street musicians became a feature of Australian life, and Italians also made major contributions to more serious music in Australia.[315] But the Italians did not make the kind of technological contributions that the Germans made.[316] All these patterns the Italian immigrants in Australia shared with Italian immigrants in the western hemisphere.

In social as well as economic terms, the history of Italians in Australia parallels that of Italians in the United States and in other countries. For example, the early immigration from Italy to Australia was overwhelmingly male—more than twenty times as many men as women in 1901.[317] Many of these men had families that they were supporting in Italy.[318] With the passing years, the repatriation of sojourners and the reuniting of families in Australia reduced the sex imbalance.[319] Italian women had higher fertility rates than other women in Australia,[320] and fertility was especially high among those women born in Italy.[321]

Italian social life was so centered around the family that circles of acquaintanceship and friendship were very narrow, and there was no meaningful *community* of Italians, nor Italian political cohesion or involvement,[322] much less political loyalty to Italy.[323] Yet Italians lived clustered together in the early years, largely separated from Australian life,[324] speaking Italian,[325] and following such traditional Italian customs as maintaining strict control over unmarried daughters.[326] Intermarriage with other Australians was rare. As late as 1933, four-fifths of all Italian-born husbands in Australia had Italian-born wives. Some of these marriages took place in Italy before migration, some in Australia, and a significant proportion were a result of single Italian men's returning to Italy to get Italian brides to bring back to Australia.[327]

Assimilation began gradually to take place with the passing years, and especially with the emergence of a second generation of Italians educated in Australian schools. English became the primary language of the children, while Italian remained the primary language of the parents.[328] Occupational mobility paralleled these social trends. Whereas the early Italian immigrants had been primarily laborers, in later years more were employers or self-employed than were employees.[329]

JEWS

The massive, worldwide wanderings of the Jews began with the conquest of Palestine and the destruction of Jerusalem by the armies of the Roman Empire in 70 A.D. Jews had lived outside of Israel before then—in Greece and in Iraq, for example, centuries before Christ.[330] But now began the era of the *Diaspora,* their mass dispersion across Europe, North Africa, the Middle East and eventually the western hemisphere. Jews were for centuries not only scattered generally, but separated from each other in different nations, and separated from the life of the people around them in each country. Strong religious convictions among the Jews inhibited their assimilation into Christian European society or the Islamic world, and discriminatory restrictions kept them from becoming integrated.

While the Jews of Europe became numerically and culturally the dominant portion of world Jewry, there were major Jewish communities scattered across North Africa, and as far across Asia Minor as Iraq. Indeed, Iraq, Algeria, and Morocco at one time each had Jewish populations larger than those ever living in Greece, Holland or Yugoslavia.[331] Over the 18 centuries between the end of ancient Israel and the emergence of modern Israel, the Jews in various parts of the world to some extent slowly assimilated—both culturally and biologically—to their respective surrounding societies. In physical appearance, Middle Eastern and North African Jews looked more like Arabs than like European Jews. Of the Jews who lived among the Berbers in Morocco, it was said that "they spoke Berber, looked like Berbers, and were Berbers in everything except their religion."[332] In short, differences in physical appearance between Jews of different lands became marked.[333] In many of the Arab lands, the Jews developed a Judeo-Arabic language that was their dominant colloquial speech by the eighteenth century. Persian was spoken by Jews in Iran and Afghanistan, Sephardic Jews from the Iberian peninsula spoke Ladino—a form of Medieval Spanish with an admixture of Hebrew,[334] which tended to be replaced by Judeo-Arabic after many of them migrated to North Africa and the Middle East following persecutions in Spain and Portugal.[335] The Ashkenazic Jews in the rest of Europe developed the colloquial language, Yiddish—an intricate mixture of several languages—primarily of German, Hebrew, and Slavic.[336]

The extent to which Jews acquired the culture of the surrounding society varied with the extent to which the surrounding society accepted them on that basis. In eastern Europe, where anti-Semitism was particularly virulent, Jews lived for centuries without making Russian, Polish, or Lithuanian their mother tongue.[337] Conversely, after the legal emancipation of Jews in Hungary, they became culturally Hungarian.[338] Similarly Iraqi Jews, who were at one time citizens with equal rights,[339] were also the most assimilated Jews in the Arab world.[340]

In short, the Jews of the Diaspora became very much differentiated—not only by nationality but ethnically and religiously within given nations. Sephardic Jews seldom married Ashkenazic Jews, whether in Europe, the United States, or Israel. Even among the small Jewish communities in India, intermarriage is rare between ethnically different Jews.[341] The reuniting of Jews from around the world in modern Israel has not eliminated these many cultural and racial differences from the centuries of the Diaspora, but has in fact made their contrasts more painfully apparent and pitted them against each other politically.[342] The achievement of a national unity despite these internal diversities has been one of many remarkable aspects of Israel.

From the early centuries of the Diaspora, Jews were predominantly artisans and middlemen—peddlers, merchants and moneylenders, and most were poor.[343] In the days of the Roman Empire, Jewish peddlers often followed in the wake of the Roman legions, selling merchandise.[344] As the empire declined, Jews also moved among the barbarians, introducing them to the products and ideas of the civilized world. As learning declined in Europe, the Jews held on to more of it than many Christians, causing the latter to develop more respect for Jews, whose knowledge was often useful to them.[345] At the same time, this prestige of the Jews among the masses was resented by church officials, who used their influence against the Jews.[346] By and large, however, the treatment of the Jews in the first thousand years of the Christian era was not as bad as it was to become in later centuries. With the rising religious fervor of Christians during the era of the Crusades, Jews became targets for wild mobs who sometimes slaughtered them by the thousands.[347] Jews lived a precarious existence throughout Europe, often paying for protection by the ruling powers[348]—protection which was sometimes given and sometimes withheld, depending upon the disposition of the sovereigns and the political expediency of sacrificing the Jews as scapegoats for general frustrations and discontents among the populace. Very similar patterns existed across North Africa and the Middle East. The triumph of Islam in the region often meant either forced conversions of Jews, on pain of death, or else their subjugation and deliberate humiliation—as in Yemen, where an 1806 decree imposed upon Jews the task of removing the carcasses of animals from the streets and cleaning the latrines, and where a 1905 decree required Jews to step off the sidewalk into the gutter whenever a Muslim walked past.[349]

Jews lived separately, first voluntarily and later by official compulsion. For example, a Polish edict in 1266 said:

> ... we command that the Jews dwelling in this province of Gaesen shall not live among the Christians, but shall have their houses near or next to one another in some sequestered part of the state or town, so that their dwelling place shall be separated from the common dwelling places of the Christians by a hedge, a wall, or a ditch.[350]

Similar edicts were issued in many parts of Europe and the Middle East.[351] The word "ghetto" originated in the Middle Ages to designate the segregated Jewish section of many European cities. Jewish ghettos were often walled off and had gates that were locked at night, when Jews were forbidden to be abroad among the Christians.[352]

Jews were restricted as to the kinds of occupations they were allowed to engage in, as well as where they were allowed to live. Jews had many artisan skills but were usually not admitted to the guilds which had monopolies of practicing such skills in many cities and towns. In the early centuries A.D., many Jews were farmers and landowners but in most countries they were forced out of these occupations by various restrictions and prohibitions. Jews found— or created—such economic roles as they could. They became middlemen of one sort or another throughout Europe, North Africa, and the Middle East—petty peddlers, junk dealers, pawn brokers, and a fortunate few became substantial merchants and bankers. Many Jews practiced their artisan skills on the fringes or in the interstices of these societies.

Their skills, work capacity, and frugality made Jews valuable additions to many economies, and the money they lent made them welcome by rulers and the nobility, who were often in need of loans to sustain their wars or other extravagances. But the peasants and the poor of Europe, North Africa, and the Middle East, like their counterparts in southeast Asia, hated foreign middlemen who prospered in their midst and were therefore presumed to prosper at their expense. Yet, as with the overseas Chinese in southeast Asia, mass expulsions of Jews often led to *higher* interest rates and worse economic conditions, so that Jews were often later allowed—or invited—back to countries from which they had been expelled.[353]

Confiscatory taxation, mass expulsions, orgies of mob violence, looting, and systematic destruction of property all took their toll on the Jews, both economically and psychologically. Jews became poor in many countries where they had once prospered. They remained strangers and prey to local bullies in countries where they had lived for centuries—sometimes longer than the majority of the inhabitants who were considered natives. "Timidity, self-consciousness, suspicion of their neighbors became characteristic of the ghetto Jew."[354] They walked with a bent posture of humility and fear— "the ghetto crouch." Nor was this reaction limited to European Jews. In Yemen as well, "Jews had learned the art of accepting insults with self-effacement,"[355] and "Yemenite Jews themselves recognized that humility and timidness were basic features of their character."[356]

Conditions varied unpredictably from time to time and from place to place, adding to the uncertainties of the Jews and leading to refugee movements from country to country as conditions became intolerable in one place or more humane policies made others more attractive. Much of the anti-Semitic policies or mob violence in Europe, North Africa and the Middle East expressed religious differences, but the pattern was very similar to the fate of the Chinese in southeast Asia, where religious differences were seldom major considerations. Moreover, even in Europe, North Africa and the Middle East, there were many worldly—and especially economic—gains to be made by using Jews as scapegoats, killing people to whom money was owed, restricting competitors, and confiscating the property of an unpopular people, either piecemeal by discriminatory taxation or all at once in sporadic edicts. In short, religious rhetoric did not imply religious bigotry as the prime motivating force, especially among ringleaders of mobs or rulers of nations.

Spain

Jews lived and prospered in Spain for centuries before the founding of the Visigoth's kingdom in 412 A.D. or the conversion of the Visigoths to Roman Catholicism in 589 A.D. As in much of the rest of Europe during this period, the Jews of Spain lived with a certain amount of toleration and even respect from the non-Jewish population.[357] For centuries, itinerant Jewish peddlers spread knowledge of a wider social world among the insular peoples of various parts of Europe and created an interest in civilized life among the barbarian tribes that had spread across Europe with the decline and fall of the Roman Empire.[358] By the time the Visigoths founded their kingdom in Spain, Jews were well-established, influential and wealthy there.[359] They engaged in a wide range of activities, including the ownership of large estates and the holding of both civil and military offices.[360]

Although the Visigoths were initially very tolerant of religious differences,[361] the conversion of their ruling monarch to Catholicism in 589 established strong church-state ties and began a policy of restrictions on Jews that developed into full-blown persecution under the later Visigothic kings, notably in the seventh century A.D. The motivation for these actions appeared to have been political rather than religious.[362] Nevertheless, many Jews fled Spain under the later Visigothic kings.

Ironically, the conquest of Spain by the Mohammedans in the eighth century A.D. restored freedom to the Spanish Jews and opened what has been called a "golden age" in their development.[363] Not only did the Jews of Spain prosper, Spain itself became the wealthiest and most cultured nation in Europe.[364] Jews became a conduit for the transmission of skills and scholarship, as well as goods, between the Moslem and the Christian worlds.[365] The Jews continued their prosperity and prominence in high places after the restoration of Christian rule in Spain. While most Spanish Jews worked in such occupations as craftsmen, small businessmen, and money lenders, some owned textile manufacturing businesses or were high level administrators and tax collectors for the Spanish monarchy.[366] Jews dominated the liberal professions in Spain.[367] While protected by the monarchy, Jews were bitterly resented by the poor and the uneducated in Spain—and were victims of sporadic riots in the fourteenth century.[368]

Spain—called *Sepharad* in Hebrew—was the home of the Sephardic Jews, who were in the cultural forefront of world Jewry, and quite conscious of that fact. For centuries after this golden age, many put the letters ST after their names for *S'fardi Tahor* in Hebrew or "pure Sephardi."[369] They continued to be called Sephardic Jews even after they settled in Holland, North Africa, the United States, or elsewhere.

In the fifteenth century, Jews were caught in the midst of internal power struggles in Spain, many were massacred in various Spanish cities,[370] and eventually a royal decree was issued in 1492 expelling Jews from Spain and confiscating much of their property. Wealth confiscated from Jews helped finance the fateful voyages of Columbus that began that year.

Many of the expelled Spanish Jews made their way to Holland, where there was religious freedom. The Spanish Jews who settled in Holland helped to make Amsterdam one of the world's great commercial ports,[371] and came ultimately to own one-fourth of the shares in the Dutch East India Company.[372]

The Sephardic Jews who settled in Algeria became the acknowledged leaders of the Jewish community there, and leaders also of the commercial activities of the nation.[373] Although the Spanish government had confiscated the wealth of the Sephardic Jews, they could not confiscate the skills and traits that created that wealth in the first place—and would create it again in many nations. Sephardic Jews retained their sense of ease, confidence, and superiority:

> The Sephardi looked down from on high upon the poor little Jew from the north, accustomed to misery and oppression, who cowered, made himself humble and hugged the wall, who had always lived with doors and windows closed, shut up in the *Judengassen* (Jewish streets) in sullen isolation, who shunned all social contact, all friendship with the non-Jew; who, always despised and unwanted, lived here and there as a veritable nomad, always ready to take off, with his bundle and his wanderer's staff. . . . After ten centuries, these brothers in Israel had ceased to recognize each other. Their encounter did not take place without hurt.[374]

Ironically, they would meet again, centuries later, in Israel and then it would be the northern European Jews who would be ascendant.

Germany

Germany, where the Jews were to meet their greatest catastrophe in the Nazi Holocaust, was throughout most of its history one of the most tolerant European countries for Jews. The German states were not free of the persecutions and sporadic violence that marked Jewish life elsewhere in Europe, but these things were simply not as bad as they were in other parts of Europe. In the eleventh century, when the first Crusades introduced massive violence against Jews, the Jews who lived along the Rhine were on such good terms with their German neighbors that they "refused to believe the warnings sent by the Jews of France that danger threatened."[375] Many German Jews therefore became part of the ten thousand Jews killed in Central Europe.[376]

Because Germany in Hebrew was *Ashkenaz*, the German Jews were called Ashkenazic Jews, and like the Sephardic Jews they continued to carry this name with them as they settled—sometimes for centuries—in other nations of Europe or in the western hemisphere. Most of the Jews of Europe and of the world are Ashkenazic Jews.[377] It was in Germany that Yiddish originated in the twelfth century and that Reform Judaism and Zionism later evolved. Frankfort on Main became a center of world Jewish culture.[378]

Jews were sometimes invited to settle in German cities[379] and at other times massacred or expelled—and then invited back.[380] Sometimes the German nobles protected them—in their castles when the Crusaders came through in 1146[381]—and sometimes the nobles turned on them. In the seventeenth and eighteenth centuries, there were "court Jews," who served kings and princes in various ways. But "the prince's death, or even his whim, could abruptly end their careers and cost them all their fortune or even their lives."[382]

German Jews attempted to assimilate into German society by adopting the language, the dress, and even some outward religious customs of their Christian countrymen. Reform Judaism in Germany featured many outward similarities to Christian churches, such as stained glass windows, mixed choirs, and instrumental music—and calling the place of worship a temple instead of a synagogue. Such innovations made little headway in eastern Europe, where the distinction between Jew and Gentile was too great to be affected by such gestures.

Over the centuries, Jews in Germany rose to positions of affluence and influence, especially after the many small German states were unified into one country.[383] By the end of the nineteenth century, there were nearly 600,000 Jews in Germany, "a prosperous community, all German-speaking and German-feeling, with more than half of them in commerce, one-fifth in industry and trade, and about 6 percent in liberal professions and public service."[384] Even the most religiously orthodox Jews considered themselves "totally German."[385] This remained true even after immigration to the United States. Nineteenth century German Jewish immigrants to America typically settled among other Germans and took part in the general community life, while retaining their own religious institutions. This was not true of later emigrants from eastern Europe, who lived lives very much apart from other Polish and Russian people, except for commercial transactions. American Jews were so pro-German as late as World War I as to bring on U.S. government prosecutions for voicing support for an enemy nation.[386]

Jews were a major part of the economic, scientific, and cultural life of Germany. They were disproportionately represented in the arts, the sciences, and the press, and even played a role in German politics. Jewish refugees from eastern Europe sought a haven in Germany. Although Jews were only one percent of the German population, they became 10 percent of the doctors and dentists, 17 percent of the lawyers and won 27 percent of the Nobel Prizes won by all Germans from 1901 to 1975.[387] Social acceptance from other Germans accompanied these advances and achievements by Jews. In the 1920s, nearly half of all Jewish marriages in Germany were to Gentiles. Thousands of Jews converted to Christianity or simply withdrew from the Judaic religion and community.[388] In short, Jews achieved some of their greatest economic prosperity, scientific and artistic achievements, and widespread social acceptance just on the eve of the rise of Hitler and the Nazis.

Anti-Semitism in Germany reached fanatical levels among the small group of Nazis in the 1920s. When the general crisis and collapse of the Weimar Republic brought the Nazis to power in 1933, the stage was set for the greatest catastrophe ever to befall the Jews, or perhaps any other people in history—the cold-blooded murder of 6 million defenseless human beings, for no other reason than simply being Jews. While this was the climactic disaster of Jewish history, it was also a repetition of a pattern that had appeared again and again in their history.

Eastern Europe

Historically, eastern Europe has lagged behind western Europe in economic development and general cultural advancement. The Jews carried the economic skills and cultural development of western Europe into eastern Europe. In order to encourage this process, the Polish ruler Boleslav issued a charter in 1264 protecting the Jews in his domain.[389] This made Poland an attractive refuge for many European Jews, not only from Germany and central Europe but also from as far away as Spain.[390] Later rulers continued this policy in order to attract more Jews and gain the benefits their skills were bringing to Poland. By the sixteenth century, Jewish academies were flowering in Poland and other Slavic areas,[391] where many Jews were living in self-governing communities. Polish Jews were in the vanguard of Ashkenazic Jewish cultural development.[392] Economically they were thriving as well:

> .... Jews could function on an equal footing with Christians. They controlled the international trade between Christian Europe and the east, and from the late fifteenth century with the Ottoman Empire; provided the nobility with clothing, dyes, and luxury items; financed kings, magnates, cities, and businesses; managed mines and customs stations; and played a leading part in the periodic fairs which took place in several major cities.[393]

In the year 1600, there were about 500,000 Jews living in Poland—far more than in western and central Europe combined.[394]

The prosperity of the Polish Jews provoked resentment among the Polish peasant masses, especially bitter toward those Jews who acted as rent collectors for the Polish nobility and tax collectors for the Polish government. By the middle of the seventeenth century, popular hatred of Jews in eastern Europe was expressed in periodic mass violence—a century and a half of "almost uninterrupted massacres of Jews."[395] Polish Jews also suffered economic, social and cultural decline.[396] When Poland was incorporated into the Russian empire, Jewish residences were restricted to specific parts of Russia called the Pale of Settlement. Jews could not live "beyond the Pale." Eastern European Jews were now worse off than the Jews of western Europe, and were cut off from the life and culture of other Europeans.[397] The Russian government attempted to assimilate the Jews by authoritarian measures: orders to Jews to cut their beards, dress like Russians, teach Russian in their schools, and send their youth away for long years of military training which included Russian non-Kosher food and Russian religious practices.[398]

Evasions and repressions followed these policies, until the middle of the nineteenth century, when Czar Alexander II began to rescind many anti-Jewish policies. But the assassination of the Czar in 1881 marked not merely the end of these policies, but the beginning of a new era of mass violence against Jews in Eastern Europe. The Russian police stood idly by as massive riots (pogroms) spread through Russia in 1881, killing several hundred Jews. The Russian government's response to these riots—and international indignation over them—was to force Jews to relocate from the smaller towns into the larger urban centers within the Pale.[399] The impossible situation of Jews in Russia and in other parts of eastern Europe provoked one of the greatest exoduses ever seen in history. In a period of thirty-three years, almost one-third of all the Jews in eastern Europe left their homelands.[400] Between three-quarters and four-fifths of the Russian Jewish emigrants went directly to the United States,[401] and many other Jews found their way to America after stopping temporarily in other countries. While only about fifteen hundred Jews per year had left Czarist Russia in the decade ending in 1880, more than fifty *thousand* per year immigrated to the United States in the next decade, and this was doubled again in the following decade. In the early twentieth century, nearly a hundred thousand Jews per year were leaving Russia for the United States alone.[402]

When Poland gained independence from Russia after World War I, its resurgent nationalism took the form of excluding Jews from many sectors of the economy where they had been working for centuries.[403] The rise of Nazi anti-Semitism in neighboring Germany during the 1930s found its echo in Polish thoughts and deeds, including anti-Jewish boycotts and pogroms. After the Nazis conquered Poland, their anti-semitic policies were well-received by the Poles, who cooperated. At the end of World War II, Poland was virtually without Jews.[404]

The United States

A long history of greater religious tolerance than in Europe made the United States especially attractive to persecuted Jews. Jews began arriving early in colonial America—Sephardic Jews, who had wandered from country to country seeking refuge in the wake of the mass expulsions from Spain in 1492. In 1654, a small group of Jews from Brazil arrived on the *St. Catarina,* sometimes known as "the Jewish Mayflower."[405] By the time of the Revolutionary War, there were about two thousand Jews in the American colonies.[406] These early Sephardic Jews were followed by German Jews in the eighteenth century. Then came the massive immigration of eastern European Jews, beginning in the 1880s.

Unlike the German Jews, who were spread out across America, eastern European Jews concentrated in New York City. Of nearly a million and a half Jews who entered the United States between 1881 and 1911, 70 per cent settled in New York City. Their greatest concentration was on Manhattan's lower east side, where more than half a million Jews were packed into one and a half square miles.[407] About half of the Jewish families slept three or four to a room and another quarter slept five or more to a room.[408] Kitchens and parlors often served as bedrooms at night,[409] and parts of an apartment often served as work places during the day for "sweatshop" labor, with its long hours and low pay.[410] The streets below were also crowded with masses of pushcarts, peddlers and customers—a packed throng through which a few wagons tried to force their way.[411] In these streets, "the crush and the stench" were suffocating.[412]

The great bulk of the early immigrant Jews from eastern Europe were manual laborers, but two-thirds were skilled workers.[413] One out of three Jewish immigrant workers earned a living in New York's garment industry,[414] where the workers were usually eastern European Jews and the owners German Jews.

Although the Jewish immigrants arrived in America with less money than most other immigrants,[415] their rise to prosperity was unparalleled. Working long hours at low pay, they nevertheless saved money to start their own small businesses—often just a pushcart—or to send a child to college. While the Jews were initially destitute in financial terms, they brought with them not only specific skills but a tradition of success and entrepreneurship which could not be confiscated or eliminated, as the Russian and Polish governments had confiscated their wealth and eliminated most of their opportunities. The Jews began to rise again in the United States, first in skilled occupations and small businesses. Their children could then be kept in high school and many began to enter the free municipal colleges of New York City. By 1916, Jews constituted 44 per cent of the students at Hunter College and 73 per cent of the students at City College. Even at Catholic Fordham University, one fifth of the students were Jews.[416]

The Jewish educational advancement paid off in professional careers. For example, Jews constituted 8 percent of the population of Cleveland in 1938, but were 18 percent of that city's dentists, 21 percent of its doctors, and 23 percent of its lawyers. In New York, where Jews were about one fourth of the population, they were 55 percent of the doctors, 64 percent of the dentists and 65 percent of the lawyers.[417]

Anti-Semitism increased along with the growing population of eastern European Jews, whose foreign ways, dress and language repelled many Americans and greatly embarrassed the more acculturated German Jews. Barriers went up against Jews in general in various occupations, businesses, and industries, as well as in social settings such as clubs or hotels. Jews crowded into those sectors that were open to them—and created their own industries. New York's garment industry was owned overwhelmingly by Jews. So was Hollywood's motion picture industry during the heyday of the great studios like MGM and Warner Brothers. But the Jews never dominated the huge American economy in any way approaching the domination of the overseas Chinese in the less developed southeast Asian economies.

By 1969, Jewish family income in the United States was 72 per cent above the national average. More than one fourth of all Nobel prizes won by Americans had been won by Jewish Americans. While Israel was the historic Jewish homeland, there were more Jews in the United States than in Israel. Indeed, Israel itself owed much to the financial and political support of Jews in America.

CHAPTER FOUR

Blacks and Coloreds

I n different parts of the world, individuals of racially Negroid ancestry have been divided into the more or less racially pure "blacks" and a half-caste group known variously as "coloreds" in South Africa or the West Indies, or as "persons of color," or by more numerous and minutely graded racial designations in Latin America. Marked cultural differences have often accompanied these differences in skin color and ancestry. Both the cultural and the biological differences have evolved from the history of Negroes as a conquered people in Africa and an enslaved people in the Western Hemisphere. Here the term "Negro" includes both blacks and coloreds.

The geography of Africa has played a major role in shaping the history of its people. The vast continent—much larger than Europe —is geographically fragmented, especially south of the Sahara desert, which in itself served for centuries as a major barrier separating Africans from contact with the civilizations of Europe and the Middle East. Like other geographically fragmented areas, such as Italy and China, Africa has had many internal differences in language and culture, acting as barriers to political or economic cohesion. The jungles, mountains, deserts, and waterfalls that give Africa its geographic distinction and beauty also doomed many of its peoples to isolated tribal lives and a fateful vulnerability to invading nations representing larger cultures.

Africa has been characterized as "particularly ill-favored by nature."[1] Although the continent of Africa is larger than Europe, it has a shorter coastline, for the European coastline is more indented with natural harbors that facilitate trade and communication. Europe also has many more navigable rivers—a vital economic asset, for ancient civilizations in Egypt, Babylonia, and China began in river valleys,[2] most of the world's great cities have arisen on rivers or harbors, and modern civilizations have developed around those cities. Africa has suffered not only from a dearth of navigable rivers and natural harbors, but also because parts of its coast were inaccessible to Africans and Europeans alike until the development (late in history) of ships capable of overcoming treacherous currents and winds. Nor were these the only natural handicaps of Africa. Much of Africa has been infested with the tsetse fly, whose parasites are fatal to draft animals. In turn, this meant that wheeled carts pulled by animals were not feasible, and that transportation was largely by the far more expensive method of human beings carrying freight in bundles or baskets. Numerous tropical diseases also afflicted humans—decimating and debilitating Africans and impeding large-scale contacts with the culture of Europe, for Europeans were even more vulnerable. Before medical science was able to cope with these diseases, a European could expect to die within a year of arrival in parts of Africa.[3]

Where large civilizations did arise in Africa, it was where these geographic handicaps were not as severe. Ancient Egypt was, of course, the most famous of those civilizations. The land of the pharoahs and the pyramids was dependent for its existence on the Nile River, one of the longest navigable rivers in the world. The large African kingdoms of the Sudan arose in a region where level plains facilitated widespread communication.[4] The east coast of Africa was less forbidding than the west coast, and early on established trade relations that reached the Middle East and Asia.[5] But these more fortunate parts of Africa were not the main source of the Africans transported by the millions to the western hemisphere as slaves or subjugated in their homelands, as in South Africa. The region of the great Niger river gave rise to a more advanced civilization than in the interior of Africa,[6] and many slaves came from that region —but such slaves were often from other African tribes subjugated by the more powerful Nigerian tribes.

THE CARIBBEAN AND SOUTH AMERICA

By the time of the massive importations of African slaves into the Western Hemisphere, slavery had long ago died out in most of Europe. Spain and Portugal were exceptions, however. In the fifteenth century, Lisbon alone imported more than 400 slaves per year,[7] and slavery was not abolished in Portugal until 1773.[8] The sugar industry in Madeira was estimated to have imported tens of thousands of African slaves during the era of the Atlantic slave trade.[9] The dominance of Spain and Portugal in the Western Hemisphere during the era of European colonialism meant that both slaves and freed men lived and developed under laws and customs that had a long tradition in the Iberian Peninsula. Portuguese Brazil or the many Spanish colonies therefore differed in this respect from the Anglo-Saxon colonies of North America, which had no such legal or social tradition to draw upon in the British Isles.

Various legal protections for slaves which had evolved over the centuries in Spain and Portugal have convinced some scholars that slavery was less severe in Latin America than in British North America, where no such legal protections existed in Anglo-Saxon law.[10] But legal protection is only one factor affecting the treatment of slaves, and differing economic, demographic, and ideological characteristics are among the other variables at work.

Empirically, the mortality rate among slaves in Latin America and the Caribbean was far higher than in the United States,[11] and there is also other, more direct, evidence that the treatment of slaves was generally as bad or worse in Latin slave societies.[12] For example, although slave marriages and family life enjoyed legal protection under Portuguese law in Brazil,[13] most Brazilian slaves did not live in family units,[14] for the overwhelming majority of Brazilian slaves were males[15]—and even when there were slave women, some Brazilian slaveowners deliberately locked up men and women separately at night to prevent pregnancies.[16] In the Brazilian economy, it was not considered profitable to raise slave children,[17] and infant mortality claimed the great majority of children born to slave women.[18] Suicides also appear to have been much more common among slaves in Brazil than in the United States.[19]

Nor was Brazil unique. In Latin America and the Caribbean in general, there were far more males than females—who were totally non-existent on some sugar plantations—and raising slave children was considered more costly than buying new adult slaves from Africa. The net result was a widespread dearth of family life among slaves, few children, and high infant mortality—all of which, together with killing overwork of adults, required constant large scale importations of new slaves from Africa, as the native-born slave population continually died off. Suicides also occurred on a large scale among slaves in the Caribbean and Latin America.[20]

The laws that impressed later scholars were by no means readily available to slaves—who could be brutally punished by slaveowners for making a complaint to the authorities—while economic considerations made slaves (including children) much more valuable in the United States than in Brazil, for example, which could import adult males from Africa at a closer distance with lower cost.

A striking difference between the British colonies and the Spanish or Portuguese colonies was that men, women and children were transported across the ocean from Britain to form something of a replica of the home society in continental North America, while the Spanish and Portuguese sent mostly men. Demographically, this meant that Canada and the United States became and remained predominantly white societies with black minorities, while much of the Caribbean has been predominantly black or mulatto,[21] as was Brazil before the massive emigration from Europe that began in the late nineteenth century.[22] Much of Spanish America, however, has been demographically dominated by *mestizos*—mixtures of whites and Indians, sometimes with African admixtures.

Race relations in the Western Hemisphere have generally varied with these demographic differences. Although white supremacy has been the dominant theme in western hemisphere societies of British, Spanish, Portuguese, Dutch, or French origin, the manner and degree to which this principle was applied in practice has varied significantly. In the classic Anglo-Saxon patterns of Canada and the United States, there has been a stark dichotomy of black and white, cutting across all political, economic, and social lines—and with "black" meaning all individuals of discernible African ancestry, regardless of the degree of racial mixture. In the Latin colonies, however, the small, vastly outnumbered white enclaves followed a divide-and-conquer strategy, making significant legal, economic, and social distinctions between blacks and mulattoes—with the latter being elaborately subdivided by skin color or presumed degrees of white ancestry.

The boundaries of whiteness have not been absolute in any of these societies, and the strictness of the definition has varied. Some people who would be considered "white" in Hispanic America would be considered "black" in the United States. In the Old South, "one drop" of "Negro blood" was said to make an individual black for all legal and social purposes, but in reality even the most racist southern states allowed individuals with less than a given fraction of Negro ancestry to be legally considered white. It is estimated that tens of millions of white Americans have at least one black ancestor.[23] However, even a man who was seven-eighths Caucasian was defined as a Negro and subjected to the racial segregation laws, as in the case of Adolph Plessy, whose landmark Supreme Court case (Plessy v. Ferguson) established the legal doctrine of "separate but equal" treatment. In much of Latin America, Plessy would have been considered white. In Brazil, "a Negro is a person of African descent who has no white ancestry at all."[24] But this definition would exclude about three quarters of all American Negroes.[25]

The term "mulatto" is likewise defined differently in the two countries. In the United States, a mulatto has one white parent and one black parent—and given the broad definition of black, that means 50 percent or more Caucasian ancestry. But the term "mulatto" has been applied in Brazil to people with less than 50 percent Caucasian ancestry, and in fact with racial proportions not very different from those of the average American Negro.[26]

Within the Negro population—including blacks, mulattoes, and other coloreds—color lines have likewise varied as between Anglo-Saxon and Latin societies. Where all Negroes were lumped together by the dominant whites, internal color distinctions were less significant for Negroes themselves. Where important distinctions were made by whites between the "blacks" and the "colored," Negroes have likewise attached greater significance to skin color differences in their own dealings with each other. While these distinctions have been socially significant throughout the Western Hemisphere, they have had less impact in the United States, for example, than in Latin America. Moreover, within the United States, skin color differences have had their greatest social impact in New Orleans, a former Latin American city whose social patterns were well established before the Louisiana Purchase of 1803, and whose "colored" population was greatly augmented by mulatto emigres from the Caribbean in the late eighteenth and early nineteenth centuries.[27]

The British West Indies likewise reflected more of the Latin American pattern, but for a different reason. Although culturally Anglo-Saxon, the demographic makeup of the islands has historically been more like that of many Latin American colonies—overwhelmingly Negro, with the small white population being predominantly male, producing a racially mixed offspring. The divide-and-conquer strategy of distinguishing blacks from coloreds therefore emerged from the dominant but outnumbered whites of the West Indies. Instead of the stark racial dichotomy of continental North America, the British West Indies emphasized skin color gradations—an emphasis still surviving more strongly among twentieth century West Indian Negroes than among American Negroes.[28]

From the earliest days of the black slave population in the Western Hemisphere, there also appeared mulatto populations—usually defined as half or more white. Many mulattoes remained slaves, but they were also disproportionately represented among free Negroes. In the United States, for example, about 8 percent of the slaves were classified as mulattoes, compared to 37 percent of free Negroes.[29] In Brazil, a majority of free Negroes were mulattoes and an overwhelming majority of the slaves were black.[30] Similarly in Barbados, a majority of free Negroes were classified as "colored,"[31] and throughout the Caribbean most free Negroes were of mixed ancestry, most slaves unmixed Africans, leading to a general tendency to call the former "colored" and the latter "black."[32] One reason for the differences of color and disparity of status among Negroes was that some slave owners freed children they had fathered by slave women, sometimes freeing the mother as well. This is not to say that most such children were freed. Rather, among those slaves who achieved freedom, this element was greatly overrepresented. Throughout the Western Hemisphere, there were consistently more females than males among the free Negro population[33]—a sex imbalance growing out of the freeing of mothers of racially mixed children.

Even under slavery, mulattoes—especially the offspring of white slave owners—had more opportunities to become house servants rather than field hands, urban slaves rather than plantation slaves, and skilled workers rather than cotton pickers or sugar cane cutters. In all these ways, they had more access to the dominant culture, and more opportunity to obtain freedom by personal favor, self-purchase through spare time earnings, or to successfully engineer an escape. The net result was that, whether slave or free, those Negroes with a higher proportion of white ancestry had advantages —literacy, job skills, urbanization, and the values of the dominant culture—to pass on to their descendants. Those descended from wealthier slave owners sometimes had money or property as well. Long after slavery, lighter complexioned Negroes continued to be over-represented among those with education, job skills, or general acculturation. Many of these attributed their advantages to genetic superiority.[34]

There are numerous gradations of racial mixture designated by a variety of names in Latin societies. The term "black" was considered insulting by the free colored populations, partly because it referred generally to slaves, and partly because of repugnance for Negroid features and African history. In later, post-emancipation times, "colored" would be considered a more polite designation for Negroes in general—but a designation increasingly rejected by Negroes who resented the implication that there was something wrong with being "black."

The relative size of the free colored population varied greatly from country to country, ranging from about 10 percent of the total Negro population in the United States and Jamaica[35] to more than half in colonial Brazil,[36] as well as in the Spanish colonies in general.[37]

Brazil

Brazil imported more than six times as many African slaves as the United States, although the surviving slave population was greater in the United States. The slave population of Brazil never reproduced itself like that of the United States, but was constantly replenished by new slaves from Africa. Among the consequences of this was a black population in which African cultures survived to a far greater extent than among American Negroes.[38] Indeed, African words and pronunciations affected the Portuguese language as spoken by the white masses in Brazil.[39] As late as the nineteenth century, at least 40 percent of the slaves in the provinces of Rio de Janeiro and São Paulo were African born.[40] By contrast, in the contemporary United States, 99 percent of the slaves were American born.[41]

The massive importation of Africans to Brazil was facilitated by its geographic proximity to Africa, but it was necessitated by a large loss of slaves (1) due to a high mortality rate under the brutal conditions of Brazilian slavery[42] (some slaves were literally whipped to death or thrown into pools of piranhas or boiled in oil[43]), and (2) the widespread achievement of freedom by slaves in Brazil. As early as the eighteenth century, there were more than two thirds as many free Negroes as slaves. By 1808, there were more free Negroes than slaves.

The Portuguese colonists in Brazil were predominantly male. This meant that sexual liaisons with black and Indian women were widespread, leading to a complex stratification of racially mixed offspring.[44] By the late eighteenth century, whites constituted less than one fifth of the population of the country, and as late as 1821 whites were only about one fourth the population—outnumbered both by mulattoes and by blacks.[45] Only the massive immigration of Europeans to Brazil beginning in the late nineteenth century produced a predominantly white population. However, the term "white" *(branco)* is used more flexibly in Brazil than in Anglo-Saxon countries, and especially so in the province of Bahia, where Negroes have historically been concentrated. Nearly one-fifth of the *brancos* in Bahia in the 1930s were mulattoes in North American terminology.[46] As in the United States, the European immigrants moved primarily into those parts of the country where slave plantations were *not* predominant.[47] As a result, there have been large regional variations in the racial composition of the Brazilian population. As of 1890, *brancos* were about one-third of the population of Bahia[48] but nearly two-thirds of the population of the state of São Paulo and four-fifths of the population of the city of São Paulo.[49]

Mining booms and attendant urban commercial development in

eighteenth century Brazil created many opportunities for the slaves to earn money in their spare time and to purchase their freedom with their savings.[50] This was an established practice, legally recognized under Portuguese law in colonial Brazil.[51] The lack of artisans among the Portuguese overlords created an opportunity for slaves to earn money by becoming carpenters or barbers, or to acquire other artisan skills. Most of the barbers in eighteenth century Brazil were slaves. Some slaves worked as clerks in their masters' stores and became acquainted with business operations well enough to conduct some on their own. Slave men and women became peddlers and some women became prostitutes.[52] In addition, there were fraternal organizations of blacks or mulattoes that made loans to slaves to buy their own freedom and repay the money in installments.[53]

Free blacks and free coloreds were subject to many legal discriminations in colonial Brazil—forbidden to enter many occupations, hold many military or civil offices, or even to wear clothing considered to be above their assigned place in Brazilian society. Still, there was some progress over time, and by the early nineteenth century, blacks and mulattoes dominated virtually all the skilled trades in Brazil.[54] The Portuguese disdained manual labor,[55] leaving these opportunities for non-whites. Many free blacks and free mulattoes became cattle-raisers, farmers, shopkeepers, craftsmen and peddlers—jobs which both slaves and white men were constrained from filling, for different reasons.[56] However, there was economic retrogression for Negroes in Brazil in the last quarter of the nineteenth century, when they faced the competition of a massive inflow of immigrants from Europe,[57] many of whom did not share the Portuguese reluctance to perform manual labor.

Throughout the history of Brazil, many mulattoes have attempted to escape racial discrimination by "passing" as whites.[58] As in much of Latin America, wealth facilitated acceptance as "white," and at one time official certificates of whiteness were for sale. In the eighteenth century, when a question was raised as to whether a certain official was a mulatto, the answer was: "He was but is not any more."[59]

In parts of twentieth century Brazil, it is said that where there was sugar, there are Negroes.[60] That is, the present geographical distribution of blacks, mulattoes, and others of various degrees of African ancestry reflect the past distribution of sugar plantations worked by slaves. In the state of Bahia, in tropical northeastern Brazil, whites were less than one-third of the population, in the middle of the twentieth century,[61] though a majority in the country as a whole.[62] Brazil today is a country of many kinds and degrees of racial mixtures, among Caucasians (mostly Portuguese), indigenous Indians, and people of Negro stock. These various racial mixtures are differently represented at different socioeconomic levels—whites at the top and blacks at the bottom[63]—and a wide range of racial combinations and degrees are socially important. But by and large, Brazil has not had the degree of racial rigidity or hostility found in most multi-racial and multi-ethnic societies.[64] While such racial hostilities in the United States have often been attributed to a legacy of slavery, the Brazilian experience at least raises questions about that explanation, for slavery persisted in Brazil longer than in any other western nation, being abolished only in 1888—a quarter of a century later than in the United States. Perhaps equally important, however, is that most Brazilians of African descent were freed *before* slavery was abolished as an institution.[65] Black and slave were not synonymous. Moreover, in direct contrast to the United States, it is precisely in the regions of Brazil where blacks are most concentrated—notably Bahia—that race relations are best, and it is the lower class whites who seem to get along best with dark Brazilians, and intermarry with them the most.[66]

At the end of the eighteenth century, there were more than 400,000 free Negroes in Brazil, and by the time slavery was abolished, there were about three times as many free Negroes as slaves.[67] This contrasts sharply with the U.S. experience, where 90 percent of the Negro population was freed as a result of the Civil War. In Brazil, at least half of the Negro population had been free for at least a generation, by the time the institution of slavery was abolished.[68]

Though racism, as such, is not as prominent a feature of Brazilian society as of other multi-racial societies, Brazil has highly rigid *class* lines and a distribution of income that is much more unequal than that of the United States, for example.[69] The small upper class is almost exclusively white. In such a country, where the top 5 percent of employed individuals receive half the national income,[70] class differences are also racial differences. Whether measured by income or property, whites are significantly more prosperous than mulattoes and mulattoes more prosperous than blacks.[71] As in much of the Western Hemisphere, this reflects historic advantages going back for centuries.

For all its more relaxed race relations, Brazil has larger black-white disparities than the United States in education[72] and in political participation.[73] Blacks are also extremely rare in high positions in the professions or other high-level occupations in Brazilia.[74] There are difficulties in trying to use terminology that will describe the same sorts of people in both Brazil and the United States. However, darker-skinned individuals seem not to have risen as rapidly in Brazil as in the United States.[75] Indeed, even mixed-blood Negro individuals have risen less in class in Brazil than in the U.S.A.[76] This suggests that racism may be less of a factor in economic advancement than is commonly supposed. Historic head starts in acculturation seem as highly correlated with economic advancement in comparing people of African ancestry in Brazil and the United States as in making internal comparisons among the Negro populations of both countries.

The West Indies[77]

The British West Indies followed an economic and social development pattern quite different from that of the British colonies on the North American continent. While Canada and the thirteen American colonies were settled by whole families and communities of whites, the population of the British West Indian colonies—principally Jamaica, Barbados, and Trinidad—consisted overwhelmingly of black slaves, controlled by a contingent of white male overseers, attorneys, and other auxiliary personnel. Giant plantations—much larger than in the United States—were the dominant mode of production, sugar was the dominant crop, and the owners of these plantations typically lived in England, leaving day-to-day control in the hands of overseers. All these features helped shape the history of blacks and coloreds in the West Indies.

Absentee ownership—in the West Indian colonies, as in the southern United States or Latin America—typically meant short-run maximization of output, with little concern for long-run effects on the slaves or on the plantation land and structures. But while absentee ownership was the exception in the United States, it was the rule in the West Indies. Resident plantation owners in the United States had an economic incentive to protect their own long-term investment in slaves and plantations, even though overseers' incentives were to concern themselves only with current output, on which their commissions or reputations depended. This conflict of interest, which was usually resolved in favor of plantation owners in the United States, was typically resolved in favor of the overseer in the West Indies, because the plantation owner in London could not monitor his day-to-day activities. West Indian slaves were therefore treated somewhat differently from slaves in the United States —usually more brutally, and with less concern for the fate of infants or pregnant women.

In the West Indies, where it was considered cheaper to buy new slaves than to maintain the existing population,[78] infant mortality was several times higher than in the American south, where resident plantation owners and their wives protected their long-term economic interest represented by new slaves. Nearly two million slaves were imported into the British West Indies before the slave trade was abolished in 1808[79]—almost five times the number imported into the United States, which had a far larger total black population. The difference was that slaves had higher death rates and lower birth rates in the West Indies. Partly this reflected more cruel treatment in the West Indies,[80] but partly too it reflected the greater biological vulnerability of African slaves to European diseases as compared to native slaves who had acquired biological resistance and immunity to such diseases. Jamaica was long a "seasoning" ground for newly enslaved Africans[81]—a place where they were broken into their new role as slaves, acquired some acquaintance with the language and culture, and some measure of biological resistance. Some of these seasoned slaves were then shipped to other places, including the United States. American slaves were thus not genetically different from those of the West Indies but were both biologically and culturally different. African cultural survivals were much more common in the West Indies, where new Africans continually reinforced their homeland cultures.

The huge size of the West Indian slave population, relative to that of free whites or free Negroes, meant that the feeding of slaves could not be done by purchases of food from the non-slave population. Slaves had to grow the bulk of their own food, and both time and land had to be set aside for this purpose. Contemporary observers noted that the slaves worked much harder on their individual plots than in the routine plantation work.[82] West Indian slaves and free Negroes together were major suppliers of food to the larger society. Barbados, for example, depended almost wholly on them for food, and huckstering was "deeply imbedded in the cultural system of non-whites" there.[83] Thus, even during the era of slavery, West Indian Negroes—both slave and free—had economic incentives to exercise initiative, as well as experience in buying, selling and managing their own affairs. This experience was usually denied slaves in the United States, who were issued rations, and who were deliberately kept in a state of dependence[84] which was not feasible under West Indian conditions.

Another consequence of the preponderance of blacks in the West Indian population was that slave uprisings were more feasible than in the United States, where the power of the predominantly white community foredoomed such rebellions. In the West Indies, however, there were not only rebellions but enclaves of escaped slaves operating as continuing communities for decades.

American slave owners preferred to hire married overseers, to minimize the problems created by sex relations between an overseer and slave women.[85] In the West Indies, however, there were very few white women and most overseers were bachelors.[86] It was a pervasive pattern among these bachelor overseers to have a slave woman as concubine, more or less openly acknowledged.[87] Moreover, the shortage of white women in the West Indies meant that other white men in the colony had a demand for Negro women—a demand satisfied in part by hiring slave women out as prostitutes[88] and partly by having free colored concubines.[89] The net result was the growth of a mulatto population—both slave children (often freed along with their mothers) and the offspring of temporary unions of sojourning white bachelors who would some day return to England for legal marriage with an Englishwoman. As elsewhere in the hemisphere, a "colored" population had advantages over the black population—both financially and in acculturation—and these tangible differences in turn led many of the racially mixed Negroes to disdain and separate themselves from the darker masses.[90] Unlike the stark black-white dichotomy of North American Anglo-Saxon societies, the West Indian society had an elaborately graded skin color hierarchy reminiscent of Spanish colonies.[91]

While whites monopolized the most lucrative and prestigious positions in the West Indies, there were simply not enough of them to restrict free Negroes to purely menial jobs. The free colored were carpenters, masons, plumbers, small businessmen, and worked in other occupations requiring skill, initiative, or education.[92] Some even became owners of estates and slaves.[93] But despite their economic standing, free Negroes were neither legally nor socially granted equality with whites, but were constantly reminded of their inferior status by discriminatory laws and by such social practices as referring to them without the usual courtesy titles of "Mr." or "Miss."[94] Thwarted in attempting to advance beyond limits set by whites and unwilling to identify with blacks, the free colored population of the West Indies became an inbred group whose values were expressed in genteel etiquette and status-giving possessions.[95]

The free colored population of Jamaica was tiny but rapidly growing. In 1722, when the total population of Jamaica was about 88,000 people, less than one percent were "free colored," compared to 9 percent white, and 89 percent slaves.[96] By 1800, however, the free colored were about 3 percent of the island's total population of 340,000, with whites now 10 percent, and the slaves still the overwhelming majority at 88 percent.[97] The colored portion of the Jamaican population continued to rise after the abolition of slavery in 1834, reaching 18 percent of the total population by 1844.[98] In Barbados, the free Negro population was about 5 percent in the 1820s,[99] and just over half were colored rather than black.[100] About 62 percent of all Barbadian slaves freed were female,[101] reflecting the common practice of freeing slave mothers and their children sired by overseers.

Emancipation in the West Indies in 1834 was followed by a period of economic dislocation and a virtual re-enslavement of the blacks by debt peonage.[102] The small minority of whites continued dominant in the colony's economy, society, and political apparatus. Many non-white West Indians sought their fortunes abroad, notably in the United States. More than one million West Indians—virtually all Negro—have moved to the United States since the nineteenth century, about 300,000 during the first three decades of the twentieth century.[103] West Indians have historically constituted the largest black immigrant group and an absolute majority of black immigrants to the United States.[104] They have been—and remain—concentrated in and around New York City. After the restrictive immigration laws of 1924, few West Indians were able to enter the United States,[105] but recent immigration law changes have led to a renewed West Indian immigration to the U.S., with Jamaicans being the largest element.[106]

The West Indian immigration to the United States—notably New York—in the first three decades of the twentieth century coincided with a massive internal migration of American blacks from the south to the urban north, with New York being a prime destination. The two groups turned Harlem from a predominantly Jewish to a predominantly black community in the 1920s, when about one fourth of black Harlemites were West Indian. The two black groups were, however, culturally very different and have remained so. The West Indians were more urban, more skilled, more frugal, and more entrepreneurial. About 9 percent of the employed West Indians were professionals, 7 percent white collar and 55 percent skilled workers, with only 31 percent unskilled, and virtually all were literate.[107] Their children outperformed American black children in the public schools.[108]

These early advantages continued to differentiate West Indian blacks from American blacks. By 1969, black West Indians in the United States earned 94 percent of the average income of Americans in general, while native blacks earned only 62 percent. Second-generation West Indians in the United States earned 15 percent *more* than the average American.[109] More than half of all black-owned businesses in New York State were owned by West Indian blacks.[110] The highest ranking blacks in the New York City Police Department in 1970 were all West Indians, as were all the black federal judges in the city.[111] There has also been an "extraordinary predominance of West Indian directors of black-studies programmes in American universities."[112] West Indian immigrants in London were not nearly so successful,[113] perhaps because they have arrived later, or because they did not have a large native black population to provide customers for their businesses, clienteles for their professions, or voting support for their political leaders. Nor are West Indians prosperous in their homelands. The per capita output (real income) of Trinidad is less than that of Puerto Rico and only 28 percent of that of the United States. The per capita output of Jamaica is only about half that of Trinidad.[114]

SOUTH AFRICA

The first permanent European settlement on the southern tip of Africa was founded in 1652. The Dutch East India Company established a station at the Cape of Good Hope, as a stopping place for its ships headed for the Dutch East Indies. Here the ships could replenish their supplies of water and food, and the sailors could have relaxation and recreation in preparation for resuming a long voyage to the east. Capetown was known in that era as "the tavern of the seas."[115] That tiny outpost grew over the centuries to ultimately become the nation of South Africa.

The small colony first established on the southern tip of Africa was populated by indentured servants—contract laborers recruited (or kidnapped) in Holland to work for some period of years for the Dutch East India Company. They represented "the chronically unemployed and floating urban underclass of the Netherlands" and proved to be "unruly and inefficient workers" in South Africa.[116] Yet they were destined to change the course of history.

The need for a dependable labor force to man the colonies led the Dutch authorities to import Chinese workers, who—like Chinese elsewhere—"enjoyed a high reputation for industriousness."[117] These were augmented by slaves—not primarily Africans, but slaves imported from India, Ceylon, and Indonesia. As in the Western Hemisphere, the enslavement of indigenous peoples—who could more easily escape or be rescued by their compatriots—was not as effective as the importation of foreign slaves.[118] So, while African slaves were being shipped out to North and South America, Asian slaves were being shipped into Africa.

By 1659, the Cape Colony had more slaves than whites. But this imbalance, and its potential danger to the security of the colony, was corrected by allowing freed white indentured servants to settle in the colony, buying land and slaves. By the year 1700, the free burghers outnumbered the slaves by 50 percent.[119] In this early Dutch colonial era, the white population was disproportionately male, and continued to be so throughout the eighteenth century, until the British began settling in their traditional style of whole families in the early nineteenth century.[120] But before that happened, widespread miscegenation between the Dutch and the non-white population—primarily the East Indian slaves, more so than the Africans[121]—produced a racially hybrid population, some of whom were absorbed into the white population, and some of whom became a separate half-caste group, known in the nineteenth and twentieth centuries as the Cape Coloreds.

In the early colonial years, the Dutch authorities welcomed additions to the free populations of the small, isolated colony, and accepted both miscegenation and mixed marriages.[122] Moreover, the Eurasian offspring of such marriages were classified and treated as Europeans, even if the marriages occurred after the children were born. By 1850, Eurasians constituted more than half of those officially classified as Europeans.[123] There were some social barriers against the hybrid Europeans, but nothing comparable to that in the United States, or in South Africa itself in the twentieth century. Moreover, they had the same legal rights as other Europeans. One of the early rulers of the colony had a noticeable trace of East Indian ancestry.[124]

The strategic importance of the Cape—on the main shipping lanes from Europe to Asia—attracted the British, who first took over the colony in 1795, relinquished it to the Dutch again in 1803, and then occupied it in 1806, making it part of the British Empire for nearly another century. British settlers added the fourth major ingredient to the South African population, along with black Africans, the Dutch, and East Indians.

The boundaries of the Cape Colony continually expanded, under both the Dutch and British, partly as a result of official imperial policy but mainly as a result of the unauthorized explorations and settlements of Dutch pioneers and nomads known as "trekboers." Their treks expanded the area of white occupation around the cape tenfold between 1703 and 1780. The trekboers, still reflecting their origins as an underclass in Holland, were described by a contemporary as a "miserable and lazy" class of whites.[125] Still, with European firearms—and sporadic colonial support in wars that broke out with local African tribes—they were able to push back, enslave, or otherwise subjugate the indigenous Africans. They became a rural ruling class—unlettered and unskilled, living primitively, but each master of an isolated farm or herd, and accustomed to rule over Africans.

The treks of these boers—ancestors of today's Afrikaners—were generally opposed by the colonial power, whether Dutch or British.[126] Rescuing or supporting them in their numerous clashes with African tribes was costly, but letting them lose or be annihilated by the Africans was intolerable politically. Colonial governments tried to restrain these freewheeling ventures with only limited effect. Around the trekboers developed a mystique of rugged individuals defying authority—and after the British takeover, defying foreign imperialist authority. By the early nineteenth century, there were already present in South Africa all the major ingredients of its later history—the mass of subjugated blacks, the divisions among the dominant minority of whites of British and Dutch ancestry and the small impotent group of East Indians and Cape Coloreds.

The imposition of British laws and values around the beginning of the nineteenth century created new frictions. The British did not share the Dutch tolerance for miscegenation[127] nor for the spread of Islam by the East Indians.[128] But the British also banned the slave trade in 1808, banned slavery itself in 1834, and applied laws to both blacks and whites. The idea that blacks had legal rights—that whites could be punished by the government for what they did to blacks—was shocking to the boers, accustomed to doing as they pleased in such matters. British judges and British missionaries were resented by the boers for interfering with their individual "rights" to subjugate the Africans in whatever way they saw fit.[129] Eventually, these frictions gave rise to the Great Trek of the 1820s to 1850s, in which organized parties called *Voortrekkers* set out heading northeast of the Cape Colony to migrate permanently beyond the jurisdiction of British colonial authorities.[130] This mass secession from British South Africa was at first a movement into vast vacant land, but then it became an incursion into the lands held by various African tribes who fought to defend it. Firearms enabled the outnumbered *Voortrekkers* to defeat the Africans and establish a series of "boer republics" based on the principle that there could be no equality between blacks and whites, not even formal equality before the law.

The victory of the boers was historic in many respects. It established independent, openly racist states, notably the Orange Free State and the Transvaal, northeast of the Cape Colony. It also welded the *Voortrekkers* into a people with a history, heroes, a mystique, and a new identity. They were now boers or Afrikaners, no longer simply Dutch (just as their language, Afrikaans, evolved to be different from its Dutch roots). By the middle of the nineteenth century, there was a white population of perhaps 40,000 people scattered over 100,000 square miles north of the Orange River.[131] The Afrikaners were a group and a power.

British power pursued the Afrikaners, first in the boer republic of Natalia, which became Natal after the British conquest of 1843. The discovery of diamonds in 1867 and gold in 1884 in areas controlled by the boers attracted the British (who had previously recognized boer independence in the Transvaal and the Orange Free State), bringing on two Anglo-Boer wars. British victory in 1902 brought the Transvaal, the Orange Free State, Natal, and the Cape together to form a new country called the Union of South Africa, independent but part of the British Commonwealth.

White supremacy was the cornerstone of this peace. The only part of the Union of South Africa in which blacks or coloreds had historically had effective political rights was the Cape. The British parliament assumed that these rights would with time spread out from the Cape to make the Union of South Africa a more tolerant place for non-whites.[132] In reality, the opposite happened, as the racism of the boer republics spread over all of South Africa. After World War I, southwest Africa was taken from Germany by the League of Nations and placed under the control of the contiguous Union of South Africa, bringing many more Africans under this regime.

From "Color Bar" to Apartheid

The Union of South Africa began its existence as a nation with a black majority which had significant rights only in the Cape area, a white minority that was more Afrikaner than British, a racially mixed "colored" group concentrated in the Cape, and East Indians from both the Dutch colonies in Asia and from India. The British were, and remained, economically dominant—owning and directing most of the business and industry of the country. The East Indians worked as small businessmen and traders. The native Africans lived primarily in rural areas.

The Afrikaners at this time still worked primarily in agriculture, but their population growth was rapidly filling up the land, forcing many to seek industrial work, especially in the newly developing

South African gold mines. A movement of Afrikaners towards the cities began with the end of the Anglo-Boer War and the founding of the Union of South Africa. But the Afrikaners proved to be unsatisfactory workers—noted for absenteeism and for quitting unexpectedly.[133] They not only lacked industrial skills but showed no great interest in or aptitude for acquiring them.[134] Work had never been a highly valued activity among Afrikaners. After generations of having black Africans doing their work for them, they had long considered it "a shame to work with their hands,"[135] or even to be employees.[136]

The mining companies resorted to importing more than 60,000 Chinese indentured laborers, and to training native black Africans, much to the anger of the Afrikaners. To add to the newly urbanized Afrikaners' resentments, blacks in Capetown at that time might share a bus seat, a park bench, or a stretch of beach with whites, and "colored" policemen might direct whites.[137] Physical proximity to blacks had never bothered Afrikaners in a rural setting where whites were overlords, exalted in an elaborate racial etiquette.[138] Associating and competing with non-whites in an impersonal urban setting was something else, however.

A violent strike in the South African mines in 1907 prepared the way for the first legislated "color bar" or racial employment barrier in South Africa—against the Chinese who were deported when their contracts expired.[139] Black Africans were next. The rise of African miners in the early twentieth century[140] was halted by the Mines and Works Act of 1911, which reserved all skilled work for whites.[141] Moreover, a ratio was specified between foremen (white) and laborers (blacks)[142]—a quota system for whites, destined to become more widespread in South Africa with the passing years. The inability of Afrikaners to maintain their historical privileges in open competition with non-whites was the key to these and later discriminatory laws. According to a noted white South African economist: "The most virulent among the white miners seemed to have been those who had not troubled to qualify themselves for promotion."[143]

The labor shortages of World War I caused South African mining companies to use blacks in higher levels of work than before, and post-war economic difficulties led the mining companies to continue the practice.[144] This provoked a general strike in 1921 that was "virtually an armed uprising" by white miners, most of whom were Afrikaners.[145] Thousands of troops, backed by tanks and bombers, were required to restore order. Estimates of the dead ranged from 150 to 220, and at least 500 were wounded. Having crushed the strike, the mining companies began lowering wages and laying off white workers. A court decision then invalidated the color bar, further undermining the position of the Afrikaners.[146] However, a political backlash swept a new government into power —a coalition of Afrikaner Nationalists and the South African Labor Party.

The new government enacted a stronger color bar, replaced black workers with white workers on the government-owned railroads, subsidized a similar replacement in municipal governments, and enacted a minimum wage law to reduce employers' incentives to use black workers.[147] Colored workers were informally eased out of many jobs as a result of government pressure.[148] Much of the racist program of this era was supported or initiated by politically left-wing individuals and groups, including socialists and Marxists.[149] Humanitarian demands for a "civilized labor policy" put further pressure on employers to pay wage rates that would price most Africans out of a job.[150] The Nationalist Party—representing at that time Afrikaner workers and farmers against British business interests—was also ready to intervene in the economy then, and many times thereafter.

Black Africans have never been allowed to compete in a free labor market. Beginning in colonial times, native Africans were forced off their land, not only by military means, but also by poll taxes that made it necessary for them to give up traditional subsistence farming or herding and enter the money economy of the whites.[151] Here they were forced to become contract laborers and prevented by stringent vagrancy laws from taking time to pick and choose their best opportunities.[152] Nevertheless, large disparities in wages between blacks and whites provided a constant temptation to South African employers to substitute the cheaper labor, even if surreptitiously.[153] In turn this provoked ever more stringent legislation to maintain white wages, jobs, and privileges.

Sometimes government intervention took the form of equal-pay-for-equal-work policies,[154] which destroyed the employer's incentive to hire blacks. Sometimes it took the form of occupational licensing in situations where only whites would be licensed.[155] Sometimes it took the form of government imposed educational "requirements" exceeding the educational level of most Africans.[156] Black entrepreneurs have also been hamstrung with government regulations forcing them out of areas with good prospects of profits.[157] Black farmers in South Africa have had to compete with more heavily subsidized white farmers.[158] Private capital has been restricted from entering the "native areas" of South Africa.[159]

South African whites have never relied on beating blacks in open market competition. They have relied much less than American racists, for example, on theories of innate genetic inferiority of blacks, and have accordingly termed themselves white supremacists rather than racists.[160]

In addition to numerous economic barriers, there have also been strict controls on where blacks could live in South Africa. The role permitted blacks in the cities was that of migrant workers, who were not allowed to settle there permanently. An overwhelmingly male black urban work force developed, with women being deliberately restricted in order to prevent the development of a permanent black urban class. But though these policies inhibited the permanent settlement of black individuals in the cities, they did not prevent the growth of permanent black urban enclaves with a large flow of individuals back and forth to the rural "native areas" of the country. Social barriers also confronted South Africa's blacks, coloreds and other non-whites. However, all these barriers had loopholes and regional variations in the stringency with which they were applied. The Afrikaner Nationalist Party proposed in 1948 to close these loopholes and to move systematically and pervasively to enshrine white supremacy with a national policy called *apartheid.* The proposal was ridiculed by the ruling United Party, a more moderate (though also segregationist and white supremacist) party supported by the British South Africans and less extremist Afrikaners, and headed by a former boer general, Jan Smuts. The surprising election victory of the Nationalist Party in 1948 marked the beginning of their political dominance in South Africa to the present day. It marked also the beginning of a greatly expanded government role in the economy and society, and the growth of a huge bureaucracy to administer increasingly detailed regulation of race relations in every aspect of South African life.[161]

Apartheid has meant the rigid separation of public facilities from buses to park benches, a banning of intermarriage and severe penalties for "immoral acts" between men and women of different races, the forcible removable of non-whites from the few racially mixed residential areas and their expulsion from the white colleges and universities of South Africa. So numerous and petty are the laws and regulations that about one third of all black African men are arrested and convicted of some offense annually.[162] Apartheid also applies segregation and discrimination to coloreds and East Indians, both of whom previously held many rights and privileges denied to blacks. Cape Coloreds lost the right to vote, for example.[163]

Apartheid also brought forth the doctrine of "separate development"—a deliberate attempt at preventing the adaptation of Africans to European languages, culture, or political ideas. The vast, barren "native areas" of South Africa were more formally made into "black homelands" controlled by tribal chiefs selected and supported by the South African government, and in 1976 one such area—the Transkei—was granted a cosmetic "independence." The doctrine of "separate development" was also applied to East Indians, coloreds, and to some extent even whites—with Afrikaner and British children in the Transvaal being taught in separate schools in different languages.[164]

Apartheid is a policy not simply of separation but of subordination, and even systematic humiliation, of non-whites. Running through its myriad applications is the principle that no white shall ever be subordinate to a non-white, nor shall they meet on a plane of equality or even apparent equality. One directive of the Minister of Bantu Administration declared that "no official shall shake hands with a black man."[165] Police raids on black areas "are almost invariably accompanied, at best, by gross discourtesy and manhandling."[166] Those few black Africans who have somehow managed to acquire a good education or a certain level of prosperity are all the more resented by white South Africans, especially Afrikaners and particularly policemen.[167]

In 1961, the Nationalist government of South Africa severed its last ties with Great Britain by leaving the British Commonwealth and declaring itself a republic. This was part of a general development of a siege psychology—and intense loyalty, among Afrikaners particularly—in the face of worldwide criticism of apartheid.

Population, Economy and Society

There are more than 18 million people in the Republic of South Africa. Black Africans constitute just over two-thirds of the population, whites about one-fifth, coloreds one-tenth and Asians 3 percent.[168] About one-third of the Africans live in urban areas[169] which have a larger black than white population.[170] About half of the country's total population still lives on the land, and this half creates only about 10 percent of the national output.[171]

Afrikaners are 60 percent of the white population,[172] and despite their emphasis on racial purity, their own racial composition is an estimated 7 percent non-white[173]—a legacy of the early miscegenation of colonial times, when nearly one-fourth of the marriages were intermarriages.[174] In the Cape Province today, between one-tenth and one-fourth of the individuals classified as "white" have non-white ancestors.[175]

Despite their political ascendancy for more than 30 consecutive years of Nationalist Party control of the central government, Afrikaners are still not economically on a parity with the British South Africans, who control most of the industry and commerce of the country. In mid-twentieth century South Africa, English-speaking whites in Durban had nearly double the per capita income of Afrikaans-speaking whites, and in Johannesburg 10 percent of the British families had annual incomes of £ 1,000, compared to less than 2 percent of the Afrikaner families.[176] Jews in South Africa are also more prosperous than the Afrikaners, as well as better educated. Traditionally, most of the British have supported the United Party, in opposition to the Nationalists, but in recent years they—together with South African Jews—have given increasing support to the more liberal Progressive Party.[177] Afrikaners are over-represented relative to the British in South Africa's police,[178] and have dominated those military posts not filled by conscription.[179] More than four-fifths of the army's permanent staff are Afrikaans-speaking.[180] Afrikaners have dominated government employment in the civil service as well, holding more than four-fifths of those entry level jobs open to whites.[181] Afrikaner domination of the higher levels of government is so complete that only one South African of British ancestry serves in an 18-member cabinet.[182]

Whites as a group have historically earned several times the annual income of blacks in South Africa,[183] and more than half the total income of the country,[184] though they are a minority of its population. Whites also own or occupy 87 percent of the country's land,[185] leaving the Africans with not only far less land but much poorer quality land, insufficient to feed themselves without the earnings of migrant workers in South African cities.[186] Over the years, as South Africa has industrialized and urbanized, its total real income per capita has risen rapidly.[187] In the cities, Africans earn more than double their incomes on "native reserves" and nearly double their incomes as employees on white farms.[188] Blacks have been receiving a slowly rising share of the national income since the 1930s.[189] During the mid-1970s, black incomes rose at a faster percentage rate than that of whites,[190] and small but increasing numbers of Africans have occupied skilled and sub-managerial positions.[191] But the painful slowness of the process may be illustrated by the fact that it was 1979 before textbooks for black school children were provided by the government; they had to buy their own before, while white school children received theirs free.[192] It was 1980 before there was a black police officer in charge of a police station.[193]

Black South Africans remain only partially acculturated to European values, language, and behavior. Only about half the urban Africans can express themselves in imperfect English or Afrikaans, and these proportions are progressively lower for urban African women and for rural Africans. Altogether, less than a third of black South Africans speak a European language. Moreover, whites often prefer to address blacks in some crude approximation of their native tongues and resent English-speaking Africans.[194] Nearly all Africans speak a Bantu language as their mother tongue.[195] Like other rural peoples, Africans have not acquired a sense of the value of time—punctuality, efficiency—that is essential to a commercial and industrial society. African customs expose the rare individual who achieves affluence to having his wealth dissipated by relatives —thereby reducing incentives to acquire it in the first place.[196] Moreover, the South African government's policies deliberately attempt to retard the blacks' acculturation by denying them permanent residence in the cities and trying to recreate tribal society and tribal authority in native "homelands."

The Cape Coloreds are about 10 percent of the South African

population,[197] and are about one-third Asian, one-third European, and one-third African in ancestry.[198] Sexual liaisons between the Hottentots and the trekboers who subjugated them added an African strain to the Eurasian coloreds produced in the early days of the Cape Colony.[199] As their names suggest, most Cape Coloreds (89 percent) live in and around Capetown.[200] Cape Coloreds are highly acculturated to European values and norms, and have been for generations. Most coloreds (89 percent) in South Africa speak Afrikaans—half speak only Afrikaans[201]—and most practice the Christian religion. Nationalist Party policy in the 1920s contemplated including the coloreds with the Europeans.[202] Only informal social barriers separated the coloreds from the whites at that time, and many of the more prosperous coloreds found entry to white society, including intermarriage, in the late nineteenth century.[203] These acculturation patterns go well back into the history of the country. Beginning in the 1830s, white missionaries operated schools for colored children, and some poor whites also attended.[204] Before apartheid disfranchised them, colored voters sometimes held the balance of power in close elections in some districts of the Cape Province.[205] Economically, the coloreds earn substantially more income than the blacks,[206] and have more skilled workers, though half of the colored remain unskilled.[207] South Africa's coloreds have been analogized to blacks in the United States:

> Both groups are descended to a large extent from slaves or quasi-slaves rather than indigenous groups that were conquered and allotted reservations under conditions that permitted them to retain substantial elements of their traditional culture. Both are of racially mixed origin, although there is a difference of degree.[208]

Internal color differences within the South African coloreds have been a divisive force,[209] as among American Negroes.[210] The lighter-skinned elite of both groups have been noted for a certain sterile gentility, a seeking of "acceptance" rather than achievement.[211] The South African coloreds are disdainful of and alienated from the black Africans,[212] and make little common cause with them politically, despite the resentments both feel toward apartheid.[213]

South Africa's non-white majority is fragmented—the Africans by tribal divisions among themselves,[214] by suspicions of the coloreds,[215] and by deep resentment of the entrepreneurial East Indians.[216] Among some of the more bitter or more politically active Africans, a counter-racism has developed against whites.[217] White South African brutalities such as the Sharpeville massacre in 1960 or the killing of Steve Biko by the police in 1977 add fuel to this anger. Yet the many predictions of the South African government's fall that have appeared over the years seem still to have little substance. The Nationalists have so changed the election laws and districts as to make it highly unlikely that any other party could win an election against them.[218] Moreover, the British who initially opposed apartheid have largely been co-opted to its support.[219] The rising anger and bitterness of the non-white protest has created a fear that any fundamental change would threaten all whites. Moreover, the strategic location of South Africa that first attracted the Dutch, and then the British, is still a weighty constraint on the policy of Western nations, especially the United States. More than half of Europe's oil supplies go around the Cape,[220] and the prospect of having an anti-Western or pro-Soviet regime at that location severely limits the extent to which Western nations can jeopardize the existing government there, however much their policies may be disapproved.

Moreover, South Africa's own economic and military power make it too formidable for any African nation to challenge. It produces 40 percent of the industrial output of the entire continent, including 80 percent of its steel,[221] and it has both the industrial and technological base to produce nuclear weapons.[222] Boycotts of South Africa enjoy a certain political popularity in the West, but boycotts have generally been ineffective against other countries, and are likely to be even more ineffective against a largely self-sufficient economy like that of South Africa, and a people like the Afrikaners who already have a siege psychology. The example of the Rhodesian transfer of political power to blacks is less apt than it might seem, for Rhodesia-Zimbabwe was not settled by Afrikaners. Even a few minor token concessions to non-whites by the Nationalist government in recent years have brought forth angry charges of betrayal by many Afrikaners.[223]

THE UNITED STATES

The first people of African ancestry were brought to colonial America in 1619. They were not all slaves (perhaps none were), but included indentured servants whose terms of servitude expired after a given number of years, leaving them free. By the 1660s, however, perpetual slavery was the fate of Africans brought to America.[224] Most of these slaves came from a narrow strip of the western coast of Africa—about half from what is now Angola and Nigeria, significant numbers from Ghana, Senegal, Gambia, and Sierra Leone, but some from as far away as Mozambique on the east coast.[225] Some came from the West Indies, which served as an intermediary point where Africans were trained for their new roles as slaves, but most came directly from Africa to North America.[226]

Altogether, about 400,000 slaves were imported into the area that would later become the United States—the British colonies on the North American continent and the vast French continental holdings later to be added by the Louisiana Purchase.[227] Most of the slaves were imported between 1741 and 1810.[228] At the time of the first U.S. census of 1790, blacks constituted nearly one-fifth of the country's population[229]—and only one fifth of the blacks had been born in Africa.[230] Unlike slaves in the rest of the Western Hemisphere, American Negroes were cut off from their African cultures early in their history. Half were American-born as early as 1680,[231] and the ability of the American slave population to reproduce itself—unique among slave populations of the Western Hemisphere[232]—meant that few Africans were imported as replacements. By the time slavery was abolished, 99 percent of the slaves in the United States were American-born,[233] unlike some Latin American slave societies where emancipation produced "African-born freedmen."[234]

While the Negro population of the United States was not formally divided into blacks and mulattoes (or coloreds), it was sharply divided into slave and free. The "free persons of color" were less than 10 percent of the Negro population in the first census of 1790. This increased to a high of 14 percent in the 1830 census, and was

11 percent in the census of 1860—the last census in which the distinction was made.[235] The overwhelming majority of the slaves were concentrated in the South,[236] whose climate and soil were suitable for the kinds of crops for which slavery was most feasible.[237] Outside the South, the picture was quite different: There were more than twice as many free Negroes as there were slaves, as early as 1810.[238] Northern blacks, though poor and socially pariahs, nevertheless had a long head start over southern blacks in their acculturation to American society. Even among slaves, those in the North were more urbanized and more likely to be house servants with opportunities to absorb the culture of the world around them:

> Northern slaves not only gained first-hand knowledge of their masters' world, but they also rubbed elbows with lower-class whites in taverns, cock-fights, and fairs where poor people of varying status mingled. . . . the cosmopolitan nature of cities speeded the transformation of Africans to Afro-Americans. Acculturation in the cities of the North was a matter of years, not generations.[239]

Actually, few slaves arrived in the North directly from Africa, but usually came from the South or the West Indies, "in two's or three's" but "rarely by the boatload."[240] The relatively small numbers of blacks dispersed among large numbers of whites speeded acculturation for both the free and the slave Negro populations of the North. This regional difference in acculturation was destined to remain an important factor in the history of black Americans.

Another historic factor was the American ideology of freedom and democracy—though often a bitter mockery to blacks, subjected to slavery, segregation, discrimination, and lynching. American democratic ideals in fact made it morally necessary to justify the treatment of blacks by a racist ideology more sweeping than anything found in less democratic societies, such as those of Latin America or even South Africa. The morality of slavery had seldom been a serious issue in most slave societies in history,[241] but because of the American ideal of freedom, the institution of slavery was an anachronism embroiled in controversy from the outset. The American Revolution heightened awareness of the contradiction, and most states outside the South abolished slavery in the decades immediately following independence.[242] Even in the South—where the financial vested interest in slavery was far greater—there were attempts to abolish slavery, led by such national figures as Thomas Jefferson, George Washington, and Patrick Henry. But the decisive figure proved to be Eli Whitney, whose invention of the cotton gin made the South the "cotton kingdom" of the world, and thereby made slavery far too profitable to be abolished voluntarily.

Most whites in the United States did not own slaves, and even those who did seldom had the number of slaves or the kind of affluence depicted in such fictional works as *Gone with the Wind*. In 1790, nearly one-fourth of all free American families owned slaves, but by 1850, that was down to 10 percent—and in both eras, the average slave-holding family had less than 10 slaves. In the South, however, nearly one-third of all free families owned slaves in 1850.[243]

Anglo-Saxon aversions to racial intermixture in the American colonies were greater than those found in Latin American colonies[244] or even among the boers in colonial South Africa.[245] Nonetheless, in colonial America as in South Africa, racial intermixture was far more common in the early years than in later history. For example, in seventeenth century Virginia, between one-fourth and one-third of the children born to white unwed mothers were mulattoes.[246] There were also some inter-racial marriages among people of financial substance[247] as well as among the poor,[248] though laws and social ostracism increasingly prevented this with the passing of time.[249]

Mulattoes in the United States, while generally more urbanized and acculturated than blacks as a group, were neither socially nor economically comparable to mulattoes in Latin America, Jamaica, or South Africa. In all these latter slave societies, where white women were scarce, mulattoes were typically the offspring of slave owners and slave women. In early colonial America, however, mulattoes were often the offspring of black men and white women[250]—a relationship viewed far less tolerantly. Moreover, mulattoes in colonial America "were usually the sons and daughters of lower-class whites rather than of rich planters and their slave concubines, as was generally the case in other New World slave societies."[251] American mulattoes were not from an upper class culture to the same extent as mulattoes elsewhere. There was less cultural difference, as well as no legal distinction, between American Negroes with differing amounts of white ancestry. Finally, mulattoes filled an important economic role in the rest of the Western Hemisphere (and to some extent, South Africa), by providing skilled manual labor in societies with no large white working class, and in which whites in general acquired a disdain for working with their hands. In the United States, there was a large white working class, eliminating any special need for mulattoes and permitting the larger society to restrict all Negroes—mulattoes or blacks—to low and menial tasks.

The Era of Slavery

Most blacks, for most of their history in America, were slaves. The experience of slavery has left its imprint on much of the later history of the American Negro. As in Brazil, the geographic distribution of blacks continued to reflect the concentration of slave plantations, long after emancipation. Approximately nine-tenths of all American Negroes were located in the South as late as 1910.[252] Work habits continued to reflect the resistance to work, and evasion of work, that had developed under slavery.[253] Slavery left its imprint on the white population as well, including the majority who owned no slaves. White supremacy remained for generations as much a watchword in the American South as in South Africa. Blacks were not conceived to have either legal or moral rights,[254] and when the federal government or individual blacks acted as if they did, mob violence, vigilante terrorism, and cynical twisting of the law in the South attempted to keep the Negro "in his place." As in South Africa, the masses of ill-educated, poorly skilled whites were the most vehement and violent in their assertions of white superiority. And, like South Africa, Brazil and other slave societies, the American South developed among its free white population an aversion and disdain for hard work, which was associated with slaves. The South was, and has remained, the poorest region of the United States—its white population being perennially poorer than other white Americans,[255] and especially so in those states of the deep South where slaves were concentrated.

De Tocqueville noted in the 1830s that, although white Americans in the South had the same racial and cultural background as those who settled other regions of the country, "the colonies in which there were no slaves became more populous and more prosperous than those in which slavery flourished."[256] Sailing down the

Ohio River between the slave state of Kentucky and the free state of Ohio—with similar climate and soil—de Tocqueville found the white population "ignorant and apathetic" on one side and full of "activity and intelligence" on the other[257]—with the land of the slave state being visibly less cultivated than that of the free state.[258] In Frederick Law Olmsted's well-chronicled travels through the South in the 1850s, he likewise found much "lazy poverty" among white southerners,[259] and when he did encounter highly efficient businesses or other organizations, they were disproportionately run by northerners, foreigners, or Jews.[260] A distinctive "southern way of life" developed during the antebellum era and endured long afterwards, even though the original settlers in the South were not initially different from the original settlers in the North or the British West Indies.[261] The South has been described as "not quite a nation within a nation, but the next thing to it."[262] As a leading Southern historian observed of the South:

> . . it is a land with a unity despite its diversity, with a people having common joys and common sorrows, and above all, as to the white folk a people with a common resolve indomitably maintained—that it shall be and remain a white man's country. The consciousness of a function in these premises, whether expressed with the frenzy of a demagogue or maintained with a patrician's quietude, is the cardinal test of a southerner and the central theme of southern history.[263]

Northern whites were not egalitarians. They were simply not preoccupied with the small numbers of blacks among them as southerners were with the large numbers of blacks among them. In 1790, blacks were 35 percent of the population of the South but only 3 percent of the population of the North—and these percentages were virtually unchanged in 1870. As late as 1940, blacks were 24 percent of the population of the South but only 4 percent of the population of the North.[264]

The purely material conditions of life—food, clothing, shelter— for slaves were not significantly worse than among contemporary white working class Americans, and were not as bad as conditions among some contemporary European peasant or working class people.[265] But slavery was much more than economic exploitation. In order to reduce escapes and force people to engage in uncompensated labor, blacks were deliberately kept illiterate, fearful of brutal punishments, and self-abasing in the presence of whites. The sudden ending of slavery in 1863 did not mean an equally sudden end of ignorance, fear, or subservience on the part of blacks—or of the expectation of such behavior on the part of whites. As in South Africa, those blacks who advanced furthest in education and prosperity were likely to be the most resented by whites, and especially by poor whites. In short, slavery not only inhibited the development of the education, work habits, or personal pride needed by free men; its ideological aftermath tended to penalize the development among blacks of these traits that were rewarded among other Americans.

Among the most tragic consequences of slavery were the forcible breakups of slave families by the sale of individuals, sometimes hundreds of miles away. Anguished partings of couples, or of parents and children, were among the many tragedies of slavery. Nearly one-sixth of adult Mississippi former slaves studied in 1864–65 had been forcibly separated from a spouse.[266] The immediate post-Civil War era saw masses of blacks searching for lost members of their families, often across hundreds of miles, and even as late as the 1880s black newspapers were filled with advertisements from people still trying to locate family members from whom they had been separated under slavery.[267] In short, many black families were torn apart under slavery, but the family as an institution remained important to blacks. Post-war studies showed that most black couples in their 40s had been together 20 years or more.[268] Moreover, most black children were raised in two-parent families during the era of slavery.[269] A high incidence of female-headed families among blacks was not a legacy of slavery but a development that emerged well into the twentieth century.

Along with the enslaved blacks, there developed a small but growing class of free Negroes. There were nearly half a million "free persons of color" in 1860, compared with about 4 million slaves.[270] Free Negroes were about equally divided between North and South,[271] while slaves were concentrated in the South, and especially the deep South.[272] While slaves were concentrated in rural areas, free persons of color were about equally divided between rural and urban areas.[273]

The fate of free Negroes depended to a large extent on the changing conditions of slavery. In the early seventeenth century, when the non-white population (free or in bondage) was so small and so acculturated as to attract little notice, free Negroes exercised most of the rights of whites of similar socioeconomic condition.[274] With the mass importation of African slaves toward the end of the century came "black codes" enacted to control both enslaved and free Negroes—the latter being seen as a danger to slavery by their very existence as examples of free black people, quite aside from whatever knowledge, incitement, or aid in escaping they might provide to their brothers in bondage.

Life was made particularly intolerable for free Negroes in areas with concentrations of slave plantations, with the result that "free persons of color" began migrating toward the upper South, toward urban areas, and toward the North, at the same time that the slave population was steadily moved in the opposite direction—southwestward to the cotton growing black belt of the deep South.[275] By 1860, the proportion of free Negroes to slaves was less than 1 percent in the black belt states of Mississippi, Alabama, Georgia, Arkansas, and Texas, while "free persons of color" were nearly half the Negro population of Maryland, more than three-quarters in the District of Columbia and over 90 percent in Delaware.[276] Rights historically enjoyed by free Negroes were increasingly restricted or abolished. They lost the right to vote, to testify in court, to live or work where they wanted to, to peaceably assemble or to bear arms, to use public facilities, or even to educate their own children at their own expense in private schools.[277] Not all these rights were lost completely in all places or at the same time. But the passing decades of the early nineteenth century saw a pervasive retrogression in the legal rights of free Negroes throughout the country, and especially in the deep South.[278]

Despite the spread of oppressive legal and political restrictions, the "free persons of color" advanced economically. Property ownership among free Negroes in Virginia doubled between 1830 and 1860.[279] Real estate owned by Negroes in Tennessee tripled between 1850 and 1860, though the Negro population of the state increased by less than 20 percent during that span.[280] Georgia, Alabama, Florida, and Maryland showed similar patterns.[281] In New Orleans, where the most prosperous community of "free persons of color" lived,[282] their property ownership rose from about $2.5 million in 1836 to more than $13 million by 1860.[283] Urban areas were the most favorable to economic advancement[284] and for acquiring education. Literacy was the rule rather than the exception among urban free Negroes,[285] even in states where they were forbidden to attend either public or private schools. Clandestine private schools for free Negro children flourished throughout the South.[286]

Cities were also centers of miscegenation. In 1860, one-fourth of the Negro population of Charleston, South Carolina, was of racially mixed ancestry, and in New Orleans the proportion was virtually one-half.[287] Free colored women in New Orleans outnumbered free colored men by more than two-to-one in the middle of the nineteenth century, at a time when white men in that city outnumbered white women nearly as much.[288] Sex imbalances were common in contemporary southern cities, leading to racially mixed children in the United States as in other nations under similar circumstances.

The historic significance of the antebellum "free persons of color" reached well beyond the era in which they were legally differentiated from the rest of the black population. The social differentiation of this class and its descendants reached well into the twentieth century, and has by no means entirely disappeared today. They were literally generations ahead of other Negroes in education, urbanization, acculturation, and economic conditions. As early as 1850, three-fifths of all "free persons of color" were literate,[289] but as late as 1900 the Negro population as a whole had not yet reached that level of literacy.[290] In the mid-nineteenth century, "free persons of color" were more urbanized than contemporary whites, and more urbanized than the black population as a whole would be until 1940.[291]

These head starts had enduring consequences. An 1868 survey in Nashville showed that "more than half of the leading 'colored men of property' in this city had been freed before the general Emancipation." A majority of the Negro delegates to the Louisiana Republican Convention in 1865 and the South Carolina Constitutional Convention in 1868 were free-born.[292] Of those delegates to the first meeting of the American Negro Academy in 1897 who had been born before 1865, most had been born free.[293] As late as the 1940s, a survey of the students at the leading black institution of higher learning, Howard University, showed that half were descendants of the antebellum "free persons of color,"[294] who were only 11 percent of the Negro population of that time. Most black college students were descendants of "free persons of color" until the post-World War II era,[295] when the G.I. bill enabled the children of the black masses to attend college. Most of the black leadership on into the twentieth century were the descendants of antebellum "free persons of color," including the black founders of the NAACP. Most black holders of doctoral degrees in the mid-twentieth century were also descendants of the antebellum "free persons of color," as were most Negroes who worked as professionals in the nation's capital.[296] The most successful high schools for blacks in the twentieth century were located in cities that had historically had the largest concentrations of antebellum "free persons of color."[297] As with other groups around the world, historic advantages in acculturation had enduring consequences for generations to come.[298]

From Emancipation to Civil Rights

The Reconstruction era after the Civil War saw a sudden rise of blacks to political prominence during the occupation of the South by federal troops. Blacks held office from the local level to both houses of Congress. Some southern state legislatures even had a majority of Negroes. In Washington, there were thirteen black congressmen and two black senators.[299] In general, these political developments had little effect on the economic condition of the mass of newly freed blacks. The white reaction to all these political developments, imposed by an army of occupation, included widespread terrorist attacks by vigilante groups, of which the best known was the Ku Klux Klan. The mass of blacks continued to live in fear of such groups for generations.

With the passing years, the hostility of southern whites toward the Reconstruction policies of the federal government continued, while the support of northern liberals waned. Finally, the Compromise of 1877 ended federal occupation of the South and returned political control of the region to southern whites. Blacks were disfranchised, driven from office, and increasingly segregated. Increasing numbers were also lynched—161 in the peak year of 1896.[300]

In the North during the same period, discrimination against the relatively small number of blacks there was declining—in voting, in public accommodations, and in housing. Most of the big northern cities—New York, Chicago, Detroit, Philadelphia, Cleveland

—had no all-black neighborhoods, nor even 50 percent black neighborhoods, for blacks were widely distributed within these cities.[301] In nineteenth century Detroit, black physicians and dentists had predominantly white patients.[302] The leading caterers in Philadelphia were black—and their clientele was white.[303] In Chicago as well, there were black businesses whose customers were mostly white.[304] In Michigan and Ohio, black politicians were elected by predominantly white voters.[305] Throughout the North, there seemed to be a basis for optimism about the future of race relations. Then suddenly, in the first decade of the twentieth century, it all began to change.

The black populations of northern cities had long been augmented by migrants from the South, but the beginning of the twentieth century saw an enormous increase in numbers, changing the social composition of northern black population. The record-breaking migration of the decade from 1900 to 1910 was nearly *tripled* in the next decade, and that in turn was nearly doubled again during the 1920s,[306] when nearly three-quarters of a million blacks migrated out of the South.[307]

The rural southern black migrants were typically far less acculturated than the older black residents of the northern cities. Like other groups of acculturated people who had gained a measure of social acceptance by the larger society, the northern blacks bitterly resented the newcomers—"uneducated and completely unaccustomed to urban surroundings"[308]—whose behavior now threatened the standing of the whole group. Black northerners, including the contemporary black newspapers, denounced them as ignorant, vulgar, rowdy, unwashed and criminal.[309] As these southern-born blacks became a majority of the northern black population, northern whites began to erect barriers against *all* blacks—in jobs, housing, and social activities. The southern vigilante terrorism of the Ku Klux Klan began to appear for the first time in northern cities. The first residential segregation law was passed in Baltimore in 1911, and was quickly copied by other cities.[310] Even in cities where blacks had been living in white neighborhoods for decades, rigid segregation now appeared, and attempts by blacks to move in among whites were met with mob violence, shootings, and bombings.[311]

The black ghettoes that were to become an enduring feature of American cities took shape during this era. Harlem was first, but as late as 1910 Harlem was still predominantly white.[312] With

almost overnight suddenness, neighborhoods with some blacks became all black, as whites fled and southern migrants poured in. In
Cleveland, for example, while the black population tripled in the
early twentieth century, the number of census tracts with *no* blacks
in them increased.[313] So did the number of all-white elementary
schools,[314] in a city where school integration had occurred in the
1840s.[315]

As northern whites erected barriers against blacks, elite north-
ern-born blacks also raised social barriers against the southern-born
black masses. Class distinctions and exclusions within the black
community became more pronounced during this era, as the educated and sophisticated elements put distance between themselves
and the black masses.[316] These social traits were often associated
with skin color differences, given the historical head start of mulattoes among the urbanized "free persons of color." Before the
great migrations, more than one-fourth of all northern urban
Negroes were recorded by the census as mulattoes[317]—half or
more white—but this proportion dropped as the descendants of
slave field hands flooded into the northern cities.

Ironically, it was precisely the same mulatto elite that excluded
other blacks which launched a nationwide attack on white exclusions of blacks, marked by the founding of the National Association
for the Advancement of Colored People in 1909. The NAACP's
continued dominance by the mulatto elite caused some other blacks
to call it the National Association for the Advancement of *Certain*
People. The NAACP agenda reflected the priorities of the elite—
equal access to white institutions and white neighborhoods, enabling them to escape the black masses. Given the poverty of the
black masses, who at this point could not afford to buy homes in
any neighborhood, or to attend any colleges or theaters, or to stay
at hotels or go to concerts, it is difficult to understand the emphasis
of the NAACP during this era on public accommodations and
restrictive covenants without understanding the class composition
of the people who ran it. Similarly, it is difficult to explain the bitter
antagonism between this group and Booker T. Washington by their
respective agendas—which were identical in content and differed
only in priorities[318]—without understanding that Washington was
"up from slavery" and had as his central preoccupation the development of the black masses in the rural south, while DuBois centered his concern on what he called "the talented tenth" of the race.

This social difference was reflected also in Booker T. Washington's easy rapport with rural southern Negroes,[319] while DuBois remained distant and aloof from the black masses in whose name he so often spoke.[320]

Despite ideological caricatures of his position, Booker T. Washington never renounced civil rights. Throughout his career he took the position that "all privileges of the law be ours"[321] but that was simply not his main thrust. He believed that "political activity alone" could not save the Negro for "back of the ballot you must have property, industry, skill, economy, intelligence and character . . ."[322] The posthumous publication of Booker T. Washington's papers revealed that he had secretly financed court challenges to Jim Crow laws,[323] while remaining publicly removed from politics, as a means of safeguarding the philanthropic and political support necessary to continue his work among rural blacks in the South. The mulatto elite saw Washington—quite correctly—as preoccupied with the descendants of slave field hands,[324] and with little interest in the fate of people like themselves.

Both in the North and the South, the black masses advanced, though slowly. At the turn of the century, nearly half of all blacks were illiterate, but that was down to a quarter by 1920 and to less than half of that by 1940.[325] Mortality rates also declined, though remaining above the national average, which was also declining at about the same rate.[326] The occupational advancement of blacks occurred not only over the generations, but also during the careers of given individuals. While about half of all young black males in 1920 were farmers and farm workers, by the time they were in their 50s and 60s in 1960, only 11 percent still worked in such occupations.[327] In 1939, the average income of black workers was approximately 41 to 45 percent of the average income of white workers, but by 1960 the percentage had risen to between 60 and 67 percent.[328] On the political and legal fronts, blacks gained some minor concessions during the early decades of the great migrations but by and large this was a period of political retrogression nationally.

During the decade of the 1960s, under "equal opportunity" laws and policies, blacks rose substantially in incomes and occupations —both absolutely and relative to whites.[329] During the 1970s, under preferential treatment or "affirmative action" policies, the relative rise leveled off—though the latter policies created far more resentment by whites, and broke up the historic alliance between black and Jewish organizations that had long fought together for civil rights.

Blacks have exhibited the classic patterns of social pathology among groups attempting to move into a modern urban economy without the skills, traditions, or experience for it. Blacks have had higher than average incidences of crime, disease, educational problems, and families on welfare.[330] Rates of crime and violence among blacks have been so high that in some years there were more black than white murder victims *in absolute numbers,* though blacks are only about 11 percent of the population.[331]

An assessment of black progress or the black position today would depend on the basis chosen for comparison. Blacks remain below the national average economically. But despite historically unique forms and degrees of discrimination and oppression, blacks are not today economically unique. Blacks do not have the lowest incomes or occupations or the highest incidence of broken homes.[332] Blacks are today one of a number of low income American racial or ethnic groups with a number of serious economic and social problems. Blacks are unique only in how far they have come and the degree of opposition they have encountered.

PART II

Analysis

CHAPTER FIVE

An International Perspective

Racial and ethnic comparisons are difficult enough, without the additional complications of making such comparisons across very different societies and for different periods of history. The purposes of such comparisons cannot go beyond these limitations. Yet even within these constraints, there are important implications to be drawn from racial and ethnic history, viewed internationally. Some of these implications reach beyond questions of race and ethnicity, and provide insights into larger questions of how whole societies function and malfunction.

GROUP DIFFERENCES

Culture

Racial and ethnic groups differ enormously in their economic performances, whether in their respective homelands—where climatic and geographic differences complicate comparisons—or in other countries under the same climatic, geographic, legal and political conditions. Generations of German and Scotch-Irish immigrants settled along hundreds of miles of the great mountain valleys of the eastern United States, stretching southward from Pennsylvania through Maryland, Virginia, and the Carolinas, but they lived both separately and differently. The Germans prospered and the Scotch-

Irish produced some of the most enduring pockets of poverty to be found among white Americans. Both groups were predominantly family farmers, and usually the Scotch-Irish pioneered a little ahead of the Germans, so that the Scotch-Irish had the first choice of the best land—and yet they never did as well with it as the German farmers. The differences in their work habits were symbolized by the difference between the log cabins that the Scotch-Irish made a prominent feature of the American frontier—because it required little skill or equipment to build[1]—and the huge barns and sturdy houses laboriously constructed by the Germans.[2] The same kinds of contrasts are found throughout southeast Asia—most strikingly between the indigenous peoples and the overseas Chinese, though various immigrants from India and elsewhere have also prospered there in the midst of poverty-stricken natives. In Brazil and Argentina, vast natural resources remained untapped and other opportunities unused by the Portuguese and Spanish settlers, until a new agriculture and whole new industries were created by German, Italian, and Japanese immigrants.[3] Again, those who were there first—and who retained political control throughout—did little or nothing with the objective conditions which others developed to unsuspected heights.

The point here is not to praise, blame, or rank whole races and cultures. The point is simply to recognize that economic performance differences are quite real and quite large. Simple and obvious as this point may seem, it goes counter to many prevailing approaches, doctrines, and conclusions.

Much of the literature on racial, national, and cultural groups attempts to be neutral on group differences. A leading scholar on race and ethnicity has "consciously tried to avoid any invidious value judgments concerning the various cultures" studied.[4] Against the historical background of bias, bigotry, and sweeping stereotypes on group and national differences, this agnosticism or cultural relativism is understandable and perhaps laudable in intent. But to ignore the large role that performance differences have played in human history is to ignore or misdiagnose important causal factors at work in that history. Cultures are ultimately ways of accomplishing things, and the differing efficiencies with which they accomplish different things determine the outcomes of very serious economic, political, and military endeavors. Much of the oppression in the world would not be possible if some groups did not have heavier firepower, more effective technology, or greater wealth, than others. Moreover, those enjoying the benefits of a particular culture's advantages have every *practical* reason to want to preserve that culture, even aside from emotional ties or "invidious" perceptions. *It is not simply a matter of how one chooses to look at it.*

Cultures need not even have different efficiencies in order for cultural preservation to be an important practical concern rather than simply arbitrary chauvinism. The Spanish language may be just as effective a vehicle for conveying ideas as the English language, and yet an overwhelmingly English-speaking society may have a legitimate stake in seeing to it that its Hispanic citizens learn English, because of large costs imposed by internal *differences* in language, even if neither language is "superior." Sheer numbers may determine the relative costs of having one group rather than another change its language or add a second language. But such decisions cannot be reduced to mere chauvinism, insensitivity, or other purely subjective attitudes or "perceptions." There are real costs involved in having a tower of Babel—independently of how one chooses to look at it. The printing of ballots, directions, and other public communications in a multiplicity of languages is only one of these costs, and by no means the largest. People lose their lives when they cannot communicate in an emergency with paramedics, firemen, or policemen. Culturally Balkanized nations have repeatedly fallen victim to internal disintegration or to conquests by more united peoples. The peoples of Africa have paid a staggering price for the geographic barriers that have fragmented that continent and made them prey to peoples from other lands. Cultural Balkanization is a man-made analogue to this cruel happenstance of nature.

Some cultures have been more technologically or organizationally effective than others during one historical epoch, and vice versa during other epochs. The relative power of Egypt and Israel are quite different today than in the time of the Pharoahs. China today no longer enjoys the great technical and organizational superiority it once had over Europe. In short, even from an efficiency standpoint, one culture is not categorically or permanently superior to another. But that is very different from denying, or averting our eyes from, major cultural advantages that may exist at any given historical juncture. The massive borrowing of particular items by one culture from another—the Europeans' abandoning of Roman numerals in favor of Arabic numerals, for example—suggests that these practical advantages are valued by most cultures, that cultural relativism is a luxury in which few can indulge. Consequential decisions cannot be equated with merely subjective status rankings.

Forcible attempts to stamp out cultures—Czarist Russia's brutal attempts to "Russify" the Jews, for example—seldom succeed, and cause needless human suffering in the attempt. Even well-meaning nineteenth century American reformers' attempts to "American-ize" the immigrants usually produced more resentment than accul-turation. But the very immigrant groups that bitterly resisted organized Americanization programs controlled by others have—selectively, and at their own pace—become thoroughly American-ized over the generations. In the process, other Americans have adopted many foods, words, and practices that were once limited to particular ethnic groups. In short, people eventually tend to recognize and avail themselves of the benefits of other cultures, whether they are a majority or a minority.

The degree to which acculturation has been a prerequisite for economic advancement has varied greatly from group to group. Those who do not require employment by others—because they are independent farmers or businessmen, or are employed by their own people—have less need to acculturate in order to prosper. The Chinese in southeast Asia have been able to maintain separate cultures and communities, and yet dominate the economies of their host countries. German farmers prospered in eighteenth and nine-teenth century America and Brazil, despite linguistic and cultural separatism. So have Italians in Argentina. Immigrant Jewish work-ers in nineteenth and twentieth century New York found Jewish employers, permitting them to continue speaking Yiddish and ob-serving their Sabbath. Even where there have been substantial linguistic and other cultural differences between employers and employees, labor contractors have bridged the language gap by recruiting and supervising the workers, and supplying them with the kinds of foods and other amenities peculiar to their culture. But for groups lacking sufficient numbers of their own employers or labor contractors, and living chiefly as urban employees, the ability to communicate and cooperate with people from other cultures is crucially important economically. Hispanics who grow up in Eng-lish-speaking homes in the United States have higher incomes and more education than Hispanics who grow up in Spanish-speaking homes.[5]

Much contemporary social philosophy proceeds as if different patterns of group "representation" in various occupations, institutions, activities, or income levels must reflect discriminatory decisions by others—that is, as if there were no substantial cultural or other differences among the various groups themselves. Yet this key assumption is nowhere demonstrated and is in many ways falsified. Even in activities in which no discrimination is possible, people are not proportionately represented. Activities solely within the discretion of the individual—choices among television programs to watch or card games to play, the age of marriage, or the naming of children—show widely differing patterns between different racial, ethnic, and national groups.

The cultural advantages that enable some groups to advance faster—and particularly to advance from poverty to affluence—need not be specific skills. The Chinese who immigrated into southeast Asia or to the United States usually had little to offer besides a monumental ability to work hard and long, and to save their money. Even with groups who had useful job skills—such as the eastern European Jews who entered the garment industry in the United States—their greatest success came ultimately in other fields, using new skills acquired by education or experience. Attitudes and work habits are often more crucial—and take longer to acquire—than do specific skills. The Chinese's aptitude for arduous and painstaking work—demonstrated in numerous manual occupations in southeast Asia and the United States—readily produced scientists and mathematicians in both places, when the opportunities arose. But groups without such traits seldom choose science and mathematics as fields of study, even when they are financially able to reach the college or university level.

As noted in Chapter 2, although there are approximately equal numbers of Chinese and Malays in Malaysian colleges and universities, the Chinese outnumber the Malays by more than eight-to-one in the sciences and fifteen-to-one in engineering.[6] Similarly, in the United States, although Hispanics with doctoral degrees outnumber Asians with doctoral degrees by two-to-one in history,[7] Asian doctorates outnumber Hispanic doctorates by more than seven-to-one in mathematics and by ten-to-one in chemistry.[8] While a

Mexican American scholar refers candidly to "our nonscientific culture,"[9] much contemporary literature proceeds as if different group representation in various occupations is nothing but a result of institutional discrimination. Black doctorates in the United States outnumber Asian doctorates nearly three-to-one in history,[10] but are outnumbered by Asian doctorates by six-to-one in mathematics and nearly nine-to-one in chemistry.[11] More than half of all doctoral degrees received by American Negroes are in education,[12] a notoriously undemanding field of study[13] and a less remunerative field of work. So are half the doctoral degrees received by American Indians, not one of whom received a doctorate in mathematics or physics in 1980.[14]

Wide-ranging disparities in fields of study are common, not only among racial or ethnic groups, but between men and women as well.[15] Nor is this a criticism of those who choose the less demanding and less remunerated fields. Behind such choices are many factors, including the quality of previous education and the amount of mathematics taken or mastered. There is ample evidence that these factors differ enormously from group to group.[16] Third-party observers can hardly claim to weigh these factors better than the individuals concerned, and so are in no position to second-guess the trade-offs chosen. But given what choices have been made, neither can disparities in occupational "representation" be automatically attributed to employers. Nor can income differences between people at the "same educational level, measured by degrees or years of schooling (omitting field of specialization or level of competence) be regarded as decisive evidence of discrimination. The prevailing assumption of equal group representation or equal income in the absence of discrimination flies in the face of overwhelming evidence of pronounced patterns that follow each group around the world.

These historic cultural differences cannot be reduced to socioeconomic "disadvantage" in "society." Black American, Mexican American, and American Indian students from families with incomes of $50,000 *a year and up* still do not score as high on the mathematics portion of the Scholastic Aptitude Test as do Asian American students from families with incomes of $6,000 *and below.*[17] Asian Americans as a group also outscore white Americans as a group on the mathematics portion of the S.A.T.[18] This is a repetition of international patterns among the same groups in different countries. The Japanese in Japan have a much higher proportion of their college population specializing in mathematical and technical fields than do American college students. And no one familiar with the perseverance of the Chinese in numerous occupations around the world and down through history should be surprised at their prominence or "over-representation" in disciplines like mathematics and science that demand such persistent application.

Among the economically important cultural differences between racial or ethnic groups are in their respective attitudes toward manual and "menial" labor. Many whites in societies in which blacks were enslaved came to associate hard, manual or "menial" labor with the race to which they felt superior. A Brazilian proverb says: "Work is for Negroes and dogs."[19] In colonial South Africa, the white man considered it "a shame to work with his hands."[20] In the United States, in the antebellum South, "to work industriously and steadily, especially under the direction of another man, is in the southern tongue, to 'work like a nigger.' "[21]—something to be avoided like the plague. German, Italian, and Japanese immigrants to Brazil, who arrived largely *after* slavery was abolished, were not handicapped by such attitudes. Nor were the many immigrants to the United States, most of whom arrived after the Civil War and the great bulk of whom settled outside the South, even in the antebellum era. Many of the immigrant groups who rose to prosperity, even past the native European populations of Brazil or the United States, did so by a willingness to apply themselves to hard, dirty and "menial" tasks. The Chinese and Japanese in the United States began almost exclusively in such tasks.

While there might be a certain poetic justice in the economic handicaps that slavery created for the white members of slave societies, the enduring stigma of hard, manual, or menial labor has produced an anti-work ethic handicapping blacks as well.[22] Blacks in Brazil and the United States showed remarkably similar historical patterns of resistance to the inherent requirements and constraints of labor markets, in the wake of emancipation from slavery—including a reluctance to accept responsibility and self-discipline,[23] and preoccupation with status aspects of work[24]—"fascination for occupations that seemingly or actually conferred status,"[25] as a Brazilian observer noted. Even the enterprising West Indian blacks in the United States have long had a "distinct aversion for manual labor."[26] Both in Brazil and in the United States, there has emerged a class of black men who have disdained regular work altogether, in favor of living off women, casual labor and petty crime.[27] In both countries, especially in the early years after emancipation, blacks have shown an attitude of ridicule toward individuals and groups who sacrificed current amenities for future economic advancement.[28] Examples of other groups who began in poverty and rose to prosperity have tended to produce anger rather than emulation, even when these were nonwhite groups such as West Indian immigrants or Vietnamese refugees in the United States.

The passing generations have also brought forth a new class of black Americans—"strivers" or "bootstrappers"—who have followed the historic pattern of others struggling upward from poverty to affluence, and taking pride in their lowly origins. But even such famous black Americans as Joe Louis, Nat "King" Cole, and multi-millionaire publisher John H. Johnson—people who have won a measure of respect from white Americans for themselves and their race—have been disdained by the old mulatto elite, preoccupied with status traditions inherited from the era of slavery.[29]

Cultural differences have been enduring over the generations, as well as prominent at a given time. The British in South Africa still have substantial economic advantages over Afrikaners, though the latter have been in the country more than three centuries and the British nearly two centuries. The Chinese continue to dominate the economies of many southeast Asian nations, as they have for centuries. The descendants of antebellum "free persons of color" in the United States still remain greatly over-represented among American Negro leaders and high achievers more than a century after all blacks were freed, and northern blacks still score higher on I.Q. tests than southern blacks.[30]

The magnitudes and persistence of cultural differences have grim implications for attempts to create programs to "solve" the "problem" of intergroup differences in income, education, etc., within a time horizon that is politically relevant to elected officials. What can be done politically in the short run is to (1) make visible, symbolic appointments from among the already more fortunate and more acculturated members of disadvantaged groups, (2) create the appearance of "concern" or "compassion" by giving well-heralded benefits earmarked for particular groups, and (3) blame all remaining differences ("inequities") on those who oppose these cosmetic and divisive policies. *Long-run* political policies are almost a contradiction in terms, in societies where politicians are elected in the short run. Even in autocratic societies, repeated drastic changes in policy toward the Jews in Europe and the Chinese in southeast Asia suggest that neither benign nor sinister policies are likely to remain stable, where race, ethnicity, and politics are combined.

Race and Racism

There is a widespread view that "race is an epiphenomenon devoid of intrinsic significance,"[31] and that South African whites, for example, "have created the 'racial problem' " there.[32] But being appalled by the policies of South Africa does not imply a belief that the whole problem is in the minds of racists, in South Africa or elsewhere. As already noted, intergroup differences are real, large, and enduring —whether these groups differ racially, culturally, or in other ways. Race may have no *intrinsic* significance, and yet be associated historically with vast cultural differences that are very consequential for economic performance, physical health, personal safety, and political stability—regardless of whether racism is a major element in people's subjective attitudes. It is widely agreed that racism has been far less of a factor in Brazilian history than in the history of the United States, and yet black-white economic differences are greater in Brazil than in the United States, where cultural differences between the races have historically been less. Race may have no *intrinsic* significance in either country, but it is correlated with very real differences in skills, attitudes, values, and experience, all of which are very consequential. Combining people of vastly different cultures in one country has never been easy, whether in northern Ireland, southeast Asia, Lebanon, or in black or white nations on the African continent. Racism is one tragic consequence of these difficulties, not the sole creator of the problem.

Racism is a term used to cover so many different kinds of behavior that it is difficult to pin down a specific meaning. "Racism" can be used legitimately as a term of moral denunciation of racially discriminatory behavior, and no confusion results so long as that is understood to be its sole purpose and significance. Confusion and illogic result when this general usage alternates with a more specific designation of racism as a belief in the genetic inferiority of various peoples. From the standpoint of moral culpability, South Africa must surely be one of the most racist nations in all history. But such racial policies in South Africa long antedate any general concern with, or awareness of, genetic theories, and even today genetic theories or beliefs do not play anywhere near the role in South Africa that they did in Nazi Germany or in the American South.

Blacks were not enslaved because of theories of biological inferiority. Such theories followed in the wake of slavery, and were not even the first rationalization used. Only after religious rationalizations for slavery began to run into difficulties were biological rationalizations substituted, both in South Africa and in the United States.[33] In Brazil, biological rationalizations for slavery were never central, for "defenders of slavery on purely racist grounds were as rare among public supporters of slavery in Brazil as they were common in the United States."[34] Non-racist slavery was common in the ancient Greek and Roman worlds.[35] In short, racism is neither necessary nor sufficient to explain slavery—or discrimination, for that matter. As noted in earlier chapters, the Chinese and the Jews have been subjected to discrimination and violence in many nations for many centuries, without any general belief that they were biologically inferior. Conversely, a man like Arthur Jensen, whose work has led him to conclude that the races are genetically different in intellectual potential, may nevertheless decide that the magnitudes involved are sufficiently small and sufficiently variable from individual to individual that it still pays to judge each person as an individual, regardless of race.[36]

The question is not about the "right" or "best" definition of the word "racism." Words are servants, not masters. The real problem is to avoid *shifting* definitions that play havoc with reasoning. The extent to which discriminatory behavior is related to biological beliefs is an empirical question rather than a foregone conclusion. On a practical level, opponents of discrimination can dissipate considerable energy fighting tangential issues if they are not clear about their priorities.

The complex issues revolving around genetic versus environmental explanations of intergroup I.Q. differences have often been reduced to ideological simplicities by those who see a stark choice between (1) accepting racial inferiority doctrines and (2) blaming tests for being biased, unreliable, or irrelevant. But here again, very real and very consequential differences can exist between groups for historical reasons, even if race has no intrinsic or genetic importance. No one seriously doubts that black Americans as a group play better basketball than white Americans or that Jews are disproportionately represented among the great violinists of the world, whether or not these results have anything to do with genes or religion. In short, high *correlations* can exist between race (or nationality, religion, sex, etc.) and some important trait, whether or not race is the *cause* of that trait. A test may be both valid and valuable as a predictor, whether or not it measures innate ability. To condemn a test for revealing consequential differences is to condemn those who are disadvantaged to remain handicapped by undiagnosed or misdiagnosed problems.

Implicit in much of the controversy over I.Q. differences is the assumption that environmental differences would be easily correctable, while hereditary differences would not. As long as assumptions remain implicit, they do not confront evidence. In reality, far more dramatic changes have been achieved in genetically determined plant and animal characteristics by selective breeding than have been achieved in environmentally determined characteristics such as regional or national differences in automobile driving habits, attitudes toward education, or respect for the rights of others. Genetically determined nearsightedness may be readily correctable by eyeglasses, while environmentally determined habits of overeating may resist numerous efforts to change. The very survival of the Jewish culture and religion is evidence of the extreme difficulty of changing environmental characteristics, despite centuries of efforts at absorption of the Jews by church and state across the continent of Europe.

Also implicit in the I.Q. controversy is the notion that mental tests are not only intellectually invalid, but morally "unfair" if they do not measure "real" or innate ability. But there is no more individual merit in having received a windfall gain in the form of brain cells rather than in the form of encyclopedias or private schooling. Each individual is born into a world he never made, with a brain he never made. His moral claims are no greater or less, whether heredity or other circumstances beyond his control gave him his advantages or disadvantages. Similarly, his value to society is the same, whether that value originated inside his head, or inside his home or school, or among his companions.

While the complex evidence on genetic and environmental components of intelligence keeps specialists embroiled in controversy, this evidence also seriously undermines many popular simplistic theories of intergroup differences, whether genetic or environmental.

The notion that some groups cannot be educated and are useful only as "hewers of wood and drawers of water" was rejected even by the leading contemporary proponent of genetic differences in intelligence, Arthur Jensen. Jensen's original 1969 article that began the current controversy argued that the academic deficiencies of disadvantaged schoolchildren were unnecessary, and could be corrected by using different teaching methods, even if such methods had no effect on their I.Q. scores.[37] Other scholars' research has suggested that I.Q. scores can also be substantially affected by environment—without claiming that the tests are therefore invalid or irrelevant. For example, black orphans raised by white families in the United States have I.Q.s at or above the national average.[38] Moreover, many European groups living in cultural isolation—whether in Europe or the United States—have had I.Q. scores as low as (or lower than) those of blacks[39]—and those groups who rose socio-economically in the United States also had their I.Q.s rise substantially, even when there was very little intermarriage to change their genetic makeup.[40] Moreover, even at a given time, there is considerable variation in I.Q. scores across a wide spectrum within each group, and considerable overlap between groups (though, unfortunately, the technical definition of "overlap" in the psychometric literature greatly understates this[41]).

In short, the issue is not whether some groups' children are unteachable, nor whether some group lacks highly intelligent individuals, but is about averages and their interpretation. Historical data indicate that these group averages themselves can change by large amounts over time. Jewish soldiers in the U.S. Army during World War I scored so low on mental tests that a leading authority considered this evidence to "disprove the popular belief that the Jew is highly intelligent."[42] But just as the Jews rose spectacularly in the economic sphere so did their mental test scores, which now exceed the U.S. national average. Other groups, such as Polish Americans and Italian Americans now have I.Q. scores at or above the national average of 100, even though their scores were usually in the low- to mid-80s back around World War I.[43] Internationally, the average I.Q. in Japan has risen by about seven points in one generation, and is today the highest for any nation.[44]

Simplistic environmentalism is equally as hard to reconcile with the factual evidence as simplistic hereditary arguments. Youngsters from different racial and ethnic backgrounds, living in the same neighborhoods and sitting side-by-side in the same schools have had group I.Q. differences as great as those between residentially and educationally segregated blacks and whites in the American South.[45] To salvage the environmental theory of I.Q. differences would require a much broader conception of environment, including cultural orientations and values going far back into history. But this broader conception of environment, reaching well beyond immediate circumstances, offers little hope of substantial change by social engineering, such as racial integration of schools. Moreover, when the unitary conception of "intelligence" is broken down into components like verbal ability, spatial conception, and mathematical reasoning, characteristic patterns emerge—Chinese Americans having better spatial conception and less verbal facility, for example, and Jewish Americans the reverse—and these characteristic group patterns simply occur at higher levels for the higher classes of each group.[46] Whether these distinct patterns are biologically or culturally determined, they do not disappear with rises in socioeconomic status. These I.Q. patterns may be part of characteristic social patterns in general. Successful Irishmen have not usually found success in the same fields as successful Jews; black American Nobel prize winners have not received their awards in the same fields as Chinese American Nobel prize winners. Groups differ in reality, and not simply in others' perceptions.

MIGRATION

Migration patterns reflect the existence and importance of differences among individuals and groups. People do not migrate randomly, either as to origin or destination, nor as to the age, sex, or other characteristics of the people migrating. There are distinct migration patterns, whether the migration is internal or international.

Origins and Destinations

A nineteenth century observer of immigrants headed for the United States noted that "the Germans have maps in their pockets and point out just the place of their several destinations," whereas contemporary Polish immigrants "do not understand where they are going . . . because it is all 'America'."[47] There was a logic behind both patterns. The Germans often came with specific skills in demand in specific industries at specific locations—brewing beer in Milwaukee, for example. But the proportion of skilled workers among the German immigrants was nearly five times as high as among the Polish immigrants, three quarters of whom were laborers with no skill to direct to a particular location. For similar reasons, the nineteenth century Irish immigrants in Milwaukee—usually unskilled— were far more likely to have drifted into town from elsewhere around the Great Lakes than to have come there directly from their homeland, a pattern more common among the German and Norwegian immigrants in the same city.[48]

Origins show patterns, as well as destinations. Indeed, the two are often linked. For example, lopsided concentrations have been common among Japanese emigrants, both as to origins and destinations. Nearly two thirds of the Japanese who emigrated from Okinawa in 1904 were from one district, and of these more than half settled in the Philippines.[49] Of those who emigrated from Okinawa to the United States in 1935, more than 90 percent went to Hawaii, but most Japanese emigrants from the Hiroshima area went to the mainland of the United States.[50] Those from the area around Nagasaki went primarily to China and southeast Asia.[51] In post-World War II Japan, 70 percent of the emigrants from Hidaka District settled in Canada, and of these 90 percent from one village settled in one area of Canada.[52]

The overseas Chinese have likewise been highly localized in origins and destinations. Of all Chinese who immigrated to the United States before World War I, 60 percent came from Toishan —one of 98 districts in one province in south China.[53] As of 1936, one province of Indo-China containing about one-fifth of the population of the country contained more than half of all the Chinese immigrants—who in turn came almost entirely from two provinces in southern China.[54] Moreover, the Chinese in Indo-China and throughout southeast Asia show a high correlation between their places of origin in China and their occupations overseas.[55] Those from one western district of Hainan Island became pepper planters and domestic servants in Indochina, while the Chinese from northwestern Kwantung Province were "principally composed of the commercial element" and those from another district of the same province "are notably agriculturists, boatmen, and coolies."[56] Forty years later, the Chinese in Vietnam showed similarly distinct occupational breakdowns by district of origin in China.[57] In mid-twentieth century Borneo, the Hailams "tend to be pig and poultry rearers, small cultivators and domestic servants" while "Cantonese and Hakkis supply most of the Chinese labor for tin mines and rubber estates."[58] Different groups have carried the matching of origins and destination further than others. Among Italian American immigrants, for example, people from the same province—or even village—in Italy often settled on the same street in the United States.[59]

Localized origins and destinations are one aspect of a larger set of forces at work in the migration process: high information costs, high psychic costs of confronting an entirely new culture and society, and a need for mutual aid, particularly in emergencies.

Information of a sort has always been available from individuals and institutions with a vested interest in promoting—or discouraging—emigration. Shipping companies, railroads, individual states of the United States and whole nations (Canada, Brazil, and Argentina, for example) advertised in nineteenth century Europe for immigrants.[60] Some European governments tried to dissuade or impede the emigration of their subjects or citizens.[61] In centuries past, capital punishment was the penalty for emigrating from China or Japan.[62]

During the nineteenth century campaigns to promote immigration, it was said that immigration agents "covered Italy as the locusts covered Egypt."[63] But although Europe was saturated with information about America,[64] there was much skepticism about its reliability.[65] What was far more effective as a transmission of information were letters from compatriots who had already immigrated to the United States:

Letters had a more continuous flow than any organized advertising. They were much more precisely directed to individuals. They were inherently more credible, coming from known persons and including as they did a wealth of individual and local detail couched in familiar language.[66]

These letters "not only spoke in glowing terms of the high wages, abundant lands, and equal opportunities that America offered, but contained a wealth of advice, information, and warning appropriate to the recipient's needs."[67] These letters were often read aloud to gatherings of people in Europe.[68] Adding to the impact of these letters were sums of money sometimes enclosed, either as gifts or aids to European relatives, or as remittances to pay for their passage to the United States.[69] Austria-Hungary received more than $80 million in U.S. money orders alone in the first decade of the twentieth century. In Sweden, remittances from America often paid for a succession of members of a single family to emigrate.[70] Most of the massive famine Irish emigration of the 1840s was paid for by money sent by families and friends in the United States.[71] While these letters were overwhelmingly optimistic,[72] they were also honest enough to keep Europeans well-advised of cyclical depressions and other changes in the American economy, with the result that the size of European emigration varied with changing conditions in the United States.[73] However, even bad times in the United States were often good by the standards of the European working class. Even from the slums, emigrants could write "glowing tributes to America,"[74] and in the nineteenth century the "meat bill of the average Negro family would surprise a French or German peasant or even an Englishman," according to W.E.B. DuBois.[75]

Some groups have had organized international networks—the overseas Chinese and the Jews being classic examples—as groups who have had to flee many countries over the centuries. Jewish welfare organizations, for example, operated in German ports to provide refreshments to Jews travelling from various parts of Europe.[76]

Technology has had profound effects on both origins and destinations. In the era of wind-driven ships, ocean voyages were time-consuming and expensive, relative to the income and wealth of the masses of working people. From many parts of Europe, for example, few working people could afford the trip to the Western Hemisphere or Australia during the era of wind-driven ships. But the northern and western ports of Europe had extensive commercial trade with North America and emigrants from these regions could find cheap passage in the empty holds of westbound vessels. The bulky agricultural and timber cargoes from west to east and the small bulk of manufactured products from east to west meant a chronic surplus of cargo space leaving Europe—space that would have to be filled either with ballast or with emigrants. Under these special conditions, passage to North America—principally the United States—was brought within the range of many European working class people during the age of sail. Thus British North America had a white working class, whereas Latin America sent a relatively few men, leading to very different racial and ethnic histories in the two regions.

Even with unusually low costs as auxiliary cargo, many emigrants had difficulty financing an ocean voyage, during an era when dependence on the wind meant uncertain sailing dates and therefore costly waits in port cities for the unpredictable arrival and departures of vessels. Moreover, the long and unpredictable voyage was a further drain on meagre resources. Many financed their voyages with financial resources from others—often by contracting to become unpaid workers for a specified number of years to repay the advance of passage money. At least half the white population of colonial America crossed the Atlantic this way.[77] Most nineteenth century Chinese immigrants to the United States crossed the Pacific with their own or family savings, or with advances made by others in China, though a few came as contract laborers,[78] much like the white indentured servants of two centuries earlier.

The invention of the steamship drastically changed origins, destinations, and magnitudes of emigration. Costs were reduced by the much shorter time required for voyages and by the predictability of schedules of departures, which meant less time waiting in seaports for the arrivals and departures of sailing ships. Moreover, because great masses of people could now afford to travel on all-passenger ships, there was no longer a need to travel to a few ports with commercial cargo traffic that would dictate destinations as well as origins. The net result was a massive increase of emigration and greater diversity as to its origins and destinations. The changeover from sailing ships to steamships was sudden and dramatic. As of

1856, 97 percent of passengers arriving in New York came by sail, but just sixteen years later virtually all came on steamships.[79] Changes in origins were almost as dramatic. Whereas more than four-fifths of all European immigrants to the United States came from northern and western Europe in 1882, by 1907 more than four-fifths were from southern and eastern Europe.[80] Destinations were also affected. The era of massive emigration from Europe to Brazil, Argentina, Australia began in the era of steamships, and the continuing immigration to the United States increased greatly in volume—from 5 million before the Civil War to 10 million in the next 30 years.[81]

It was only after the massive immigration of the steamship era that Brazil and Argentina had predominantly European populations, and that Australia became settled beyond a few coastal areas. The economic and social transformations of Brazil and Argentina by emigrants from Europe have already been noted in Chapter 3. The United States was also affected, though not as dramatically, by emigrants who were, for the first time, predominantly non-English speaking, non-Nordic, and non-Protestant, raising grave doubts at the time as to whether they could ever be successfully assimilated.[82]

From an economic perspective, migration is an investment. It represents costs—both financial and psychic—paid in the short run in order to reap some benefits (also both financial and psychic) in the long run. Like any other investment, it is more likely to be made, or made in larger amounts, by those to whom the costs are least or the future returns greatest. Young adults without family responsibilities, large accumulations of belongings, or long-fixed living patterns have lower costs moving to a new society and culture. The costs to their health or the risk to their lives by a taxing voyage are also less. Similarly, the benefits of migration will accrue to them for a longer time in the future than to someone who migrates when he is already elderly. Migrations—both internal and international—have tended to be dominated by young adults in the physical prime of life. During the great age of European emigration, for example, most emigrants went in their teens or early adult life.[83] Within the United States, the great northward migration of southern blacks was also principally a migration of young adults.[84]

Costs have varied by sex as well as by age. The dangers of sexual molestation on board ship were so great in the early nineteenth century that some young women slept sitting up on their belongings instead of lying down on the planks provided.[85] Lack of privacy for undressing also made steerage crossing psychically more costly for women than for men.[86] A 1911 report of the U.S. Immigration Commission said: "No woman with the smallest degree of modesty and with no other convenience than a washroom used jointly with men, and a faucet with cold water, can keep clean amidst such surroundings for a period of twelve days and more."[87] Sailors on the emigrant ships were notorious for annoying and touching women who were travelling alone.[88]

For similar reasons, internal migrations to unknown cities with unknown dangers were also more costly to single women than to single men. Accordingly, migrations in their early or exploratory stages have tended to be disproportionately male as well as disproportionately young adults.[89] Indeed, this has been one of the indices of exploratory or temporary migration, as distinguished from a permanent resettlement of whole families. The emigrants from Europe were predominantly young men,[90] and those from China and Japan still more so.[91] Large-scale migrations concentrated among young adults can have a huge demographic impact on such people. In the United States during the 1920s, for example, nearly half of all black males in Georgia between the ages of 15 to 34 migrated out of the state.[92]

In special cases, where survival itself is at stake, there is little cost and much benefit for all in leaving a place where the dangers of imminent death are high. The Irish fleeing the famine of the 1840s, the Jews fleeing the pogroms of the 1880s or the Chinese "boat people" fleeing the genocidal policies of southeast Asian Communists in the 1970s were flights of whole families. Refugees tend to be more sex balanced than other emigrants and temporary sojourners more predominantly male than either.

The benefits of migration vary with the difference between conditions in the place of origin compared to the place of destination. Migration can be increased by bad times at the place of origin or good times at the destination, or decreased by the reverse. For behavioral analysis, the definition of "good" or "bad" times that matters is that of the people involved. For example, third-party observers may be appalled by the treatment of blacks in South Africa, but there is a net migration of blacks into South Africa from surrounding nations whose economic conditions are not as good.[93] Similarly, in the American South during the era of widespread lynchings, blacks often had a net migration into the areas where lynchings took place,[94] when the economic benefits seemed tangible and the danger that a given individual would be lynched seemed remote to those making the decision. What is "good" or "bad" also depends on what already exists at the point of origin. Rich people seldom migrate,[95] for they have much to lose and little *more* to gain. The very poorest in some countries are also less likely to migrate, for they either cannot finance the trip or have little reason to expect to do better elsewhere.

Massive migration is often accompanied by a substantial *return* migration. Like the original migration, return migration may be temporary or permanent. In the nineteenth century, many British skilled workers "moved back and forth across the Atlantic as the relative movement of the trade cycle suggested that earnings would be better on one side or the other."[96] In the early twentieth century, there were "a quarter of a million seasonal emigrants to Germany each year" from Galicia alone.[97] German, as well as British skilled workers began in the 1870s to "shuttle back and forth across the Atlantic in response to wage movements in America and the homeland."[98] As the relative price of travel has declined with technological progress, it has become feasible for lower-skilled, lower-income people as well to have seasonal and cyclical migration patterns. Puerto Rican migration to the mainland of the United States has assumed that character in the post-World War II era.[99]

In addition to seasonal and cyclical migration, return migration is sometimes intended to mean a sojourn of some years' duration followed by a permanent repatriation. This has been the pattern of many overseas Chinese in southeast Asia[100] and in the United States in the nineteenth century.[101] Italian emigrants likewise have sojourned in many countries,[102] those from the United States often returning "arrayed like signori,"[103] and bringing with them American values—such as education—as well as American wealth.[104] Inevitably, however, some portion of migrants—internal or international—return home with disappointed hopes—for example, Italian immigrants to nineteenth century Brazil,[105] Jewish refugees from fifteenth century Spain vainly seeking safety in Portugal and then being forced to flee that country as well.[106] No doubt every migration has included varying proportions of disappointed migrants forced ultimately to return or to continue wandering elsewhere.

Whatever the basis for return migration—or whether or not the intention to return is even carried out—it tends to reduce assimilation. The overseas Chinese, regardless of their residence or even citizenship, remain essentially Chinese.[107] If repatriation does not in fact occur, this resistance to assimilation may erode after the first generation.[108] But where new *reinforcements* of the separate culture continue to arrive, the assimilation process is slowed or stopped. In many southeast Asian countries, the immigration of Chinese *women* reduced the high rate of intermarriage of Chinese men with local women and therewith slowed the assimilation process.[109] Large, continuing contingents of Puerto Rican migrants to the mainland of the United States, together with a large back-and-forth migration to the island of Puerto Rico, has likewise slowed the assimilation process of Puerto Ricans in the United States, most of whom still grow up in Spanish-speaking homes.[110] For similar reasons, Mexican Americans in the American southwest also retain Spanish as their mother tongue after more than half a century of large-scale immigration to the United States.[111] A similar pattern existed among the Italian immigrants to the United States during the early twentieth century, when they retained their own language and their own citizenship far more than most other emigrants.[112] Conversely, the drastic reduction of immigration to the United States by wars and by highly restrictive immigration legislation during the 1920s has been credited with increasing the rate of assimilation of groups whose foreign cultures were no longer reinforced by new arrivals.[113]

Migrants differ by personal, as well as cultural traits. They differ not only from the general populations in their countries of origin and destinations, but also from members of the same ethnic group already living in the country of destination. In general, migrants tend to be more able, more motivated or to have more schooling.[114] Black, white and Asian male immigrants to the United States usually begin earning less than their respective counterparts already in America—but after more than a decade, overtake and then surpass them in income. Foreign-born black males overtake native black males after 11 years and foreign-born white males overtake native white males after 13 years. Male emigrants from the Philippines take 13 years to overtake native-born Filipino Americans, and males from Mexico take 15 years to overtake native-born Mexican American males, while Japanese male emigrants require 18 years to overtake Japanese American males. White Cuban male refugees take 18 years to overtake native-born American white males. Chinese American males are the exception, in retaining their advantage over Chinese immigrants, even after the latter have been in the United States for 20 years, though the gap is very much reduced by then.[115]

Immigrants in the classic sense of people attracted to new opportunities would be expected to be a more selective group than refugees fleeing to whatever haven might be available. Black immigrants to the United States have tended by and large to be true immigrants rather than refugees, and so have Mexicans and Filipinos—the three groups who first overtake their domestic counterparts. Contemporary Cubans and Chinese have been mostly refugees from totalitarian regimes, and their greater difficulties in closing the income gap are consistent with the thesis that refugees are less selected. Japanese American immigrants are somewhat anomalous in taking 18 years to overtake native-born Japanese Americans, though it should be noted that the latter earn substantially higher incomes than the average white American, and so are more difficult to catch.

Roughly similar data from Canada, Great Britain, and Israel tend to confirm these conclusions. Foreign-born males (mostly American, British, Irish or other European) overtake native-born Canadian males in about 16 years—about the same as for white immigrants to the United States.[116] Foreign-born white males in Britain earn slightly more than native British white males.[117] In modern Israel—a country founded largely as a haven for refugees —the "earnings crossover occurs very late, between thirty-five and forty years in the country."[118]

Generations

The extent to which ethnic characteristics persist in the generations after migration is by no means determined by the extent to which there is self-conscious "identity" in the individuals or groups concerned. One may even repudiate one's cultural roots and still exhibit them. An observer in Thailand noted "a prominent Chinese merchant whose face was unmistakably Chinese and whose father was a Chinese although his mother was Thai," who "took immediate offence" at being called "Chinese," in spite of the fact that "his shop signs were in Chinese, that he spoke two Chinese dialects, that he kept his accounts in Chinese, and sent his children to a Chinese school." In his own mind, he was a patriotic Thai citizen and "made large contributions to the defence forces."[119] Indeed, many of the anti-Chinese laws in Thailand were drafted by government officials who were themselves part Chinese,[120] just as anti-Semitic laws and mass expulsions of Jews from Spain in 1492 were in part the work of Jews who had converted to Christianity.[121] The former Jews continued to use the same skills and traits they had before conversion to achieve high positions in the Spanish economy and society —and often faced the same hostility as Christians that they had once faced as Jews.[122]

With the passing of sufficient numbers of generations, substantial assimilation has nevertheless proceeded, even among the overseas Chinese in Asia and the Jews in Europe. In the Philippines, by the twentieth century, the full-blooded Chinese were greatly outnumbered by people of mixed Chinese and Filippino ancestry,[123] who formed "one of the most capable, prosperous and powerful elements of the Filippino people."[124] With the development of Filippino nationalism, "the leaders who declaimed against the Chinese most violently had almost invariably Chinese blood in their veins."[125] In Europe over the centuries, many Jews converted to Christianity—individually and in groups, voluntarily and on the threat of death—and were absorbed into the general European population.[126] In early twentieth century Germany, a growing proportion of all marriages of Jews were intermarriages—reaching nearly half in the 1920s—and in addition there were hundreds of converts to Christianity and a general weakening of the hold of Judaism on the younger generation.[127]

Differences between generations are often as great as differences between ethnic groups. Second-generation Puerto Ricans in New York in 1950 and again in 1960 were in white-collar occupations more than twice as often as first generation Puerto Ricans.[128] The same difference existed between first- and second-generation European immigrants in Boston in 1910.[129] Second generation Mexican Americans earned 20 percent higher incomes than first-generation Mexican Americans in the same age brackets.[130]

Generations are often thought of as age groups that follow after one another. But they may also represent groups of the *same* age at the same time, but with different places of birth. The comparisons above, for example, are of different generations at a given point in time. Groups with relatively large continuing migration—Puerto Ricans, Mexicans, Chinese, West Indians—may have large numbers of age contemporaries who are of different generations, in terms of settlement and acculturation in America. There may also be substantial age differences between successive generations, which complicate economic or other comparisons.

However generations are defined, there is usually some tangible economic progress in the United States from the first generation to the second generation. Where substantial economic differences exist among age contemporaries of the same group, this is clearly an acculturation phenomenon within the group, rather than a change in discrimination by employers, who seldom know or care about these internal differences in other groups.

While the second generation is usually objectively better off than the first generation, they are often more resentful of remaining disparities from the general population, more delinquent and more violent. Among the nineteenth century immigrants to America from Europe, most were grateful to have reached the United States and to live better than they or their parents had ever lived before. It was the American-born children of the immigrants who resented having lower incomes and poorer living conditions than other Americans, and it was the second generation who formed the delinquent gangs, the violent mobs, and sometimes professional criminals. The same pattern reappears today among Chinese immigrants to the United States from Hong Kong, with the added irony that many of the younger Hong Kong Chinese are Maoists, admirers of the very system that forced their parents to flee from China. Among American Negro migrants from the South, riots seldom occurred in the early northern ghettoes occupied overwhelmingly by the first generation out of the rural South, though they suffered more poverty and economic and social barriers (the presumed "causes" of violence) than later generations. It was the growth of *second generations* in the North that marked the beginning of major riots—first in Harlem in 1935 and then in Detroit in 1943. The massive ghetto riots that spread across the nation during the 1960s were likewise largely the work of second-generation black youths, with southern-born blacks seldom being involved.[131]

Substantial economic differences between different generations of the same group at the same time suggests something of the large market value of experience and skills relevant to the economy in which they work. Generational differences in residential segregation and intermarriage rates also suggest that acculturation—not group labels alone—greatly affects the response of the larger society in the social as well as the economic area. But the disappointments of the first generation (often expressed in return migration) and the resentments of the second (often expressed in violence) suggest something of the psychic difficulties in seeing this mundane fact. By contrast, fully acculturated members of the same group may be all too painfully aware of how much further the newcomers have to go.

POLITICS AND ECONOMICS

A complex interaction of economic, political, cultural and historic forces produces the rich and bewildering kaleidoscope of racial and ethnic history. Analysis, however, requires that these influences be dissected separately. This does not imply a belief that they operate in isolation from each other, or in pure form, any more than the systematic study of chemistry implies that pure elements and pure compounds exist in splendid isolation in the real world. It merely implies that we need the aid of systematic procedures to understand highly complex processes.

Economic and political issues involving race and ethnicity are often both exciting and urgent. But for that very reason, it is necessary before considering the substance of these political and economic issues to clarify the basic terms and definitions with which these issues are discussed.

Defining Concepts

One of the most common concepts encountered in discussions of race and ethnicity is *discrimination*. Yet it is seldom defined. Various overlapping, and sometimes contradictory, meanings of discrimination are used, sometimes in the same analysis. Among commonly used meanings of discrimination are:

1. Paying one group less for a given economic performance than another group would receive for the same economic performance, quantitatively and qualitatively.

2. Charging one group more for an economic good with a given production cost than would be charged another group for the same good at the same cost of production.
3. Refusing to engage in transactions at all with one group while engaging in transactions with another group offering no better terms nor performing any better economic service.
4. Perceiving individuals from different groups so differently that they are offered different terms—or one is offered terms and the other is not—even when they are objectively the same.
5. Paying or charging different amounts to individuals from different groups, regardless of the reason.
6. Different "representation" of different groups in different jobs, colleges, jails, or other institutions, regardless of the reason.

The first three definitions are consistent with each other but are inconsistent with the last two. Where groups differ in performance characteristics, corresponding differences in employment, pay, or promotion would not be discrimination by the first three definitions, but would be according to the last two. Definition No. 4 is a special case of "unconscious discrimination" (sometimes called "institutional racism") in which the discriminator is consciously treating everyone alike whom he regards as having the same qualifications, but is simply biased in his assessments of qualifications of individuals from different racial or ethnic backgrounds. The first four definitions can be combined into a single definition of discrimination as *the offering of different transaction terms—including no terms at all—to groups who do not differ in the relevant criteria* (skill, credit rating, experience, test scores, etc.). Situations 5 and 6 while sometimes accepted as *prima facie* evidence of discrimination, do not in themselves constitute discrimination. No one regards the over-representation of black Americans on professional basketball teams as constituting discrimination against white Americans. Nor can the over-representation of Chinese pilots in the Malaysian air force be regarded as discrimination against Malays, in a country where Malays dominate the top military and civilian political posts.

An intellectual and moral difficulty arises when *groups* are paid correctly in proportion to their respective productivities, but *individuals* who deviate substantially from their own group's average are not. The alcoholism, fighting, and other characteristics of nine-teenth century Irish immigrants to the United States were factors in employment advertisements that said, "No Irish need apply." But a perfectly sober, peaceable, and otherwise valuable Irish worker was excluded just as much as the worst drunken, brawling incompetent. Insofar as the job opportunities that were open, and the pay offered, represented a correct assessment of the *average* Irish immigrant of that era, there was no discrimination against Irish Americans *as a group*. There were instead internal windfall transfers among the Irish—the least productive being overpaid and the most productive underpaid. This is an important social phenomenon and moral issue in itself, but it is not group discrimination. A group's below-average income or occupational status cannot be explained by these offsetting internal transfers. To explain its substandard economic position by discrimination is to show that the group as a whole was underpaid or overcharged. Perhaps Irish Americans as a group were in fact discriminated against and a substantial part of their poverty at that time might be explained this way. The point here is not to attempt to pass judgment on Irish immigrants but to make the distinction between group discrimination and individual windfall losses and gains.

While discrimination is usually conceived of in economic terms as discrimination against workers, consumers, tenants or credit seekers, there is also political discrimination against all these groups and also against school children, defendants in court, and others who have contact with governmental institutions. Indeed, political discrimination may make it more difficult to measure economic discrimination. One of the ways in which groups may come to have different productivities is by receiving different qualities of school-ing provided by the government. Much direct political discrimina-tion is disguised by phrasing it as a "preference" for one group rather than discrimination against another. Such "preferences" for indigenous, non-Chinese people have been common in southeast Asia since World War II brought independence and similar "pref-erences" for designated racial, ethnic, and sex groups have more recently become part of political and judicial policy in the United States.[132] "Preferences" and "discrimination" are, however, sim-ply the same act expressed in different words. Preferences for A, B, and C constitute discrimination against X, Y, and Z.

Exploitation is a still more emotionally charged term—and still more elusive as to its specific meaning. Sometimes it seems to be implicitly defined by purpose or intent—that one transactor means only to "take advantage" of the other or to use the transaction solely for his own gain. The problem with this definition is that such intentions are usually reciprocal. The employer offers a job solely for the purpose of benefiting himself, with no real intention of benefiting the worker any more than he has to, in order to get him to agree to work. But the worker likewise takes the job solely for the purposes of benefiting himself, with no real intention of benefiting the employer any more than is necessary in order to keep his job. Moreover, investors may provide the necessary capital without caring about either employers or employees, but wanting only to receive a return on their investment. Another way of looking at all this is that individuals who have no emotional ties to each other may nevertheless voluntarily cooperate in a complex economic process, to the extent that each feels himself sufficiently benefited to make it preferable to the available alternatives. Societies in which economic cooperation is largely limited to those to whom one has emotional ties tend to be very poor societies,[133] given the limited circle of family, friends and patrons.

If exploitation cannot be defined by intent, it may be defined by results. Among the many shifting conceptions of "exploitation" is that it means unusually large benefits are derived by one transactor, at the expense of unusually small benefits by the other. This definition is sometimes used in economic theory.[134] Unfortunately, this particular definition has very limited usefulness in the real world. Serfdom, slavery, peonage, or other *involuntary* transactions—including the driving of indigenous peoples off their land by colonizers—might provide examples of exploitation in this sense, but *repeated and voluntary* transactions that are less beneficial than other transactions that are available are difficult to conceive, much less discover empirically.

A group may be very much discriminated against—blacks in South Africa, for example—without necessarily being exploited. Undoubtedly better education and more job opportunities would make black South Africans more productive and more highly paid, but the question of exploitation deals with whether their *current* productivity, with all their current disadvantages, is underpaid. The many interferences of the South African government in the economy make exploitation in that sense possible as well, but the point here is simply that discrimination and exploitation are two different phenomena, and evidence of the former is not evidence of the latter. Nor is this merely a matter of verbal fastidiousness. Profoundly different policies would be needed to deal with exploitation as compared to low productivity deriving from restricted opportunities for education, skills and experience. Minimum wage laws, for example, would simply increase pay levels among the exploited but would price low-productivity workers out of a job, making them worse off than before. The South African government has in fact resorted to minimum wage laws expressly in order to price blacks out of jobs that the government wanted reserved for whites.[135] Moreover, the migration of more than a million blacks from other African nations into South Africa,[136] likewise suggests that exploitation is not the real issue, even in one of the world's most discriminatory nations.

Consumers can be exploited, just like workers—and other economic phenomena may also be confused with exploitation of consumers, just as in labor markets. "The poor pay more"[137] for many consumer goods, including housing, and poor racial and ethnic groups in the United States are classic examples of this. The question is whether this represents higher than usual profits or higher than usual costs. Higher than usual *markups* may be found, but higher than usual profits very seldom. Where losses from nonpayment of rent, credit defaults, shoplifting, and vandalism are higher than usual, prices are also likely to be higher than usual, even when profits are no higher than elsewhere.[138] Perhaps the decisive evidence that profits are no higher in neighborhoods where "the poor pay more" is that supermarkets and other businesses are typically *withdrawing* from these neighborhoods, despite claims that they are "exploiting" the customers there. Again, whether or not something is called exploitation is not a matter of mere verbal fastidiousness but of consequential policy decisions. Forcing down prices, rents, or interest rates by law would make sense if exploitation were the cause of their being higher in low-income neighborhoods, but if these higher prices simply reflect higher costs or greater risks of default, then forcing them down by law accelerates the withdrawal of businesses, the abandonment of rent-controlled apartment houses, and a drying up of credit.

Political terms need clear definitions as much as do economic terms. *Democracy* is one that is especially liable to be used in shifting senses, sometimes referring to a political process (majority rule) and sometimes to a desired result (freedom, equality, legal rights, due process, etc.). But whether or not majority rule in fact leads to various social or political results is an empirical question, not a foregone conclusion. The issue cannot even be addressed unless the process and the results are defined separately. Racial and ethnic minorities are, by definition, not the majority that rules. In countries where some racial or ethnic groups are disfranchised—South Africa, for example—they may be a numerical majority of the population without being a majority (or even part) of the electorate.

Some democratic nations have, during some periods of history, advanced the political rights and socioeconomic conditions of disadvantaged racial and ethnic groups. The United States after World War II is an example.[139] But it is equally easy to cite counter-examples where the growth of democratic decision making marked major retrogressions for disadvantaged racial and ethnic groups. The vast expansion of the vote to the common man during Andrew Jackson's presidency in the United States[140] marked a new wave of dispossessions of American Indians from their lands,[141] and growing discrimination against "free persons of color" throughout the United States.[142] After the American Civil War, unpopular southern state governments, established on the power of the bayonets of an occupying army, gave Negroes political rights, but the return of popular government after the army withdrew—and especially after the spread of the franchise to the masses of poor whites—marked the beginning of the disenfranchisement of the blacks, and racial segregation and discrimination on an unprecedented scale.[143]

The American experience was by no means unique. Non-whites in South Africa enjoyed more rights when imperialist Britain ruled the land than when "Herrenvolk democracy" put political power in the hands of South African whites. In southeast Asia, the Chinese likewise had more legal rights and protections during the era of imperialism. The emergence of independent governments, responsive to local public opinion, marked the growth of anti-Chinese laws, policies, and mob violence throughout southeast Asia.[144] In short, democracy as a political process may or may not lead to more freedom and equality, for particular racial and ethnic groups or for the society at large.

Rights are a political—more specifically, legal—term in frequent use in discussions of racial and ethnic groups. Whatever the philosophical complexities of rights in some ethical or moral sense, political or legal rights refer simply to the availability of government power to safeguard some behavior or relationship. Property rights mean simply that the government will supply force to dispossess or punish anyone who makes unauthorized use of something legally assigned to someone else. Rights against the government—such as in the Magna Carta in Britain or the Bill of Rights in the United States—mean that power can be used against government officials who abuse their authority, and their edicts can be invalidated.

Rights may be general ("life, liberty, and the pursuit of happiness") or special, with respect to individuals (property rights) or with respect to activities (the right to bear arms). Specific racial or ethnic groups may enjoy rights not held by others—voting rights for whites only in South Africa or rights to preferential hiring held by a number of administratively chosen groups under "affirmative action" policies in the United States.

Rights are often assumed to be benefits to those on whom they are conferred. But the very existence of *waivers* of rights suggests that rights have cost to their recipients, and that these costs can in some cases exceed the benefits.[145] Where certain rights cannot be waived, it is by no means clear that they are a net benefit. For example, special rights for young workers in the Soviet Union make Soviet managers less willing to hire them.[146] Transactors in general are less apt to transact with those who have more rights.[147]

The creation of rights is politically attractive. It is often a very low cost way to "do something" about a social "problem." Unlike other measures which may entail large expenditures of tax money and thus provoke voter anger, the creation of rights may cost the government little more than paper and ink. What these rights cost the recipients or the society at large is a larger question for later discussion. Here it is sufficient to define the term and understand what it means in a political context, as distinguished from a moral context. Racial and ethnic groups who receive special rights may or may not be benefited by them.

A concept central to economic reasoning is the *market*. A market is not a specific set of institutions but simply the freedom to choose among existing institutions or to create new institutions, contracts, or relationships to meet one's economic purposes.[148] The presence or absence of this freedom to engage in economic transactions on terms negotiated between the transactors has had enormous impact on racial and ethnic groups. While a market may seem to be an inchoate agglomeration or a mass of confused activity, it has its own systemic logic, leading to results often quite different from those intended by the transactors.

The power of the market may be demonstrated by how often, how repeatedly, and how pervasively the South African government has had to intervene in the operations of the market to prevent or slow the economic rise of black South Africans. Yet the South African government was elected by the very same whites whose economic competition in the market led to the rise of blacks to positions considered too high for them. Racism may be just as pervasive in the market as it is in the political system, and yet the *cost* of putting it into practice as discrimination may differ considerably between the two systems, as we shall see.

Power is a term used both in politics and economics. Power is not simply the ability to get something done, but to get it done despite the resistance and opposition of others. It takes no power to give away money, for others can always be found to take it. It does, however, usually take power to occupy a foreign nation, for their armed forces will usually oppose it.

The power of A is a loss of freedom by B. When A can reduce B's options, he has power over B. An armed robber can reduce the victim's options to "your money or your life." Confusion occurs when A is credited with power because he *increases* B's options. If A is giving away money, B may come to him, or even be pleasant to him, for that reason, but B has simply chosen to behave that way. He has as much freedom as he had before A appeared. There is nothing that he did before that he cannot continue to do.

An invading race of colonizers may reduce the indigenous population's options to subjugation or annihilation—"to hell or Connaught," in Cromwell's phrase. A politically dominant group may reduce others' options to relinquishing their economic transactions or face jail for violation of laws against Chinese retailers, African skilled workers or racially mixed housing or factories.

Power has so often been abused (whether or not in a racial and ethnic context) that its pejorative connotations are politically useful for condemning situations, transactions, groups or institutions whose salient characteristics are *not* power. For example, politicians who want to use political power against groups or businesses often begin by accusing them of having—and abusing—"power" that consists of nothing more than attracting transactions adding to the public's existing options as customers or workers. The "power" of money lenders (such as the Jews in Europe or the Chinese in southeast Asia) has often consisted of nothing more than a willingness to lend at high interest rates to people whom others would not lend to at any interest rate (or only at even higher interest rates).

Effects and Limits of Politics

Political control and discrimination cut across differences in economic efficiency, restricting economic opportunities for hated groups, confiscating the fruits of their efforts or even enslaving them or practicing genocide against them. But however important these considerations may be for particular groups in particular times and places, what is remarkable from a broader historical perspective is how often the hated and politically subordinate groups have prospered economically beyond the level of those with political power.

No major country in southeast Asia has allowed equal rights for its Chinese minority, and yet the Chinese have prospered economically while the numerical and political majority has remained poor. This has also been the story of the Jews in Europe, who have sporadically been reduced to destitution by governments that confiscated their wealth—but could not confiscate the skills and traits that produced that wealth before and would produce it later again. Discrimination against the Italians in Argentina did not prevent the Italians from advancing economically beyond the native Argentines —for example, having more "representation" than the Argentines in various businesses in Buenos Aires.[149] In short, *discrimination has been pervasive, but not pervasively effective.*

Nor is the degree of discrimination decisive: Japanese Americans have historically encountered more discrimination than Puerto Ricans in the United States, but earn more than double the income of Puerto Ricans and substantially exceed the incomes of Anglo-Saxons in America. It is difficult to know in what units to measure the degree of intergroup hostility, but there have been many occasions in southeast Asia when the number of Chinese massacred in a few days has exceeded the total number of blacks lynched in the entire history of the United States.[150] The number of Armenians slaughtered by the Turks in 1915 was still larger, and the Jews who perished in the Nazi holocaust was largest of all. It may be significant that many of the great mass murders have been of "middlemen" minorities—groups usually economically better off than their murderers.

Political activity is one avenue to group economic advancement, and to many it seems the most promising avenue. Group cohesion, expressed in political pressure and bloc voting, is often regarded as axiomatically the most effective method of promoting group progress. Political cohesion may take many forms: voting together for one party, voter favoritism toward candidates of one's own racial or ethnic background, or making political appointments largely to members of one's own group.

Historically, Irish Americans have been pre-eminent in all these respects and have also been the most politically successful of all American ethnic groups. The great American municipal political machines of the nineteenth and twentieth centuries have been largely Irish political machines. Yet the Irish were the *slowest* rising of all European immigrants to America. The wealth and power of a relatively few Irish political bosses had little impact on the progress of masses of Irish Americans.

Other groups without either the political cohesion or the political success of Irish Americans have nevertheless advanced from poverty to prosperity more rapidly. Italian immigrants arrived in the United States about two generations after the Irish, and yet overtook them economically. Italian American voters have historically been little swayed by Italian candidates, often voting against them for candidates from other ethnic backgrounds. Even the most famous Italian American politician, Fiorello H. La Guardia, lost the Italian vote to his Irish opponent in 1940.[151] Jewish Americans have voted for non-Jewish liberals—including the German American Senator Robert F. Wagner and Catholic priest Father Drinan —as readily as for Jewish liberals.[152] The Chinese have deliberately avoided politics entirely during their rise from poverty to affluence, both in southeast Asia and in the United States.[153] After reaching a level of prosperity and general acceptance, then some few Chinese have chosen political careers. The same has been true of Japanese Americans.

In Brazil and Australia, the Germans have likewise stayed away from politics, and have prospered economically. Relatively few

Germans have risen to political prominence in America, but many have risen to economic prominence, including dominant figures in many industries.[154] Italians have likewise had little political prominence in Argentina, Brazil, Australia or the United States, though they have risen from poverty to prosperity in all these countries. In South Africa, the Afrikaners are dominant in politics but the British are dominant in the economy.

Historically, the relationship between political success and economic success has been more nearly inverse than direct. This is understandable as rational individual career choices. For those with less entrepreneurial orientation or experience, political, civil service, and military careers are relatively more attractive—whether they are Afrikaners compared to the British in South Africa, the Irish compared to the Jews in the United States, or the various peoples of southeast Asia compared to the overseas Chinese there. Even when politics, the civil service, and the military were open to all, the more entrepreneurial groups have typically avoided these careers because they have had better options elsewhere.

A serious problem with trying to advance a group economically through heightened group "identity" or militancy is that one group's chauvinism almost invariably evokes counter-chauvinism from other groups. The Chinese in southeast Asia prospered more peacefully when they were fragmented communities of Cantonese, Hailams, Fukkienese, etc., than after they began to be gripped by Chinese nationalism with the rise of Sun Yat-sen and a new China in the early twentieth century. Chinese nationalism provoked Siamese, Indonesian, etc., nationalism[155]—leading to heightened hostilities and increased discrimination against the overseas Chinese. In the United States, the rise of strident political and sometimes paramilitary "black power" movements in the 1960s led to a "white backlash" in the 1970s and 1980s that included strident political and paramilitary movements—many in parts of the United States where such movements had never had a foothold before, and among more educated middle-class people than ever took such extremists seriously before.

Extremists and counter-extremists often have a symbiotic relationship. The alarm that each creates in the other's group increases the group consciousness and chauvinism on which both feed. Even bloody clashes in the streets between opposing extremists can be mutually beneficial politically, regardless of who "wins" or "loses" the encounter in physical terms, for each has provided the other with an opportunity to publicly demonstrate his loyalty and dedication to his own racial or ethnic group. Both gain at the expense of moderate elements attempting to calm emotions and work out a *modus vivendi*. Once the forces of polarization pass a certain point, even the moderates are drawn toward more extreme positions, for now all specific issues recede before the ever larger looming question: "Whose side are you on?" At this point the situation may become irretrievable in terms of a resolution of issues. Northern Ireland, South Africa, and Lebanon are examples of polarization to the point where there may be no possible set of conditions simultaneously acceptable to the contending racial or ethnic groups.

More generally, political incentives reward leaders who show themselves more dedicated to their group than other leaders, more uncompromising, and more convinced that all the group's dissatisfactions are due to the reprehensible actions of other groups. Those who ascribe any part of the group's past difficulties to their own actions or inactions, or who put any responsibility for future development on the group itself run the risk of being considered less loyal or less dedicated to their own people. A Filipino official of the 1930s who argued that Filipinos should "develop the economic efficiency of the Chinese" if they wanted to supplant them in the economy "brought upon his head a storm of Filipino indignation."[156] Few other officials have made that political mistake since, either in the Philippines or elsewhere in southeast Asia. Most have ascribed intergroup economic differences to Chinese "exploitation."

Politics makes it politically difficult to correctly diagnose problems in public, and without correct diagnosis, correct prescription is unlikely. Political approaches to economic problems must be (1) emotionally acceptable to those whom leaders address, and (2) must offer "solutions" that at least plausibly lie within the political domain. Therefore, whatever the real complex of forces at work or the relative weights of various factors, political leaders tend to emphasize—sometimes exclusively—those factors for which a law or policy can be formulated, and those factors which lend themselves to the moral condemnation of other groups. Factors such as intergroup differences in demographic characteristics, geographical distribution, skill levels or cultural values tend to be ignored, however demonstrably important they may be in a cause-and-effect sense.[157] In short, political "solutions" tend to misconceive the basic issues. However, these misconceptions may serve the political leadership well, even if they are counterproductive for the racial or ethnic group in whose name they speak. Black civil rights leaders in the United States often earn annual incomes running into hundreds of thousands of dollars, even if their programs and approaches prove futile for the larger purpose of lifting other blacks out of poverty. In Thailand, the abortive attempt to drive the Chinese out of the rice-exporting business by establishing a government monopoly has not achieved its goal, but has succeeded in diverting profits to "the Thai soldier, police official, or politician" whose cooperation is now necessary to allow the Chinese entrepreneur to continue performing a service which only he can perform.[158]

Benefits earmarked for a particular group are especially helpful for that group's political leadership, even if these benefits are less valuable than alternative benefits the group might have obtained by alternative policies benefiting the society as a whole. Moreover, the attempt to obtain earmarked benefits may arouse far more opposition from other groups, therefore reducing the likelihood or the magnitude of such benefits, but they are still in the interest of the group's political leaders. If the group benefits as members of the larger society, that is no feather in the cap of racial or ethnic leaders. Conversely, if earmarked benefits are offset or outweighed by the group's losses through the adverse effect of these benefits on the national deficit, inflation, or other consequences, it is still in the interest of group political leadership to pursue this course.

Some racial or ethnic groups with an entrepreneurial bent evolve a leadership from individuals who have succeeded in entrepreneurial enterprises rather than political careers. This has been the pattern of Chinese communities in southeast Asia and in the United States. Where influential businessmen take this civic role, the policies they advocate are often quite different from those advocated by professional politicians or leaders of protest organizations. For example, the leaders of American Chinatowns have urged the police to treat street hoodlums roughly—including vigorous use of billy clubs—even though the hoodlums might be Chinese and the police white.[159] Black community leaders, however, follow opposite policies—vying with each other in decrying police use of force. Both sets of leaders respond to their respective incentives, which are quite different. Businessmen as unpaid civic leaders with no political careers in prospect have an incentive to reduce crime and other community problems by whatever means seem most effective. But blacks pursuing political or protest organization careers cannot afford to allow their rivals to seem blacker-than-thou. The differences are differences of incentives rather than of race. Chinese political leadership—as among Communist movements in southeast Asia—features the same demagoguery as politically-motivated leadership in other racial and ethnic groups.[160] Traditional Chinese business leadership in that region follows more pragmatic policies for the same reasons that other business-origin leadership has elsewhere—for example, the Japanese in the United States or the Jews historically in numerous countries where there were no political careers open to them.

The effectiveness of political means of advancing a racial or ethnic minority depends not only on the actions of its own leadership, but also on the nature of the larger society and the characteristics of the political process itself. Political approaches suffer from the sheer volatility of politics in general, and democratic politics in particular. Historically, policies toward the Chinese in southeast Asia and the Jews in Europe have shifted drastically within a generation, and similar shifts have occurred with respect to various American ethnic groups. Japanese immigrants to the United States, for example, were initially welcomed as hard workers, but within a decade were hated as business competitors, discriminated against both by laws and by informal practices, eventually interned in concentration camps under a flimsy pretext as enemy aliens during World War II, but less than a generation later they were able to live in white neighborhoods, about half now intermarry with whites—and they now receive preferential treatment as a disadvantaged minority, while earning incomes nearly one-third higher than the average American!

Whatever the merits or demerits of a particular political policy, it is almost certain to change, perhaps drastically, and often unpredictably. A shift of 10 percentage points in the voting can bring a new administration that changes policy 180 degrees. This volatility reduces the reliability of politics as a factor in long-run progress.

Effects and Limits of the Market

Analysis of either economic or political processes must begin with an awareness of substantial and consequential differences among groups, including racial and ethnic groups. These differences may be in values, in economic performance, in the degree of willingness to obey rules, or in many other characteristics. From an economic perspective, these differences can create valuable complementarities. A nation of peasant farmers—whether in eastern Europe or southeast Asia—can benefit from the addition of a group of organizers of markets for their crops and sellers of miscellaneous manufactured goods used by peasant families. By the same token, groups like the Jews in Europe and the overseas Chinese in Asia obviously found it to their advantage to migrate to places where they could perform these functions. But from a political perspective, the more desperately needed these middlemen were, and the more valuable their contributions to the economy, the greater the disparity in income between them and the peasant masses—and the more they were hated as "exploiters." The market and the political system often render opposite verdicts on the same situation. Because the political system holds ultimate power over the economy, the political verdict can be used to override the economic verdict—as in the many expulsions of Jews and Chinese at various times and places in history. The economic reality of hardships to the general population caused by the departure of the Jews and the Chinese in many cases forced political authorities to relent and let them back in, or even to try to entice them back.

One of the reasons for the different verdicts rendered by political and economic systems is that political systems give expression to *beliefs,* often at negligible cost, while economic systems are constrained by the hard realities and thus impose substantial costs for being wrong and confer substantial benefits for being right. For example, Japanese immigrants to the United States in the early twentieth century were initially paid less than white workers doing the same work in the agricultural fields where they were concentrated. In reality, however, the Japanese workers were harder workers, and this reality made them a better economic bargain for employers. Once the higher productivity of Japanese labor became known throughout the market, this pay differential not only disappeared under competitive pressures, but turned eventually into higher rates of pay for Japanese workers than the white workers received.[161]

One of the enduring misconceptions about the market is that its effective operation depends upon the goodwill of those transacting in it. But no such assumption is implied in economic analysis of markets, nor have market economists relied on any such beliefs.[162] Adam Smith's 1776 classic analysis of markets, *The Wealth of Nations,* repeatedly assumed *ill-will* on the part of businessmen.[163] In early twentieth century America, Jewish and Polish immigrants sought each other out for economic transactions despite seething hatred between the two groups.[164] The Chinese could never have advanced through the market to prosperity, either in southeast Asia or in the United States, if they had depended on the goodwill of the surrounding majority.

One of the most massive efforts based on ill-will occurred in the American South immediately after the Civil War, and its failure indicates something of the power of market competition. White southern employers and landowners attempted to band together to keep down the pay rates of black laborers and sharecroppers. Since this was perfectly legal at the time, such plans were openly discussed in the southern press. On the face of it, these white employers and landowners had every conceivable advantage: Blacks were destitute, illiterate, wholly inexperienced, unorganized, and the law had little or no concern for their rights. Yet the cold fact is that black income rose at a higher rate than white income in the generation after the Civil War.[165] Egregious frauds were perpetrated here and there, especially in the first year after the Civil War, when some plantation owners even concealed the Emancipation Proclamation from blacks and continued to work them for nothing,[166] but what is remarkable is how quickly and completely the cartels broke down.

Even an illiterate worker, unable to count his money, could tell when friends or relatives elsewhere were living better. White employers and landowners who paid more or had better working or living conditions quickly found themselves with a large supply of black applicants, while employers and landowners who had taken the fullest advantage of vulnerable blacks found themselves having great difficulty getting people to work for them. Competition forced wages up and changed working and living conditions to the benefit of blacks.[167] The southern press was filled with outraged complaints by white employers and landowners that other whites had not stuck by their agreements and that blacks were getting unreasonably high pay as a result.[168] What these southern whites regarded as excessive pay for blacks was, of course, still very low pay received by unskilled workers who required much supervision. However, as black workers and sharecroppers accumulated more experience and therefore became more valuable, their wage rates rose at a higher rate than among whites, as might be expected because of their acquisition of basic human capital that others already had. The terms of sharecropper contracts also changed, as blacks acquired more discretion in managing their farms as they gained more experience.[169] In short, competition produced changes that few—if any—whites were in favor of. The effectiveness of a competitive market is in no way dependent upon the goodwill or honesty of transactors. That is the whole point of analyzing a *market,* as distinguished from surveying or averaging the opinions, intentions or stereotypes in the minds of transactors.

In the political sphere, however, popular beliefs carry much more weight. Where the overseas Chinese or the Jews were *believed* to be harmful to the economy, they were expelled, regardless of the reality. Because American laws and ideology limited political intervention in the economy during the nineteenth century, the economic reality of rising levels of capability among blacks was reflected in increased pay, more discretion as tenant farmers, and improving housing conditions.[170] By contrast, in South Africa, where political decision making superseded economic decision making to a greater extent, the rise of blacks was far more effectively stopped.[171] In both countries, individuals and groups hostile to laissez-faire capitalism were in the forefront of the drive to impose color discrimination politically. The rise of populist radicalism in the American South at the end of the nineteenth century marked a sharp decline in the rights of blacks and a sharp rise of discrimination, segregation, and lynchings.[172] Southern populist politicians who thundered against the banks and the corporations also thundered against the "niggers."[173] On the west coast of the United States, socialist Jack London and labor union chief Samuel Gompers spearheaded anti-Chinese political campaigns.[174] In South Africa as well, socialist and trade union leaders (sometimes the same individuals) initiated demands for "color bar" legislation and backed their demands with massive violence.[175] The Nationalist Party of South Africa has long had an anti-capitalist ideology,[176] and Afrikaners considered as "abuses of capitalism" the tendency of the market to allow blacks to rise above their "place" as conceived by whites.[177]

Much of the literature on race and ethnicity claims that "stereotypes" cause various groups to sustain serious losses as employees, consumers, borrowers, or renters. The conclusion often reached is that intellectual and moral opposition to these stereotypes is urgently needed, and that each person should be judged as an individual. Stereotypes have costs that vary greatly with the circumstances. There are often negligible costs to expressing racial or ethnic stereotypes among friends and peers. But while there may be negligible costs incurred in *expressing* stereotypes in a social setting, or even in *voting* on the basis of stereotypes in a political context, *acting* on stereotypes or other misjudgments in a competitive market means incurring serious costs and even jeopardizing one's own economic survival. The same competitive forces that destroyed the white employer cartels in the post-bellum South also forced the ceding of more autonomy to black sharecroppers, despite the pervasive stereotypes about the Negro's incapacity to manage.

Biased assessments are not the only reason for discrimination. An employer who knows perfectly well that a given individual is the best qualified applicant for a job may nevertheless not hire him if that applicant is from a racial, religious or other group that the employer dislikes in general, or dislikes seeing in responsible jobs. Sometimes the employer's reluctance to hire is based on the reactions he expects from customers or co-workers, whose antipathy may be based on differences in race or ethnicity rather than job performance. Similarly, a landlord who knows that a given prospective tenant is a responsible and understanding person may nevertheless not rent to him if either the landlord or the other tenants dislike associating with persons of that individual's race or ethnicity. The same principle applies to customers of particular restaurants, hotels, or stores, where either the management or the other customers may object.

Depending upon the kind of market, such attitudes may lead to segregation, with or without inferior opportunities being accorded one group. Nineteenth century American employers, for example, discovered from experience that including Scotch-Irish and other Irish workers in the same work crews was an invitation to violence,[178] especially when they had to live together for long periods of time while building railroads or canals. Generations later, the same was found to be true of Italian immigrant work gangs, when the workers came from different parts of Italy.[179] Today, when segregation is illegal in the United States, the same result is often accomplished obliquely by having labor contractors of a given ethnicity supply the workers—who then all turn out to be of the same ethnicity. This is especially common with Mexican agricultural workers in the southwest. Again, intergroup antipathies are especially significant in situations where people live together for substantial periods of time. It has long been common among migratory work gangs, and remains particularly important today in housing.

In principle, it makes no difference whether there is actual antipathy between groups, or whether there is simply a preference for the companionship of people from one's own group. The latter may in part reflect cultural similarities that reduce knowledge costs and risks in personal relationships or business transactions. Hasidic Jews in New York's jewelry industry, for example, have for generations made transactions among themselves in precious gems without any contracts, because of their complete reliance on each others' word —but to do so with members of the general population would be to invite disaster. The classic case of group antipathy in the United States—segregation and discrimination against blacks in the South during the Jim Crow era—included both bias and antipathy, but the point here is simply that these are separate factors and can occur separately.

Where a real cost is inherent in certain associations—whether because of antipathy or cultural differences—the competitive market will not eliminate the patterns that have evolved to deal with these costs. Where separate work gangs or housing segregation arise spontaneously in this way, the market will not undo these patterns unless and until the people themselves change in either characteristics or attitudes. Indeed, even forcible intervention by the government may fail to achieve its goal—as, for example, when people re-segregate themselves socially in statistically "integrated" housing or schools. Conversely, where the characteristics and attitudes are not sufficiently different for people to incur the costs of segregating themselves—as in northern U.S. cities toward the end of the nineteenth century—there may be open housing patterns despite a complete absence of open housing laws, despite the legality of racially restrictive covenants at that time, and despite the political powerlessness of the small black urban population. The drastic changes in this housing pattern in the early twentieth century followed changes in the characteristics of the northern black population, and consequently in the attitudes of the white population, in the wake of the great migrations of unacculturated southern blacks. In San Francisco, where this migration from the South arrived decades later, the changes in housing patterns and racial attitudes also occurred decades later.[180]

A competitive market puts a price on discrimination but does not eliminate or even continuously reduce discrimination based on antipathy, as it would tend to do with misjudgments. In the case of misjudgments, those firms (or other transactors) whose beliefs happen to be closer to the truth, would acquire a competitive advantage over those who were more mistaken. For example, those early twentieth century American farmers who paid Japanese immigrant farm workers as much as whites acquired a competitive advantage over those who paid less, because the Japanese workers were in fact more productive than the white workers and an employer who attracted more of them was better off economically. For this reason, competition quickly forced up the pay of Japanese farm workers, both absolutely and relative to that of whites. Where antipathy is involved, however, the employer (or other transactor) is willing to accept lower financial gains as the price of his aversion. Less prejudiced employers may earn slightly higher profits, but this differential will not automatically be eliminated through competition, for "psychic income" can make up for the difference in money income —within limits, for the firm must still make enough money income to survive. Still, the cost of discrimination becomes prohibitive at the point where the firm cannot survive. Even the most racist owner of a professional basketball team would have little choice but to hire blacks.

It need not be the actual decision maker who has the antipathy that causes discrimination. If employees object to working with someone from a different racial or ethnic background, the employer has an incentive to take that into account. If existing employees' morale, output or quit rates change because of the introduction of unpopular new employees, this represents a decline in productivity, even if the new employees are just as able as the old. While this situation *can* lead to discrimination, it need not in all cases. Insofar as the old employees can be replaced by more of the new employees from a different group, the threat or likelihood of their quitting or having reduced morale loses its effectiveness. Even in the antebellum South, when white workers at the Tread-gear factory in Virginia refused to work alongside black slaves, they were simply replaced with more blacks. But for this reaction to occur, there must be immediately available qualified replacements for the whole range of jobs involved.[181]

For racial and ethnic groups whose range of job capabilities extends into skilled, managerial, and entrepreneurial positions, an unwillingness of other workers to work with them has far less effect. Even if both workers and employers do not want to work with Jews, Jewish employers can employ Jewish workers and compete in the product market. Indeed this pattern has historically emerged with the Jews, the Japanese, and the Chinese, among other entre-preneurial groups. But where the range of skills in a given group is insufficient to man whole firms, they are at the mercy of others who may or may not agree to work with them.

Where antipathy is involved, it need not be based on any assumption that the resented group is inferior. Jews and Chinese have often been resented in countries around the world because their higher efficiency was seen as threatening. Even where a whole group is considered genetically inferior, it is often precisely the demonstrably capable members of that group who are particularly resented. For example, "it often angers the poor Whites in South Africa to see well-dressed Africans, or to hear them speak in a cultured manner."[182] Similar reactions to well-bred blacks have been common among many American southern whites at various times in American history.[183]

The discussions of markets thus far have been implicitly in terms of competitive markets. But markets may be noncompetitive for a number of reasons. Regulated public utilities—electric, telephone, and gas companies—are usually monopolies in their respective markets. Some enterprises are legally nonprofit: schools, hospitals, and foundations, for example. Purely private monopolies have been quite rare in American history and few cartels have held together without government regulation.

The cost of discrimination in a competitive market are the foregone profits lost by passing up transactions that would otherwise be remunerative. The threat that one's competitor will engage in these transactions can jeopardize the survival of a given firm. But in an insulated, non-competitive market such losses may be less, or even zero. A regulated utility that discriminates in hiring may have to pay higher costs of searching for and attracting qualified workers, since they pass up a certain fraction of such workers because of their race, religion, national origin, or other group identification. To hire 100 qualified workers may therefore imply searching out 150 qualified workers, if one-third are rejected for belonging to the "wrong" groups. These extra costs of production can be passed on to the firm's customers with the permission of the regulatory commission. It is not simply the fact that public utilities are monopolies that reduces the cost of discrimination. It is because they are *regulated* monopolies that discrimination costs are low or nonexistent. An unregulated monopoly would make a larger profit by nondis-criminatory hiring, but the regulated monopoly's profit rate is con-trolled by the government, so it cannot make a larger financial profit anyway. It can instead use its monopoly position to gain various nonfinancial perquisites—including discrimination.

Unions are a major factor in making labor markets noncompeti-tive. They have both direct and indirect effects on discrimination. Directly, they have at various times excluded various groups from membership—in the United States, the Irish, the Italians, the Chi-nese, and blacks perhaps most pervasively of all. Some unions have limited entry to relatives of existing members. This, in effect, ex-cluded members of other racial and ethnic groups. Like all prefer-ential treatment, it is also discrimination when looked at from the point of view of those *not* preferred.

Employers' self-interest has often put them on opposite sides from labor unions regarding racial and ethnic exclusion. The larger the supply of labor, the more the employer can select abler workers and the less likely wages are to rise. Employers and union members may be of the same race and ethnicity, and share the same bias and antipathy against other groups, but their respective *costs* of translat-ing subjective prejudice into overt discrimination are very differ-ent, leading to opposite behavior. Even in South Africa, employers have attempted to hire more Africans, and in higher positions, than the racist ideology or even government regulations would permit.[184] The development of racial exclusion in South Africa followed the development of militant labor unions there in the 1880s,[185] and union activity—including mass violence—spearheaded the progressive extension of discrimination against Africans, which ultimately culminated in rigid apartheid.[186] The first major "color bar" legislation in South Africa was passed in 1911, as a means of forestalling more union violence, which had included dynamiting, bloodshed and sabotage.[187]

In the United States as well, employers have often attempted to hire members of unpopular racial or ethnic groups and have incurred the bitter opposition of labor unions as a result. Chinese laborers were hired in California to help build the transcontinental railroad. Mexicans have been—and still are—imported to do agricultural field labor. During World War II, industrialist Henry Kaiser imported literally daily trainloads of blacks from the South to work in his factories.[188] None of this was motivated by altruism, but both employers and employees seized opportunities to advance themselves economically. Unions representing people who were there first, or who felt themselves somehow entitled to more than the newcomers were making, of course viewed this as an economic threat and sometimes a racial affront. Ironically, black American skilled workers were able to continue working at their trades in the South long after they were barred from such trades in the North, because labor unions had greater difficulty in establishing themselves in the South. Again, it was not simply the amount of prejudice which was economically decisive, but the *cost* of translating that prejudice into overt behavior. Non-union southern employers would have lost more by refusing to hire black skilled workers. Northern unionized employers could not have gained as much by hiring black skilled workers, who would have had to be paid the same artificially high union wages as white workers.

In addition to their own direct discrimination, labor unions also make it cheaper for employers to discriminate. The cost of discrimination to an employer consists of the lost profits which he could otherwise receive by hiring from a larger labor pool, getting more selective workers at lower cost. Where unions have forced wage rates up above the level they would have reached in a competitive market, employers demand fewer workers while the supply grows, as more job applicants are attracted by the higher pay. In short, a chronic surplus of applicants is created by artificially high wage rates. A chronic surplus of workers allows employers to exclude any kind of workers they do not like—including by race or ethnicity—without suffering the kinds of financial losses that such discrimination would entail in a competitive market.

CHAPTER SIX

The American Experience

The historic movement of millions of immigrants and the great variety of racial and ethnic groups that constitute its population today make the United States a unique study in race and ethnicity. The very concept of ethnic "minorities" is misleading in the United States, where there is no ethnic majority. While Caucasians from a large majority—87 percent—of the population of the United States,[1] ethnic breakdowns among whites (and blacks) remain significant, and there is nothing approaching an ethnic majority. A majority-minority characterization would have been valid in colonial America, when more than three-quarters of the inhabitants of the 13 colonies were of British ancestry,[2] but by the time of the first U.S. census in 1790, they were only about half of the population.[3] While it is fashionable to talk as if there were still an Anglo-Saxon majority today, they are in fact only 14 percent of the American population. They are the largest single group in the population, but are not even close to being a majority.

Even these data understate the ethnic heterogeneity of the American population. Each of these groups contain many individuals whose ancestry is a mixture with other groups. More than two-thirds of all Americans who give their ancestry as English also list other ancestries. So do nearly four-fifths of all American Indians.[5] For the United States as a whole, only 45 percent of the population consists of people of a single ancestry (as far as they know[6]), while 38 percent know their ancestry to be multiple, and 17 percent do

TABLE 6-1

ETHNICITY	NUMBER	PERCENT
British	29,548,000	14
German	25,543,000	13
Black	23,465,000	11
Irish	16,408,000	8
Hispanic	9,178,000	5
Italian	8,764,000	4
French	5,420,000	3
Polish	5,105,000	3
Russian	2,188,000	1
Unidentified	17,556,000	9
Other	85,130,000	42

Source: U.S. Bureau of the Census[4]

not specify.[7] Racially, Anglo-Saxon dominance is a myth.

Sometimes it is the Anglo-Saxon culture that is considered oppressively dominant, requiring all others to abandon their heritage as the price of acceptance or progress in American society. Historically, however, Japanese, German, and Jewish immigrants began their rise to prosperity while barely speaking English, retaining many cultural traits and living in isolated communities.[8] More generally, cultural adaptation in the United States has been a two-way process—the general culture containing many features once peculiar to particular ethnic groups. American popular music is based on music once peculiar to blacks—the blues and jazz. Nothing is more American than frankfurters and hamburgers, but both are named for cities in Germany because they originated with German Americans. American slang has likewise incorporated ethnic peculiarities. The habit of addressing someone as "man" originated with blacks and the phrase "go for broke" originated with Japanese Americans. Nothing is more American than cowboys and the old west, but these cowboys used ranching practices that originated with the Spaniards when they occupied the southwest, and the American pioneers crossed the western plains in covered wagons that were once peculiar to German farmers in Pennsylvania.

What is loosely and misleadingly called an "Anglo" society or culture in the United States is in fact a mosaic with prominent features of Semitic, Hispanic, Negro, Asiatic, and other origins. The American clothing industry was essentially created by Jews, as were most of the great motion picture studios. The American beer industry and piano industry are the creations of Germans. Contract gardening in California was created and dominated by the Japanese. Even organized crime in America has had a distinct ethnic flavor, being dominated in historical succession by the Irish, then the Jews, and then the Italians. The great American political machines of the nineteenth and early twentieth centuries were almost invariably Irish political machines—and their attitudes and practices derived from the peculiar history of Ireland.[9]

The illusion of a dominant majority and peculiar "minorities" is fostered by the practice of comparing some given group with "the national average" in income, I.Q., longevity, crime, or other variables. But in a highly diverse country like the United States, with regional and other variations overlaying and complicating the ethnic mosaic, the so-called "national average" is nothing more than a statistical amalgamation of wide-ranging diversities. No group is as unusual as it may appear to be when compared to the national average. Every ethnic group is similar to some other ethnic group in income, I.Q., fertility rate, etc. Black-white comparisons, for example, often show great disparities, but in fact blacks do *not* have the lowest incomes,[10] I.Q.'s,[11] occupational status,[12] or educational levels,[13] among American ethnic groups, nor the highest levels of alcoholism[14] or of female-headed families.[15] Blacks are simply one of a number of groups in the same region of the distribution.

Precisely because race and ethnicity have often involved powerful emotions and sometimes dramatic and violent actions, there is a tendency to regard all inter-racial and inter-ethnic differences as due to race or racism. But American racial and ethnic groups differ enormously in characteristics ranging from age to regional distribution to diverse cultural backgrounds. Many of these characteristics have a major impact on the economic conditions of racial and ethnic groups, even though they attract much less attention than race or racism.

ECONOMIC DIFFERENCES

The majority-minority vision of American society is belied by ethnic income differences, which are spread across a wide continuum, rather than showing a national norm with a few exceptions.

Among non-white Americans, some groups (Japanese and Chinese) earned more than whites, some (Filipinos and West Indians) earned about the same, and others (Indians and native blacks) earned substantially less. Still other groups with a majority classified as white (Puerto Ricans and Mexicans) earned substantially below the national average.[17] In short, non-white groups are spread across the income spectrum, just as white groups are. On the whole, whites earn more than non-whites, but only because, statistically, about 90 percent of non-whites in the United States are native black Americans—not because non-white groups are all consigned to lower economic positions. Japanese Americans earn higher incomes than Americans of German, Italian, Irish, Polish, or Anglo-Saxon ancestry. So do second generation black West Indians.[18]

Historically, there is little question that non-whites have encountered more economic and social barriers than whites in the United States. The pervasive Jim Crow laws that confronted generations of blacks in the South were unique, but the worst years of anti-Asian laws and policies on the west coast were a close second—featuring vigilante violence as well as legal discrimination and public hostility.[19] Yet what is surprising is the cold fact that there has been little correlation between the degree of discrimination in history and the economic results today. It would be hard to claim that Puerto Ricans have encountered as much discrimination as the Japanese—who have about *double* their incomes. It would be even more difficult to claim that Puerto Ricans have historically encountered a level of discrimination comparable to that of blacks, who have higher occupational status and 20 percent higher incomes.[20] There may well be color prejudice against the multi-colored Puerto Ricans, but it would be hard to claim that it is stronger than color prejudice against black West Indians, who have 50 percent higher family incomes.[21]

TABLE 6-2

ETHNICITY	*1969 FAMILY INCOME %	**1977 FAMILY INCOME %
Jewish	172	**
Japanese	132	—
Polish	115	119
Chinese	112	—
Italian	112	114
German	107	111
Anglo-Saxon	105	113
Irish	103	110
National Average	100	100
Filipino	99	—
West Indian	94	—
Cuban	80	88
Mexican	76	73
Puerto Rican	63	50
Black	62	60
Indian (American)	60	—

Source: U.S. Bureau of the Census and National Jewish Population Survey[16]

  * Median family income of each ethnic group divided by the median family income of the U.S. population as a whole.

  ** Comparable data for Jews are not available for both periods, but using Russian-American data as a proxy for Jewish data, as is commonly done in the literature, shows an income percentage of 146 for 1968, 140 for 1970 and a 1977 income percentage of 143.

It may seem difficult to reconcile the demonstrable color prejudice which has applied to all non-white groups, for at least a substantial part of their history in the United States, with the equally demonstrable fact that various non-white groups today equal or exceed the economic level of various white groups. Part of the answer is that the translation of subjective prejudice into overt economic discrimination—or of discrimination into poverty—is by no means automatic. The historic prosperity of the hated "overseas Chinese" in southeast Asia, or of the Jews who have faced centuries of anti-Semitism in Europe, is perhaps the most dramatic evidence of this. In addition, however, prejudice itself is not fixed either in scope or intensity.

American racial and ethnic attitudes and behavior have changed in many ways during the post-World War II era. Jews were restricted or excluded from many university faculties before the war,[22] but in the postwar era their representation on such faculties rose far beyond their proportion of the population.[23] Professional sports which totally excluded black athletes before the war came to be dominated by black athletes after the war—baseball, football, and above all, basketball. Anti-Japanese laws, which flourished in California before the war were resoundingly defeated in a postwar referendum.[24] Attitude surveys over the years have shown major reversals of public opinion on race and ethnicity,[25] and rising rates of intermarriage substantiated the reality of these changes.

Historically, the degree to which various groups have encountered prejudice or social acceptability has varied greatly over time —as indicated by such things as changing residential segregation patterns and changing intermarriage rates. Only in recent years has the intermarriage rate for any non-white group approached 50 percent. It has generally been the more prosperous and better educated non-white groups who have had the highest intermarriage rates and the least residential segregation. About half of all *current* marriages of Japanese in Los Angeles County and in Hawaii are inter-racial marriages[26]—almost invariably with whites.[27] Historically, this has not always been so, for only about 2 percent of Japanese marriages in Los Angeles during the 1920s were intermarriages, and a generation later still only 11 to 12 percent of their marriages were intermarriages.[28] The Japanese are also no longer residentially segregated,[29] and neither are the Chinese.[30] At the other extreme, only about one percent of blacks who are currently being married have brides or grooms of a different race, and even outside the South the intermarriage rate of blacks is only about 4 percent.[31] Blacks are, in addition, far more residentially segregated than most other ethnic groups—except Puerto Ricans.[32] In short, social acceptance seems to be correlated with economic success, both at a given time and historically. This has been true of white groups as well as non-whites. As of 1910, Italian immigrants were more residentially segregated than blacks in many cities.[33] The ethnic intermarriage rate of the nineteenth century Irish in Boston was less than one-fifth of their marriages,[34] while most Irish husbands today have wives who are not Irish.[35] For most American ethnic groups—white and non-white—social acceptance seems to have come *after* their economic rise, and was not a cause of that rise. Looked at another way, lack of social acceptance has not prevented either white or non-white groups from rising out of poverty.

One of the most obvious reasons why some groups earn higher incomes than others is often ignored: They work more. More than half of all Chinese American families have more than one income earner,[36] while only about one-third of the Puerto Rican families have multiple income earners.[37] More than 20 percent of all Puerto Rican families have *no one* earning an income.[38] Puerto Rican women remain outside the labor force far more so than either black or white American women.[39] In the prime earning years (age 25–44) less than half as many Puerto Rican women as non-Hispanic white women are working. These are the years when the highest proportion of black women (61 percent) and the lowest proportion of Puerto Rican women (22 percent) are working.

Another factor of major importance that is often ignored is that groups differ greatly in age, and therefore in work experience. Age has profound effects of its own—independently of race and ethnicity—on incomes, unemployment rates, crime rates, fertility, and a host of other social variables.

Raw age differences alone are not the whole story, however. Income variations and educational variations between the more prosperous and the less prosperous groups are concentrated in their *older* members. That is, the younger members of the various groups are much more similar in incomes and education, reflecting more equal opportunities in more recent times, as well as a growing acculturation in the more disadvantaged groups. First, as to income: the differences among young males (18 to 24) are much smaller—absolutely and in percentages—than among those in their peak earning years (45 to 54). Indeed, in these younger brackets, a low-income group like the Puerto Ricans actually earns more than a high-income group like the Chinese. In general, low-income groups reach their peak incomes early, while higher-income groups peak later on, as they continue to rise to higher positions with experience. Among the younger workers, those who have been in

TABLE 6-3

ETHNICITY	MEDIAN AGE		
	Entire Group	*Income Earners*	*Family Heads*
Jewish	46	—	50
Polish	40	—	—
Irish	37	—	—
Italian	36	—	—
German	36	—	—
Japanese	32	41	46
Chinese	27	39	44
Filipino	26	37	43
Black	22	41	43
American Indian	20	38	42
Puerto Rican	18	34	36
Mexican	18	—	—
West Indian	—	43	45

Source: U.S. Bureau of the Census and National Jewish Population Survey[40]

college or have other training may not have as much job experience as others who have been at work, so that it takes some time before higher skills offset the effect of greater experience among their less trained contemporaries.

The combined effect of age and education can be seen in the fact that Jewish family heads are not only fourteen years older than Puerto Rican family heads, but in addition average six more years of schooling[42]—the difference between failing to complete the ninth grade and reaching the third year of college.

Disadvantaged groups are rising in educational qualifications, not only absolutely but also relative to the general society. This is reflected economically in the fact that younger members of disadvantaged ethnic groups earn incomes more comparable to their peers than do the older individuals who came along in less favorable times. Among young husband-wife families outside the South, black family income was 78 percent of white in 1959, 91 percent in 1969, and 96 percent in 1970.[43] When both husband and wife

TABLE 6-4

ETHNICITY	MEAN INCOME OF MALES 1969	
	AGE 18–24	AGE 45–54
American Indian	82	53
Blacks	83	54
Chinese	66	100
Filipino	91	69
Japanese	83	107
Puerto Rican	101	62
West Indian	96	74

Source: U.S. Bureau of the Census[41]

work in both races, the black couples earned 4 percent more than the white couples in 1970[44] and 5 percent more in 1971.[45]

The United States is a regionally diverse country, in which the average income in some states is more than double what it is in others.[46] Obviously the regional distribution of ethnic groups affects their average income in the nation—obvious, but often ignored. In 1969, blacks and Puerto Ricans had very similar incomes nationally, but only because half the black population was in the South, a low-income region where few Puerto Ricans lived. Blacks outside the South earned significantly higher incomes than Puerto Ricans in the same places.[47] The relative economic positions of the two groups—and the whole question of the role of color in the American economy—could be misunderstood if regional distribution were not taken into account.

American ethnic groups have varied widely in their regional distribution patterns, largely for historical reasons going back to the era of mass immigration.[48] But however various ethnic groups came to be located where they are, their economic fate is tied to the fate of the industries and occupations of those regions. In addition, those who have migrated face the special adjustment problems of migrants, as well as representing a special kind of person compared to others in the same group. American Indians in the urban northeast are almost a decade older than Indians in the rural midwest—and have two less children per family.[49] Blacks in the North have higher incomes than blacks in the South.[50]

In addition to the impact of demographic and regional factors, ethnic groups also differ because of cultural differences that existed long before they ever set foot on American soil. These include not only specific skills—the Germans producing beer, pianos, and optical equipment, and the Jews clothing and retailing—but whole patterns of orientation toward the economy, the society, and life in general. Groups who shared the same immigrant slums, and whose children sat side-by-side in the same schools, nevertheless had entirely different patterns of development in America—patterns reflecting traditions from thousands of miles away and from centuries past.[51] When the Irish were poor immigrants, the men often worked building railroads and the women as maids, but when the Jewish immigrants went through equally desperate poverty, they almost never worked at either of these occupations, which would have conflicted with their religious observances and their conception of the family.[52] Black West Indian immigrants have had far lower crime rates than other blacks living in the same ghettoes—and lower crime rates than white Americans, for that matter.[53] Apparently the "root causes" of crime due to "social conditions" in the ghetto did not affect the West Indians. The Irish have had rates of alcoholic psychosis that were 25 times the rate among Italians and 50 times that among Jews.[54] These differences hardly seem explicable by the "pressures" of American life, when great differences in drunkenness or alcoholism can be found in the same three groups in Europe in centuries past.

FAMILIES

American ethnic groups differ in the age at which they marry, the degree to which they form and maintain families intact, the size of families, and the values conveyed by the families to their young.[55] This affects not only the economic prospects of the women but of their husbands as well—the men of one group having family responsibilities that force them to take jobs early in life, while men of the other group can wait until they complete college and enter the work force at a higher level. Moreover, early marriage contributes to a large number of children—twice as many among Mexican American as among Japanese American women at the end of their child-bearing years.[56] Groups also differ in the extent to which they form families at all. For example, only 9 percent of white males in the 25- to 64-year old bracket are single, while 16 percent of black males in the same bracket are single.[57] This has economic as well as social effects. Married men—and especially those with dependent children—have higher rates of labor force participation and lower rates of unemployment.[58] A group with a disproportionate number of single men without dependents would tend also to have fewer men working and lower incomes for this reason, as well as for other reasons.

Among the families that are formed, some are broken by divorce or desertion, others never had two parents in the home at one time, due to unwed pregnancy, often among teenage girls. While comparative data on female-headed families covering the spectrum of American ethnic groups are difficult to find, some rough picture may be formed by the following data from heterogeneous sources:

TABLE 6-5

ETHNICITY	FEMALE-HEADED FAMILIES (%)
Chinese	7
Jewish	7
German	8
Filipino	9
Polish	9
Italian	10
Japanese	10
Irish	12
Mexican	12
American Indian	18
West Indian	24
Black	31
Puerto Rican	34

Source: U.S. Bureau of the Census and National Jewish Population Survey[59]

These wide-ranging differences have major implications for the way each group's children are raised. For example, more than four-fifths of all white children live with both their parents. But among black children, less than half live with both parents.[60]

Black female-headed families have had declining real incomes during a period when black husband-wife families have had rising real incomes, both absolutely and relative to white families.[61] It would be very difficult to explain those opposite trends by the attitudes of white employers. But the two kinds of families may well represent different cultural values that have economic consequences. There are other indications of this as well. For example, by the late 1960s young black males from families with a library card and newspapers and magazines in the home reached high-level occupations as frequently as white males of the same description who had the same education and home background.[62] The large occupational differences still continuing between young black and white males reflected large cultural differences that existed before either reached the employer. Many attitude surveys have concluded that low-achieving groups have the same values or aspirations as high-achieving groups,[63] but answering survey questions costs little effort while economic advancement may cost years of sacrifice and hard work. What is relevant is the willingness to *pay a price* to achieve goals. Large behavioral differences suggest that the trade-off of competing desires vary enormously among American ethnic groups.

The number of children per family has an important effect on its current economic conditions and on its future prospects as well. Mexican American families have higher incomes than black families, but lower *per capita* income than blacks. Among the consequences of this are that Mexican Americans live in substandard housing to a greater extent than do blacks,[64] and send a smaller proportion of their children to college.[65] It is not simply the average number of children in a given racial or ethnic group that is important, but their distribution as well. About one-third of all black children are born to women who never reached the ninth grade,[66] and almost half of all Puerto Rican children are born to women who never reached the ninth grade.[67] The handicaps faced by the younger generation born into families with ill-educated parents are not simply the poverty that may exist there, but also the inability of such parents to provide them with the values or orientation—much less experience—that lead to upward mobility.

Those who do have the education, values, experience, and contacts to pass on to their children often do not have many—or any —children. Blacks with a college education or professional occupations have historically had too few children to reproduce themselves. Similarly, more than half of all college-educated Puerto Rican women near the end of their childbearing years have had no more than two children, including one quarter who have had no children at all.[68] Looked at another way, more than 90 percent of all black children are born to women who never completed a single year of college.[69] So are 99 percent of all Puerto Rican children.[70]

It is a general pattern in American society for higher income groups to have fewer children than lower income groups. But this pattern is accentuated among disadvantaged racial and ethnic groups. Black, Mexican, or Puerto Rican low-income classes have even more children than equally low-income members of the general population, while their high-income members have even fewer children than equally high-income members of the general population.[71] Whatever the causes of this social phenomenon, its economic consequences are profound. Much of what the successful members of each group have achieved—often at great sacrifice— dies with them, instead of being passed on as a legacy of the race. Much of the hard struggle up from poverty to prosperity has to be repeated from the beginning in each generation, because those who have succeeded economically fail to reproduce themselves, while a large, disproportionate share of each new generation is born to people living in poverty and without the skills, education, acculturation, or personal contacts that would enable their children to have a reasonable chance at economic advancement. In short, enormous amounts of "human capital" are lost in each generation among those ethnic groups most in need of it. Their attempts to achieve economic parity would be greatly handicapped by this alone, even if there were no discrimination whatsoever.

EDUCATION

Educational differences among American ethnic groups have been very large for a very long time. Rates of illiteracy among immigrant groups have varied from virtually zero to virtually one hundred percent.[72] Among the children of immigrants in the early twentieth century, more than half the southern Italian children were behind their normal grade in school, while only one-fifth of the Dutch children were behind their normal grade. And while more than one-fourth of the Dutch children were *ahead* of their normal grade, less than a tenth of the Italian children were.[73] The proportion of school children who completed high school was more than one hundred times greater among the Germans and Jews than among the Irish and Italians.[74] Even in the middle of the twentieth century, the I.Q. score difference between Japanese and Mexican children sitting side-by-side in the same schools in the United States were as large as the difference between black and white school children attending separate schools in the segregated South.[75]

All that is unique about our times is the extent to which we ignore earlier times, and regard our racial or ethnic differences as unprecedented. In reality, today's intergroup differences are not only smaller than in the past, but are continuing to narrow. The proportion of high school dropouts among blacks was twice as high as among whites in 1967,[76] but this ratio was nowhere near the differences between the Germans and the Irish in the early part of the century. Moreover, by 1972 the black dropout rate was only 66 percent higher than among the whites.[77]

Qualitative differences in education usually add to the quantitative differences. Groups with above-average amounts of education —Jews, Chinese, Japanese—also have higher-quality education. Jewish college students are disproportionately represented in the more selective colleges, and specialize in such demanding (and highly paid) fields as law, medicine, and biochemistry.[78] The Chinese and Japanese are over-represented in difficult and well-paying fields such as mathematics and the natural sciences.[79] Chinese and Japanese college and university faculty members have the Ph.D. more often than either black or white faculty members, and the degrees are usually from higher-rated departments.[80] Conversely, groups with below-average quantities of education—blacks, Puerto Ricans, and Mexicans—also have lower qualities of education. All-black schools in the South have historically had far less resources and poorer standards than white schools, and black colleges have lagged far behind other institutions of higher learning, whether measured by objective criteria such as SAT scores, library resources, departmental rankings or faculty scholarship[81]—or measured by evaluations of observers.[82] Puerto Ricans and Mexicans not only have fewer years of schooling, but perform less well during school[83] and even the very few who go on to higher education attend less demanding colleges.[84]

In short, statistics on years of schooling understate the educational differences between racial or ethnic groups. One consequence of this is that comparisons of individuals with the "same" education and from different ethnic backgrounds often show substantial income disparities that are then taken as a measure of intergroup discrimination. In a few cases where qualitative measures of education are available, taking quality differences into account drastically changes the conclusions. Black faculty members with a Ph.D. earn slightly less than white faculty members with a Ph.D., but usually *more* than white faculty members with a Ph.D. in the same field from a department of the same quality ranking.[85]

Groups with lower-quality educational preparation tend to go into easier colleges and easier subjects in a given college. A far higher proportion of blacks than whites receive their doctorates in education. Asians, on the other hand, receive a higher percentage of their doctorates in science and engineering.[86]

A case could be made that Chinese and Japanese faculty are underpaid, when quality of education is taken into account. These Asian faculty members receive about the same incomes as black or white faculty members, but have more and higher-rated degrees, are concentrated in higher-paying fields, and publish more articles than either their black or white colleagues.[87] When all these qualitative factors are held constant, Chinese and Japanese faculty members receive thousands of dollars less than others with the same qualifications.[88] This could be a result of group discrimination, a general leveling tendency, or a result of the foreign birth and consequently lesser English fluency of many Asians, which would tend to lower their market value as teachers. This last consideration would apply more to the Chinese (about half of whom were foreign born[89]) than to the Japanese (most of whom are native born).[90] The faculty data cited do not separate the two, but census data show that Japanese with two or more years of postgraduate work earn even more than other Americans of the same high educational level, while the Chinese earn less than similarly educated professionals in the general population.[91] Whatever the true explanation of the patterns, the main point here is that gross educational data often lead to opposite conclusions from data that include qualitative differences.[92] Group income differences can be either overstated or understated as a result.

A more fundamental question may be raised as to the historic importance of education as a means of raising a group from poverty to affluence. Often it is taken as axiomatic that education is the key ingredient in the dramatic rise of such groups as Jews, Chinese and Japanese—and its lack the crucial factor in the poverty of today's low-income groups. Plausible as this may seem, the evidence does not support it. The Chinese, the Japanese, and the Jews were all rising economically before any significant proportion of them even completed high school.[93] *After* they had achieved a measure of prosperity through business success (including farming, in the case of the Japanese), *then* they could afford to send their children on to college and postgraduate education to become doctors, scientists, and other well-paid professionals. To groups without the entrepreneurial backgrounds of the Jews, Chinese, and Japanese, education is of course more important as an avenue of upward mobility. But that is no reason to perpetuate a myth about history. Even today, West Indians have the same amount of schooling as other blacks in the New York City metropolitan area, but earn 28 percent higher incomes there.[94]

Along with the myth of the historic importance of education in groups rising out of poverty, there has been a presumption that good education itself requires a particular kind of home environment. Books and magazines in the home, and much verbal interaction between parents and children, are assumed to be prerequisites to good education, along with parental "involvement" in the school as an institution. But the children of Japanese American immigrants had none of these "prerequisites" during the era of their high educational achievements. Their farmer parents were not intellectuals, and the children usually spoke to their parents only when spoken to.[95] As for parental involvement, Jewish, Japanese and Chinese immigrant parents all avoided going to the school and felt very uncomfortable with their broken English and unfamiliarity with American ways. Their input into the educational process consisted of telling their children to obey the teacher.[96] Black parents of children attending good quality black schools have likewise had little to say about how such schools were run, except to back up whatever the teacher did.[97] Whether or not these are the ideal roles for parents, the roles that are often projected as "prerequisites" today have no basis in history.

CIVIL RIGHTS

No discussion of American ethnic groups would be complete without consideration of the civil rights revolution of the 1960s. For much of American history, many laws explicitly discriminated by race—against Negroes, Asians, Hispanics and American Indians. The Fourteenth Amendment to the Constitution outlawed some of the most gross discriminations, but the doctrine that "separate but equal" facilities met the constitutional requirements enabled many segregated—and highly unequal—facilities to survive on into the middle of the twentieth century.

The 1954 Supreme Court decision in *Brown v. Board of Education* outlawed school segregation, and in rapid order numerous other segregated public facilities as well, notably in the South. A decade later, the Civil Rights Act of 1964 outlawed numerous discriminatory practices by state and local governments and by private institutions. Changing public opinion, institutional efforts at opening doors to all and growing rates of intermarriage underscored a new attitude toward racial and ethnic differences. The poorest American ethnic groups—blacks, Puerto Ricans, Mexican Americans, and American Indians—began to enter higher level occupations in greater numbers than before. Yet not all of this can be attributed to declining discrimination. Disadvantaged groups were themselves changing. Growing proportions of Mexican Americans completed high school, especially among those in the second and third generations.[98] Black enrollment in colleges doubled.[99] The Chinese and Japanese overtook whites in years of schooling.[100]

These are only specific indications of much more sweeping changes in many American ethnic groups over the generations— changes ranging from personal cleanliness to knowledge of English to reduced violence—all of which have facilitated their economic advancement and social acceptance.[101] Yet the political interpretation of group advancement has made it appear to be simply the product of the larger society's grudging acceptance in general or anti-discrimination laws in particular. It is true, for example, that the number of blacks in higher level occupations increased substantially in the years immediately following passage of the Civil Rights Act of 1964. But it is also true that the numbers of blacks in such occupations increased substantially in the years immediately *preceding* passage of the Civil Rights Act of 1964. The number of blacks in professional, technical and similar high level occupations more than doubled between 1954 and 1964.[102] The continuation of this pre-existing trend after the Civil Rights Act is hardly decisive evidence of the efficacy of political action.

Where political action has been demonstrably effective has been in *negating* the effects of state government action by the federal government. In short, government-created harm was reduced. The whole array of discriminatory practices by state governments, notably in the South, came under attack by the federal courts, national legislation and national administrative policies during the era of the civil rights revolution. As a result of the federal crackdown on southern state voting discrimination, for example, the number of black state officials elected in the South increased nearly eight-fold from 1964 to 1975.[103]

Where the federal government has attempted to move beyond this essentially negative role to produce positive benefits for disadvantaged racial and ethnic groups, the record has been far less impressive. One of the most controversial of these attempts has been "affirmative action" or preferential hiring policies. This concept evolved into "numerical goals and timetables" (job quotas) in federal guidelines issued in December 1971.[104] Two years before that date Puerto Rican family income was 63 percent of the national average, and 5 years afterwards it was *down* to 50 percent.[105] Black family income followed a fluctuating path[106] and Mexican American family income declined slightly as a percentage of the national average.[107] Whatever the complex of factors behind these numbers, at the very least, they offer no positive evidence of benefits from affirmative action.

While "affirmative action" results were unimpressive in gross terms, a finer breakdown shows disturbing counterproductive trends. The least fortunate blacks, for example, grew worse off economically, while those already more fortunate rose rapidly. Black males with 8 to 11 years of schooling, and less than 6 years of work experience earned 79 percent of the income of white males of the same description in 1967 (before quotas) and this *fell* to 69 percent by 1978 (after quotas). During the very same span, black males who had completed college and had more than 6 years of work experience rose from 75 percent of the income of their white counterparts to 98 percent.[108] By 1980, college-educated black couples were earning more than college-educated white couples.[109]

However paradoxical these sharply opposing trends may seem, they are a logical consequence of the incentives and constraints created by affirmative action policies. While government pressures to hire from designated groups created an incentive for employers to include representatives of such groups among their employees, continuing government scrutiny of their subsequent pay, promotion, and discharge patterns made it especially risky to have employees from these groups who did not work out well. In short, the tendency was to increase the demand for "safe" employees from the government-designated groups—individuals with a college education or substantial work experience—and to *reduce* the demand for those lacking such education and experience. In the academic world as well, black faculty with outstanding credentials fared substantially better than white faculty with the same outstanding credentials, but black faculty without a doctorate or publications earned less than white faculty of the same description.[110] More generally, the proportion of all black income going to the top fifth of blacks increased, while that going to each of the bottom three fifths all declined.[111]

This was only one of many social programs in which, in the *name* of the poor and the disadvantaged, those who were already well off were made still better off—while the ostensible beneficiaries were either neglected or made worse off. Nor was this pattern unique to blacks or even to the United States. Preferential treatment of Thai-owned businesses in Thailand caused many Chinese there to acquire a Thai partner, preferably one with influence with the government.[112] This presented new opportunities for Thais who were already more fortunate—but not for the Thai peasant out in the rice paddies.

Much discussion of the effect of political policies in general, and civil rights activities in particular, proceed as if one were measuring the progress of an unchanging minority, whose advancement could then be attributed to the policies in question. But the civil rights revolution occurred during—and was probably facilitated by—substantial changes among blacks, Hispanics and other groups. Most of the rise of black income relative to white income from 1940 to

1960 was due to migration out of low-income areas[113] and much of the rise since then to rising job qualifications, including education.[114] If past progress is falsely diagnosed, current and future policies based on those false diagnoses can be ineffective or counterproductive—yet bitterly divisive.

There are powerful incentives to continue the political crusades of the past, even after their beneficial effects are exhausted. Part of the reason is inertia. A large civil rights establishment, inside and outside government, has to find work to do,[115] and must convince itself and others that this work is vitally important. More generally, there is a fatal fascination with the prospect of morally regenerating other people or (failing that) smiting the wicked. Whether that will in fact advance the economically disadvantaged is another question entirely.

IMMIGRATION

Patterns and policies related to immigration have gone through dramatic changes over the years in the United States, as in other countries. Initially an open admission policy led to large scale immigration—almost all from Europe—reaching a peak of nearly nine million people during the first decade of the twentieth century, when immigrants constituted ten percent of the American population.[116] The first numerical ceiling on immigration to the United States was instituted in the 1920s, cutting the number of immigrants in half. The Great Depression of the 1930s cut immigration still further, down to about half a million people for the entire decade.[117] World War II reduced the number of immigrants to less than a thousand people per year during 1942, 1943, and 1944. While the postwar era saw sharp increases in immigration, the numbers never approached those of the late nineteenth and early twentieth centuries.

The composition of the immigration has changed as dramatically as the numbers. Nearly three-quarters of all immigrants to the United States from 1820 to 1979 were from Europe. But the decade of the 1970s saw nearly twice as many immigrants from Asia as from Europe (34 percent versus 18 percent) and a still higher proportion (45 percent) were from the Western Hemisphere.[118] There were almost as many legal immigrants from Mexico as from all the countries of Europe combined—and massive illegal immigration from Mexico makes it virtually certain that more Mexicans than Europeans entered the United States during the 1970s. However, recent changes in immigration patterns are part of a long history of changes in the numbers and origins of immigrants to the United States. As noted in Chapter 5, the change from wind-driven to steam-powered ships caused a revolution in the origins of European immigrants, raising difficult questions about the very different cultural characteristics of the "new" versus "old" European immigrants. The still newer immigration sources of our times raise very similar kinds of questions.

As also noted in Chapter 5, immigrants in general tend not only to rise in American society, but even to exceed the incomes of native-born Americans of the same ethnic background. But this does not mean that this long process is costless, either to them or to the surrounding society. More important, the succeeding generations born on American soil may form very different attitudes and exhibit very different behavior. For example, while the immigrant generation may be content and grateful to have improved their economic condition by moving to the United States, the second generation has only the American scene as its standard of reference, and may become resentful and embittered if their group's incomes, occupations, and general living conditions are below those of other Americans. Therefore, even an economically rising group may have a sharp upsurge of delinquency and crime among its youth, as happened among the Jewish and Italian immigrants in the late nineteenth and early twentieth centuries, and among Mexican immigrants and Cuban refugees more recently. The hidden costs of immigration thus include vandalism, disruption of schools, violence and murder, as well as economic costs that fall disproportionately on the poorer elements of the American population, with whom the newcomers compete for jobs.

Immigrants often begin in the United States at the bottom of the occupational ladder, even when they have the skills or aptitudes to move up later, as they acquire more information and contacts in the American job market. Cuban refugees in Miami, for example, often began in menial jobs formerly held by blacks, and then many Cubans made a spectacular economic rise. Less fortunate immigrant groups often begin and remain in low-level occupations, becoming permanent competitors with low-income Americans, whose already high levels of unemployment are a tragedy to themselves and to the taxpayers who support them. Where the immigrants are illegal, employers can hire them for less than the minimum wage, without their going to the authorities to complain. Thus illegal immigrants nave an advantage in competing for work where low-skilled Americans have been priced out of the market by law.

The problem is more complicated than immigrants' "taking jobs" from Americans. There is no fixed or pre-determined number of jobs, as implicitly assumed by those who see immigrants as simply displacing Americans on a one-to-one basis. As immigrants increase the total output in the economy, they correspondingly increase aggregate consumer demand, which is one of many economic variables whose interactions determine how many jobs there will be. But an increase in *any* factor of production (labor, capital, land, etc.) tends to raise the productivity and rewards of *complementary* factors, while reducing the demand and reward for *competing* factors. It is therefore hardly surprising that suppliers of capital welcome more labor—in the United States, as in South Africa, Brazil, or elsewhere —while the suppliers of labor (notably labor unions) seek to restrict the numbers and categories of labor admitted.

Governmental programs in various countries have tried to compromise the opposing political pressures by admitting foreign workers only after an official determination that there are not "enough" domestic workers to fill the available vacancies. This approach repeats the implicit assumption of fixed numbers of jobs, where there are in fact complex interactions of economic forces. If there are not "enough" workers *at a given wage,* then the normal effect of market competition is to cause wages to rise until more workers are attracted. At the same time, the rising cost of labor causes employers to seek more labor-economizing ways of accomplishing a given task. These two trends continue until the increasing number of workers and the reduced number of jobs come into balance—*at a higher wage rate.* But this rise in wages is aborted insofar as immigration policy admits foreign workers to fill vacancies that domestic workers will not fill at existing pay scales.

In a modern welfare state, there may be a considerable gap between the wage rate that would, for example, attract Americans to hard agricultural work, while welfare and unemployment benefits are available, and a wage rate sufficient to attract destitute people from Mexico. The net result of immigration policies to admit "enough" workers may be that agricultural employers get cheaper labor than otherwise, while American taxpayers end up supporting idle Americans who are perfectly capable of performing the same tasks—but not at wages too low to compensate them for what they would give up in various welfare state benefits. From the standpoint of the economy as a whole, excess numbers of people are being supported, beyond what is necessary to produce a given total output, even if immigrants have not directly taken jobs from Americans.

Attempts to control immigration—either quantitatively or qualitatively—encounter both practical and political obstacles. The physical accessibility of the United States, across a largely un-guarded border with Mexico or across a relatively short water route from the Caribbean, would require far more immigration person-nel, and more vigorous law enforcement, than has evolved histori-cally in generations of dealing primarily with Europeans who faced the far more formidable geographic barrier of the Atlantic Ocean.

Controlling the new flow of immigrants is also more difficult politically. Any attempt to restrict immigration according to the very different historical records of various groups in adjusting to American society encounter automatic and vociferous cries of "rac-ism." Any serious attempts at guarding the border—for example, barbed wire to deter, or jail sentences to punish, illegal border crossers—run into humanitarian objections that sway courts and politically influence legislators or administrators. The net result is that there are only negligible penalties, and negligible deterrence, for illegal immigrants from Mexico, the largest source. Those caught trying to sneak across the border from Mexico are usually sent back, and often try again the same night.

Refugees from Caribbean dictatorships like Haiti or Cuba pre-sent a very different problem, for sending them back can in some cases be a virtual death sentence. But to let them stay means en-couraging many others to follow. Often these are people with no skills of significant value in the economy and having cultural back-grounds (including violence and crime) that augur ill for adjust-ment to American society. Even in those few cases where people are jailed for immigration violations, the average sentence is only about six months, and the average time actually served only about four months.[119]

Much of the opposition to effectively enforced restrictions and selectivity is based on the historic role of the United States as a haven for immigrants, symbolized by the bold words on the Statue of Liberty: "Send me your tired, your poor, your huddled masses . . ." But the United States was not unique in having such an open door, nor is it unique in changing such a policy under changing circumstances. Canada, for example, had essentially open-door immigration until 1895, and severe restrictions on immigration began only in 1931.[120] Some South American countries and Australia actually subsidized immigration in the nineteenth century.[121] But immigration is no more exempt from diminishing returns than is any other human activity. As these countries filled up and the benefits of further immigration declined, while the social and economic costs created by the immigrants became more manifest, they all turned to both quantitative and qualitative restrictions.

American policy on immigration, like that of other countries, tries to attract more highly skilled people, admit political refugees, and to reunite families by letting relatives of its citizens enter more or less freely. The real problem is that very large numbers of immigrants enter illegally, in disregard of official policy, and therefore without either quantitative or qualitative controls. The issue confronting the United States is not simply what immigration policy to follow, but whether *any* policy will be effectively *enforced.*

CHAPTER SEVEN

The Third World

W hat is popularly called the Third World is larger than the first world of affluent nations (Western Europe, the United States, Canada, Australia and Japan), and the second world of Communist-bloc countries, combined. Most of the human race lives in the Third World. In that sense, it is an immensely important reality. In another sense, however, the Third World as a concept is a creature of vague and inconsistent definition—lumping together countries that are highly disparate in economic, cultural, political, racial and ethnic terms. Poverty is supposed to be the defining characteristic of the Third World, but substantial geographic regions and social classes in the Third World are far from poor, and some whole countries in the Third World are closer to the living standards of Western Europe than to those of other Third World nations. Sometimes the Third World is defined racially, with the white nations being rich and the non-white poor. But non-white Japan has a higher per capita income than Great Britain, the Soviet Union, and various other nations of eastern and western Europe, as well as such predominantly white South American countries as Brazil and Argentina. Saudi Arabia and Kuwait likewise have higher per capita incomes than various white nations. Moreover, when the Third World is conceived in terms of people rather than nations, it so happens that it contains more whites than blacks.[1]

While the boundaries of the Third World are difficult to define with both meaningfulness and precision, it remains true nevertheless that substantial regions of the world, substantial numbers of nations and substantial proportions of the human race live at economic levels that would be considered poverty in Western Europe, the United States, or Japan. The reasons for this poverty, possible ways of alleviating it, and the prospects for achieving prosperity in the Third World are therefore important concerns.

Because poverty is one of those things that is simply the absence of something else—wealth, in this case—a special care is necessary in analyzing it. Other concepts that are simply the absence of something else—baldness or a vacuum, for example—refer to an absence of things that occur spontaneously in nature, like hair or air. Wealth does not occur spontaneously in nature. Its presence, rather than its absence, requires explanation—especially since most of today's wealthy nations were poor nations only a few centuries ago. The real question is—What confluence of circumstances produced the fortunate conditions that a relatively small part of the human species enjoys today? To what extent can these peculiar combinations of historical circumstances be analyzed, recreated, or grafted onto other societies? To what extent do other societies desire those particular things that are considered not merely desirable, but essential, in the societies that produced them?

But before even considering these crucial questions, it is necessary to deal with other views so widely and insistently propagated that they are certain to haunt any discussion in which they are not specifically addressed. It is widely believed that overpopulation and/or colonial exploitation explain Third World poverty, and that transfers of tax money from more prosperous nations are essential, not merely for dealing with episodic emergencies, but for promoting economic growth among the poorer nations. All these views require careful scrutiny and analysis.

POPULATION

One of the oldest explanations of poverty, both domestically and internationally, is overpopulation. Even before Malthus' *Essay on the Principle of Population* in 1798, others had argued that families and nations could have too many children to prosper. Overpopulation is a concept whose familiarity is often accepted as a substitute for definition. But like any concept of "over" or "under," the key question is, *relative to what?* Are poorer countries overpopulated relative to their land, their natural resources, or food?

Land

From time to time over the centuries, there have been outbursts of writings raising alarms about the limitations of space on the planet, relative to the growing population. Some of these writings have centered on the poorer countries, where this problem is assumed to be more acute. Photographs of crowded and shabby slums in poverty-stricken nations often insinuate this viewpoint without the burden of explicitly establishing causation. Dramatic concepts, like "standing room only" or "the population explosion," also use insinuation as a substitute for evidence. Extrapolation is another very effective substitute for evidence. Malthus' extrapolations of supposedly geometrically growing population and arithmetically increasing food supply did much to dramatize and fix in the public's mind the concept of overpopulation—*before* there was any census data or other hard evidence in most of the countries of the world. Using extrapolations, one could show that if the temperature has risen a few degrees since this morning, a continuation of this trend would have us all burned to a crisp before the end of the month. The question is whether such reasoning should be the basis for alarm, analysis, or public policy.

To get some idea of how crowded the planet is in actuality, imagine that every man, woman and child on earth were placed in the state of Texas. There are 4,414,000,000 people in the world[2] and Texas has 262,134 square miles of land area.[3] That works out to approximately 1700 square feet per person. A family of four would thus have 6800 square feet—about the size of a typical middle-class American home with front and back yards. In short, every human being on the face of the earth could be housed in the state of Texas in one-story, single family homes, each with a front and back yard.

What of the teeming masses of the poor that we see and hear so much about, crowding the streets of Calcutta or the slums of Puerto Rico? It should be noted, first of all, that *rich* people are never called "teeming masses," no matter how many of them there are per square mile. Wealthy Park Avenue neighborhoods have concentrations of people that will compare with slums around the world. The fact that the crowding and the poverty both strike us vividly in many slums in no way establishes the former as the cause of the latter. The reverse is more likely: poor people cannot afford much space in urban areas, where land tends to be more expensive.

The more general question of crowded cities has little to do with total population or "over"-population, relative to the land area of a country. From an economic standpoint, crowding is what cities are all about. Many of the features of a city—the variety and scale of businesses, amenities and entertainments—are economically feasible only when drawing upon a large population as customers and workers. There may be ample land in a country whose cities are crowded—or "over"-crowded, to those who do not like it. When the population of the United States was half of what it is today, its cities were *more* crowded than now. The growth of public transportation and private automobiles has enabled people to spread out farther from the city and still be part of the pool of customers and workers that make large-scale enterprises possible.

When Irish, Italian, and Jewish immigrants were packed five or ten to a room in the slums of New York, one could travel through a hundred miles of open countryside in America without seeing a living soul (and still can today). To many well-meaning observers, it seemed obvious that the urban poor should spread out. But the immigrants wanted the jobs and the other features of a city, including the companionship of other people from a familiar culture in a strange land. Numerous efforts to get them to relocate in the countryside failed, and the few who did go often either failed as farmers or found themselves unable to cope with the isolation or other features of agricultural life. Even the Jews who became successful in an urban setting failed totally in farming communities in America[4] as in Argentina.[5] So did highly educated urban German immigrants who attempted to farm in mid-nineteenth century America.[6] The poverty and crowding of various immigrant groups in the urban slums had nothing to do with any lack of land in America.

Internationally as well, there is little or no relationship between poverty and population density. As Table 1 shows, there are high-income, low-income, and medium-income nations with high population density, low population density, and medium population density. Ethiopia has almost the same number of people per square mile as the United States (61 and 65, respectively), but averages

TABLE 7-1: POPULATION DENSITY AND
INCOME

		POPULATION PER SQUARE MILE		
		500 or more	*100–499*	*Less than 100*
PER CAPITA INCOME (Nations in each column listed in order of income)	*More than $5,000*	West Germany Belgium Holland Japan	Kuwait Denmark France	Sweden United States Canada Australia Austria Libya Saudi Arabia
	$1,000–5,000	Great Britain Singapore Barbados Jamaica Taiwan Lebanon	East Germany Spain Israel Greece Italy Ireland Poland Costa Rica	USSR Iran Iraq Argentina South Africa Brazil Mexico
	Less than $1,000	El Salvador India Bangladesh	Turkey Cuba Malaysia Morocco Philippines Egypt Indonesia China Uganda Pakistan Burma	Colombia Algeria Chile Guyana Bolivia Liberia Congo Tanzania Kenya Afghanistan Ethiopia

Source: The World Almanac and Book of Facts, 1981

less than a hundred dollars in annual per capita income. At the other extreme, Singapore has more than 10,000 people per square mile, and its income per capita is more than 30 times higher than that of Ethiopia. Prosperous Japan, with an income higher than that of many European nations, has more people per square mile than India, one of the poorest nations on earth.

An argument could be made that it is not land but arable land that is most relevant, since deserts and mountains may have little economic significance. But while this seems plausible, the deserts of Kuwait and Saudi Arabia contain the petroleum that puts them among the wealthier nations of the world. However, even if one

were to use arable land as the standard, it would change no fundamental conclusion. Japan, for example, compares even more unfa-
vorably to India on the basis of arable land than of land in general,
but it is India that has famines. Similarly, famine-stricken Ethiopia
has many times more acres of arable land per capita than Singapore
or Great Britain. As a distinguished specialist in under-developed
economies has pointed out, "famines and food shortages occur
mostly in sparsely populated subsistence economies with abundant
land."[7] These include Sumatra, Borneo, central Africa and the
interior of South America. Even in a densely populated area such as
West Malaysia, more than half the land remains uncultivated, even
though it has the same fertility as the portion that is cultivated.[8]

Famines occur because of an absence of sufficient food reserves
needed in a country during various natural or man-made disasters
(drought, war, floods, etc.), and because a poor nation's transportation system is often insufficiently developed to permit quick distribution of massive amounts of food before starvation takes its toll.
These episodic famines are ghastly human tragedies, but they have
little or nothing to do with the total population of the world or even
of the starving country—relative to land or its capacity to grow food
under normal conditions. Very densely populated places like Taiwan, Hong Kong, and Singapore report no famines.[9] Moreover,
even in famine-stricken countries, relief food supplies may be rot-
ting on the docks in ports while people are starving in the interior,
because the transportation and distribution system cannot move a
large enough volume of food fast enough to save the dying. Mid-
dleman distributors, though often decried as mere parasites, perform a function that can literally be a matter of life and death.

For some purposes, sparse population can be an economic handi-
cap. Many kinds of fixed, costly investments—sewer systems as well
as steel mills—are economically feasible only when the costs can be
spread over large numbers of users. If there are simply not enough
people within any given area being served, the cost is too great per
unit of benefit or per unit of output. This does not mean that
"under"-population is a general cause of poverty, though it can be
one factor. The spread of countries through all the cells of Table
1 suggests that population density alone tells very little about
wealth or poverty. All the countries in the upper left-hand cell have
more than 5 times the per capita income of all the countries in the

lower right-hand cell while also having more than five times as many people per square mile. But at the same time, all the countries in the upper right-hand cell have more than five times the per capita income of all the countries in the lower left-hand cell, while having less than one-fifth as many people per square mile. There is no strong correlation either way.

Nor has the growth rate of population had the dire economic consequences in history that it has in theory. For example, between the 1890s and the 1930s, Malaysia was transformed from a sparsely populated country of hamlets and fishing villages into a nation with cities and modern economic development. While its population rose from one and a half million to about six million people, this much larger population had both a higher standard of living and greater longevity. Hong Kong and Singapore have also had rapid population growth since 1950, along with increases in real income. As for the western world, its population has quadrupled since the mid-eighteenth century, while real income per capita has risen five-fold. Much of this increase in western living standards took place while its population was growing faster than in today's Third World.[10]

Natural Resources

Natural resources are another concept so familiar as to *seem* to require no definition. Yet it is a slippery and treacherous notion. For example, a large and alarming literature proclaims that we are running out of natural resources in general, or some specific resource (like petroleum) in particular. By simplistic extrapolation, that would seem to be inevitable, just as such extrapolations would also lead us to be alarmed about running out of space or being burned to death by rising temperatures.

A natural resource is something occurring in nature that *we know how to use* for our purposes. Our knowledge is as integral to the concept of a natural resource as the physical thing itself. An inventory of natural resources two centuries ago would not have included petroleum or hydroelectric power, because no one knew how to use such things. Once natural resources are seen in this light, it no longer follows that there are fewer natural resources with the passing centuries. Moreover, even for something known to be a natural resource, the amount whose existence is known can continue to increase over time. There are, for example, larger known reserves of petroleum in the United States today than there were 40 years ago.[11]

In some ultimate sense, natural resources are finite, just as land is finite. Too often there is a hasty inference from finiteness that we are, in some practical sense, "running out" of the thing in question. (John Stuart Mill as a young man once worried that, because of a finite number of musical notes, we were "running out" of music;[12] at that point Brahms and Tchaikovsky had not yet been born, and jazz not yet conceived.) But many natural resources may become obsolete—superseded by better alternatives—long before they are physically exhausted. In practical terms, we will never run out of them.

Differences in wealth among nations bear little relationship to differences in natural resources. Japan has no petroleum and imports most of the natural resources needed to produce its large industrial output. Yet it has a much higher per capita income than Mexico, which has abundant minerals, fertile soil, large petroleum deposits, and rivers capable of producing much hydroelectric power. The Japanese simply have high levels of skill, discipline, organizational capability, and other traits that enable them to outperform Mexicans economically, whether the two groups are in their respective homelands or both in California, where they have been for a similar period of time and began in very similar occupations.[13]

The natural resources of a given nation are likewise utilized very differently by different groups of people. All the things that were natural resources to Europeans existed in the Western Hemisphere before Columbus, but the indigenous populations—misnamed "Indians"—had not used those resources to achieve the economic and technological level of the Europeans, as indicated by the fact that the latter succeeded in forcing them off their lands, often against a numerical superiority of brave and resourceful Indians. In Argentina, some of the finest wheat-growing land in the world did not prevent the Argentines from *importing* wheat for generations, until a new set of peoples from different cultures and with different values and skills turned it into one of the world's great exporters of wheat. In southeast Asia, the Malay peninsula contained rich tin deposits long before the Chinese arrived to develop them, but the native Malays did little with these deposits. The same story could be repeated, with local variations, for much of Africa and the Middle East.

Food

A best-selling scare book, *The Population Bomb,* says on its cover:

> While you are reading these words, three children are dying of starva-
> tion—and twenty-four more babies are being born.[14]

As a propaganda device, juxtaposing two striking phenomena
can successfully insinuate that there is some cause-and-effect relationship between them, however little logic or evidence there may
be to support this conclusion. Famines have had no demonstrable
relationship to the number of children in the world, or the number
being born. Because famines often involve a race between relief
supplies being distributed through a primitive area and the ravages
of hunger, people die of starvation and disease while there are food
surpluses in the world, or even in their own country. But the idea
that we are running out of food enjoys a certain plausibility that has
kept it going for two centuries, despite overwhelming empirical
evidence against it.

When Malthus first wrote on population at the end of the eighteenth century, there was extremely little hard evidence on the
subject. No national census had ever been taken in Great Britain.
Malthus' statements about the American population's doubling in
25 years were based on an earlier estimate made by Benjamin
Franklin, long before the first American census.[15] As for the less
developed parts of the world, reliable population statistics for them
have been difficult to get, even in the twentieth century.[16]

As data became available in the nineteenth century, they showed
that in fact the food supply was growing faster than the population.[17] This has continued to be true in the twentieth century,[18]
even at the height of the "population explosion" hysteria. Like
most data, these have fluctuations over time, so that those who have
a vested interest in hysteria—which sells both books and political
programs—can point to such things as a 2 percent decline in the
world's food supply from 1965 to 1966.[19] But, as against this
one-year "trend," food per capita is generally higher today than a
century ago, when there were far fewer people on earth. Vast
amounts of uncultivated land, even in very poor countries like India

or Malaysia, suggest that the problem of famine and malnutrition is not one of "over"-population but of inadequate food storage facilities, distribution difficulties, and many natural and man-made barriers. Moreover, countries with virtually the same birthrate differ by several hundred percent in income per capita and in economic growth rates.[20]

Overpopulation hysteria is both philosophically and politically congenial to the outlook of those who see the world's problems in general in terms of the foolish many needing to be directed by the wise few, like themselves.[21] India, for example, instituted a massive compulsory sterilization program in 1975–1977 in which hundreds of thousands of people were "sterilized against their will, often brutally and in insanitary conditions."[22] Many Western officials and intellectuals are likewise calling for "strong leadership" to control population growth in less developed countries. This leadership almost invariably means various degrees of authoritarianism wielded by the westernized elite against the general populace.

Deficiencies of food, ranging from malnutrition to famine, are often more a result of political policies than of population size. An exporter of food like Tanzania has been turned into an importer of food, amidst widespread hunger, by the grandiose social experiments imposed by Tanzanian President Julius Nyerere.[23] Many Third World nations forbid the use of tractors, harvesters, and other agricultural machinery,[24] on the dubious assumption that machinery reduces jobs. Famines have been produced (in sixteenth century Belgium) and exacerbated (in eighteenth century India) by price controls.[25] Fortunately, the nineteenth century authorities in India learned from the catastrophe of a century earlier, and met a new threat of famine in 1866 by following opposite policies:

Far from trying to check speculation, as in 1770, the Government did all in its power to stimulate it . . . In the earlier famine one could hardly engage in the grain trade without becoming amenable to the law. In 1866 respectable men in vast numbers went into the trade; for the Government, by publishing weekly returns of the rates in every district, rendered the traffic both easy and safe. Everyone knew where to buy grain cheapest and where to sell it dearest and food was accordingly brought from the districts which could best spare it and carried to those which most urgently needed it.[26]

An economically effective policy like this could be followed, without fear of political repercussions, because India was ruled by British colonial officials. It was also the era when laissez-faire economics had its widest acceptance. Today, it is difficult to imagine an elected government letting a market operate freely during a famine—amidst inevitable charges by their political opponents that prices were "unconscionable"—even if they knew that that was in fact the fastest way to get the famine over with and save the most lives.

IMPERIALISM

The history of man's relationship to those of his fellow men who have less economic substance or military power has seldom been a pretty story. For all the glory of the Roman Empire, whose historic achievements still benefit much of mankind, it was a system resting ultimately on overwhelming power, used with ruthless brutality. Nor have the non-Western portions of the human species been exempt from such behavior: "The contempt of the aristocratic black Watutsi for their Bantu serfs, or of the Matabele for their Mashona 'dogs' was an even more extreme feeling of superiority than that felt by backveld South African farmers regarding their Bantu laborers."[27] The Chinese disdained all non-Chinese as barbarians in the days of their imperial glory, and Mandarins visiting the overseas Chinese community in the Philippines in 1603 "behaved exactly as if they were on Chinese territory and administered a flogging to any one of their race they considered deserving of it."[28]

In short, the arrogance of power has known no boundaries of race, or place, or time. Imperialism is no exception. Neither is it unique. However, it has been a widespread phenomenon for much of the non-European world for much of the past three centuries— and the visible differences in race have added to the emotions on both sides, though in reality the British treated the Irish at least as badly as they treated Africans or Asians. Even decades after the decolonization that began with the end of World War II, the economic and political aftermath of imperialism remains an important factor in world history, and the causes and effects of imperialism remain matters of controversy.

Although imperialism is thousands of years old, there have been many attempts to create special theories for the imperialism of the capitalist era or of European nations. These theories require scrutiny, not only for the question of their validity, but also as clues to the kind of thinking that shapes policies and attitudes in the Third World and elsewhere. Finally, the actual effects of imperialism must be examined, as well as its enduring legacy—in the West as well as in the less developed world.

Theories

Perhaps the earliest theories of capitalist imperialism were those of the mercantilists—a motley collection of intellectuals, politicans, and pamphleteers who helped shape European economic policies in the seventeenth and eighteenth centuries. The mercantilist conception of wealth has long been discredited among professional economists, but it continues to dominate popular and political thinking to this day. To the mercantilists, wealth was a differential gain of one at the expense of another. They were preoccupied with the *transfer* of wealth, rather than its creation. Some mercantilists regarded imperialism—and even slavery—as means by which a country might be enriched, at the expense of others.

Adam Smith's 1776 classic, *The Wealth of Nations,* rejected the whole mercantilist conception of wealth, and numerous corollaries, including the economic benefits of imperialism to the imperialist power. Adam Smith—and the classical economics tradition that built upon his foundations—regarded wealth as production, which could increase for all nations simultaneously, so that one did not have to gain at the expense of another. Smith considered imperialism to be unprofitable, for generally the imperialist's fleets and armies "acquire nothing which can compensate the expense of maintaining them."[29] *The Wealth of Nations* in fact closed with a plea to Britain to withdraw from the American colonies—currently seeking independence—and to be cautious about taking on any new colonies from a vain notion of national glory:

> If any of the provinces of the British empire cannot be made to contribute towards the support of the whole empire, it is surely time that Great Britain should free herself from the expence of defending those colonies in time of war, and of supporting any part of their civil or military

of imperialist wheel,"[58] "the imperatives of corporate control
raw materials and markets,"[59] or the "surplus product" of
talism,[60] serve as substitutes for evidence or analysis. Mundane
nomic facts—that most of the razor blades sold in France are
erican-made[61] are given sinister interpretations, when they are
ly what would be expected on the basis of Adam Smith's 200-
old writings about the international division of labor. A high
portion of cameras sold in the United States are made in Japan,
no one considers the United States a colony of Japan.

unning through most modern theories of imperialism and neo-
nialism is the old notion of the mercantilists, that one country's
chment is another country's impoverishment. According to
-colonialist theory, the "conflict between the rich and the poor
now been transferred on to the international scene."[62] Thus the
ulous profits" of Western capitalism show "the enrichment of
side of the world out of the exploitation of the other."[63] As in
t uses of the word "exploitation," the term is not defined con-
ely. Somehow the neo-colonial theorist has determined a "fair
e"[64]—a feat that has eluded economists for centuries—and
ws that Third World countries are paid less than that for their
r and raw materials. The empirical documentation which so
nds on non-essential points is, on this crucial point, replaced
hetoric that insinuates, rather than defines or empirically sub-
tiates—for example, the "intricate inter-connections of the
t imperialist monopolies,"[65] "the empire of finance capital" as
ast sprawling network of inter-continental activity . . . manipu-
g whole industries and exploiting the labour and riches of
ons for the greedy satisfaction of a few."[66]

s in Lenin's theory, "crises that were tearing at the very heart
apitalism"[67] are averted by "overseas employment of growing
tal surpluses" (undefined), and the exploitative profits received
e "enabled the capitalist classes of the metropolitan countries to
some of the crumbs to their working classes and thereby buy
n off"[68] to prevent the revolution predicted by Marx.
hatever the factual or intellectual inadequacies of neo-colonial-
neory, it serves some very important political and psychic func-
s. It explains—even if incorrectly—why the economic collapse
apitalism that Marx so confidently expected within his lifetime
till not occurred a hundred years later, without even raising the
ibility that Marx might have been fundamentally wrong in his

establishment in time of peace, and endeavor to accommodate her
future views and designs to the real mediocrity of her circumstances.[30]

While Smith disdained national glory, he considered it a factor
in wars[31] and in imperialism.[32] More of a factor, however, was that
special interests gained from imperialism, even if the colony were
"turbulent," difficult to govern, and wholly unprofitable to the
imperialist nation as a whole.[33] Modern research seems to confirm
Smith's conclusion. Full-blown imperialism—formal occupation
and administration of another country—rarely repaid the costs,
except for a few special cases like Malaya or the Congo. But for
special interest groups or individuals—"energetic traders, enterprising (corrupt?) officials, manufacturers of cheap, colorful wares"
—it always paid.[34] As a distinguished modern economic historian
has pointed out:

> One does not need a business class or an economic system to create a
> demand for empire. All one needs is a few interested people who can
> reach the ears or pockets of those who command.[35]

One of the most massive exercises in imperialism—the "frantic
scramble" of European nations for colonies in Africa—was, except
for South Africa and the Congo, a struggle for "some of the most
unremunerative territory on the globe."[36] Individuals and businesses may have found fortunes, with European taxpayers covering
the costs of conquest and administration. But that is very different
from saying that Europe became enriched by acquiring African
colonies.

One of those whose name is often invoked in discussions of
imperialism is Karl Marx. But the actual writings of Marx and
Engels reveal a very different view of imperialism from that of
latter-day Marxists. While Marx found much that the British did in
India "brutal,"[37] "sickening," and "actuated only by the vilest
interests,"[38] he nevertheless concluded that the net effect of introducing Western economic advancements would be to bring India
out of a "stagnatory" and "vegetative" kind of life.[39] Marx had no
romantic view of less developed countries: "I share not the opinion
of those who believe in a golden age of Hindustan."[40] In a similar
vein, Engels regarded the capture of an Algerian resistance leader

by the French colonialists as "very fortunate,"[41] even though he regarded the French as "brutal" and "highly blamable" for their actions in Algeria.[42] Again, the central point was that he saw the introduction of European civilization as a step forward for the colonial peoples:

> All these nations of free barbarians look very proud, noble, and glorious at a distance, but only come near them and you will find that they, as well as the more civilized nations, are ruled by the lust of gain, and only employ ruder and more cruel means. And after all, the modern *bourgeois,* with civilization, industry, order, and at least relative enlightenment following him, is preferable to the feudal lord or to the marauding robber, with the barbarian state of society to which they belong.[43]

Although these Marxian writings have been a source of embarrassment to some latter-day Marxists,[44] they are consistent with the general Marxist view that (1) what matters are not people's subjective motivations but their objective effects,[45] and that (2) particular social systems—including slavery, capitalism, and imperialism— may be "historically justified" during particular eras, even though they may be superseded later by better systems.[46]

As the passing decades failed to produce either the increasing misery of the proletariat or the decisive crisis of the capitalist system predicted by Marx, he and Engels used imperialism as an explanation of how these phenomena had been postponed.[47] These passing remarks of Marx and Engels later became the cornerstone of V. I. Lenin's theory of imperialism. Lenin's message can be summed up in his own words. In the era of "the parasitism and decay of capitalism" a few powerful imperialist nations "plunder the whole world" and "out of such enormous *super-profits*" they bribe their own workers and labor leaders.[48] While thus keeping the workers quiescent, imperialism also disposes of surplus capital—"the prodigious increase of capital, which overflows the brim," in Lenin's words,[49] and which would otherwise lead to internal economic crises in capitalist nations, according to Marxist theory.

Like the brilliant propagandist that he was, Lenin inundated the reader with statistical data on *things that were not at issue*—that capitalist industry was growing,[50] that banks had large and increasing deposits,[51] which they invested in many places[52] and then glided swiftly from these facts to conclusions which had neither

empirical nor analytical support. A crucial table by to establish his central doctrine that the otherw "surplus" capital of capitalist nations was being in developed colonial world. However, his definition regions included "Asia, Africa, and Australia" as "America" (i.e., the whole Western Hemisphere effectively prevented the reader from knowing w oped or underdeveloped parts of these vast on were in fact receiving capital investments. If dev nations were simply investing in other developed, —shuffling their capital around amongst them whole scenario of net outflows of capital from ca avert "crisis" would collapse like a house of card be back where we started, wondering why the does not cause the collapse of capitalism, as Mar dicted.

A finer breakdown reveals what Lenin's sw concealed—that modern capitalist nations tend primarily in other modern capitalist nations. The example, invests more in Canada than in all of A together—and it invests more in Europe than it Moreover, investors living in the Third World ing in the United States or Europe to investing tries. Western investments are often an overwh of all investments in a poor country, but may nev small part of Western investments worldwide.

The end of the colonial era after World War I other things, voluminous writings on *neo*-colonia this literature, imperialism has merely change substance. Under neo-colonialism, according Kwame Nkrumah, a newly independent state wi trappings of international sovereignty" continu nomic system and thus its political policy . . . side."[54] This means "control of nominally i World countries by giant financial interests" in Leninist predecessor, this literature tends to do things that are not the least bit at issue—that the and imports,[56] or many overseas branches of A while dealing with the points of controversy th insinuates rather than confronts. Reiteration of

analysis of the situation. It explains why the capitalist employees who were supposed by Marxists to become progressively more miserable over time seem on the contrary to be progressing from generation to generation. Above all else, it explains for those in the Third World why their economic performance is so far below that of Western nations, for reasons which reflect no inadequacies on their part but only moral deficiencies on the part of others. In short, it is the perfect political explanation, however little economic sense it makes.

Despite the thesis that imperialist nations have grown wealthy by impoverishing other nations, in reality nations that were *already* wealthy and powerful have often used that wealth and power to subjugate other countries and peoples, for a variety of reasons that have motivated such behavior for thousands of years. Economic rationales have sometimes been used by promoters of imperialist schemes, and these political statements have then been seized upon as "admissions" by those claiming that imperialism grows out of capitalist economic imperatives. It is significant, however, that two major capitalist nations denuded of colonies as a result of World War II—Germany and Japan—have been among the most strikingly successful in economic development in the postwar world.

The Legacy of Empire

In one respect, Marx was quite correct: What matters in a cause-and-effect analysis of history are not people's subjective motivations but the actual results. In Engels' words, "what each individual wills is obstructed by everyone else, and what emerges is something that no one wills."[69] What emerges from imperialism is thus not a question of the greed of some or the corruption of others but of concrete consequences of highly complex interactions.

It is necessary to begin with the conditions that existed in Third World countries before the imperialists came—conditions that made them vulnerable to conquest in the first place. To say that colonialism or neo-colonialism is what *prevents* development in a Third World nation[70] because of "external forces which have a vested interest in keeping it undeveloped"[71] is to beg the question as to why it was undeveloped for centuries before the imperialists arrived. Indeed, this question goes beyond the colonized areas of the past few centuries. Why was Britain so readily conquered by

Roman legions who were vastly outnumbered by the military forces of the native Britons? And did this conquest in fact impoverish and weaken Britain or did it ultimately advance British development? Indeed, the conquest of Britain by the Roman Empire followed a pattern that was to be repeated many centuries later, when Britain and other nations spread their empires through the Third World.

Before the Roman invasions, Britain was divided among thirty tribes of barbarians.[72] Britain was at that time on "the ultimate fringes of the world"[73]—at least the civilized world as it existed in Europe. Like other isolated peoples, they were backwards. Among other things, they practiced human sacrifice[74] and fought fiercely, among themselves—though their military equipment was obsolete by continental European standards.[75] Their agriculture likewise lagged behind that in the Roman world.[76] The effect of isolation can be seen in the fact that it was the interior tribes who were most primitive. While coastal tribes grew crops, the interior tribes lived on milk and meat, wore animal skins, and shared one wife among several men.[77] Despite the protection provided by the rough seas around the British Isles, the primitive and disunited Britons were successively invaded by a number of more advanced tribes from continental Europe, even before the Romans came. In the first century B.C., Belgic tribes invaded Britain, subjugating many parts of the island, building towns and introducing coins for the first time. They took over with ease wherever they went.[78] But while the Britons were unable to challenge them, the Romans were.

Julius Caesar coveted the British Isles, for its "natives, though uncouth, had a certain value as slaves for rougher work on the land, in mines, and even about the house."[79] In 55 B.C., Caesar led a raiding expedition whose fleet met disastrous weather in unfamiliar waters.[80] Nevertheless "discipline and armor once again told their tale" for the Roman expedition, which returned in triumph to Rome with captured British slaves marching behind them in the procession.[81] A century later, under the emperor Claudius, the Romans returned as full-scale invaders and eventually conquered most of the island. The oppression and atrocities of the Romans provoked a massive revolt, in which a barbarian army of eighty thousand men[82] faced no more than twenty thousand men[83] on the side of the Romans. But again, the superior discipline, organization, and armaments of the Romans prevailed.

In the centuries that followed, the Romans conquered Britain politically, economically and culturally as well. Britons began to wear the Roman toga, speak Latin, and have arcades, baths, and sumptuous banquets.[84] Under the Romans, towns developed, roads were built, and trade flourished.[85] The more efficient Roman plough was used for farming,[86] pottery and metal work were imported,[87] and new building methods used and taught.[88] Roman capital helped develop the British economy.[89] Like other less developed regions, Britain was an exporter of raw materials.[90] For nearly three hundred years, Britain under the Romans "enjoyed in many respects the happiest, most comfortable, and most enlightened times its inhabitants had ever had."[91] As Churchill said, "We owe London to Rome."[92] This was part of a more general British indebtedness to Roman civilization:

> In culture and learning Britain was a pale reflection of the Roman scene . . . . But there was law; there was order; there was peace; there was warmth: there was food, and a long-established custom of life . . . . Some culture spread even to the villages. Roman habits percolated; the use of Roman utensils and even of Roman speech steadily grew.[93]

Moreover, Britons retrogressed after the Romans withdrew in the fifth century A.D.:

> From the year 1400 till the year 1900 no one had central heating and very few had hot baths . . . . Even now a smaller proportion of the whole population dwells in centrally heated houses than in those ancient days. As for baths, they were completely lost till the middle of the nineteenth century. In all this long, bleak intervening gap cold and dirt clung to the most fortunate and highest in the land.[94]

After Rome withdrew its legions from Britain, the island again became prey to marauders and invaders from continental Europe, culminating in the Norman conquest of 1066, which became the basis for medieval and then modern Britain.

Much the same story could be told, with local variations, in the Third World. Here the motivations of the conquerors were similar to those that led the Romans to conquer Britain—greed, glory, military bases, and promotion of the careers of a few leaders. The larger question, however, is not the subjective motivation but the historic effect of these ventures. For this, it is again necessary to look at the colonized societies as they existed before the imperialists came.

Much of sub-Saharan Africa, North and South America, and southeast Asia consisted of small, tribal societies, living at a relatively primitive level of organization and technology. For example, "almost no African community south of the Sahara managed to harness draft animals to pull plows and wagons until European newcomers introduced these new methods of traction in the nineteenth and twentieth centuries."[95] The pre-colonial technology of the region was incapable of using wind or water power for milling grain. Tribal warfare, military raids, slavery and serfdom were widespread throughout the area.[96] Literacy was unknown outside of Ethiopia.[97] Similar conditions existed in the Western Hemisphere in pre-Columbian times: "The plow was totally unknown in the New World until it was introduced by Europeans, and draft animals were not used in farming."[98] There were no wheeled vehicles among pre-Columbian Indians, though there were some wheeled toys in Mexico.[99] Slavery and human sacrifice were also prevalent in some parts of the Western Hemisphere,[100] as in pre-Roman Britain. The most advanced military forces in the Americas, the Aztecs, fell easy victim to Spanish invaders for reasons similar to those that caused the Britons to be defeated by the Romans—differences in military organization and in the quality of armaments.[101]

Not all parts of the colonized world were primitive, nor did the coming of Western civilization always represent progress in all aspects of life. But by and large European colonialism brought to the Third World what Roman imperialism had brought to Britain: (1) a reduction or cessation of internal fighting that had plagued these regions for centuries, holding back economic and social progress, (2) a unified system of law as a framework for stable expectations and the security and individual planning that law makes possible, (3) features of a more advanced system of technology and organization, and (4) contact with a wider world, enabling creative potential to emerge from the restrictions of insularity. Nowhere did these benefits exist unalloyed. Everywhere they were mixed with the arrogance, insensitivity, and often brutality that have marked conquerors of virtually every race and culture.

Much of southeast Asia, as noted in Chapter 2, was first agglomerated into progressively larger units by the colonial powers in the region, for their own administrative convenience. There was no nation of Indo-China before the French came, nor any Malaya before the British. There were numerous petty rulers, marauding bands, and hundreds of pirate ships on the seas. Racial, ethnic, and tribal differences fragmented much of the region into parts too small for economic prosperity or cultural progress. It was only after European imperialism created law, order, and consolidation that large scale influxes of the overseas Chinese began—bringing in new crops, industries, organizations and ideas, along with those being introduced from various parts of Europe and more advanced Asian civilizations, such as India and later Japan. Pre-colonial Africa was likewise plagued by marauding tribes, such as the Bemba of Zambia, who "terrorized all the tribes on the boundary of their kingdom" and ruled brutally:

In nearly every village are to be seen men and women whose eyes have been gouged out; the removal of one eye and one hand is hardly worthy of remark. Men and women are seen whose ears, nose and lips have been sliced off and both hands amputated. The cutting off of breasts of women has been extensively practised as a punishment for adultery but . . . some of the victims . . . are mere children. . . . Indeed these mutilations are inflicted with the utmost callousness; every chief for instance has a retinue of good singers and drummers who invariably have their eyes gouged out to prevent them running away.[102]

The Zulus of southern Africa were another marauding tribe. Zulu warriors acquired military advantages by developing better fighting organization and implements, and "were thus in a position to live a semi-parasitic existence on surrounding peoples":

They raided their neighbors for cattle, for women, and for children, whom they incorporated into the tribe, thereby increasing its manpower, with the result that these warrior communities quickly snowballed and spread their power over vast areas of southern Africa. . . .[103]

Nor were Africans unique in their depredations and oppressions. In the Western Hemisphere, both the Aztecs and the Incas brutally treated the many subjugated tribes that formed the majority of the people in their empires.[104] The Aztecs, for example, cut the hearts out of living sacrificial victims.[105] Indeed, the "pre-Columbian racism"[106] of Western Hemisphere Indians helped facilitate the Spanish conquest, as many subjugated tribes joined forces with the Spaniards to help overthrow their indigenous overlords.

In Africa, as in pre-Roman Britain, it was those along the coasts who had the more advanced societies, with "strong and highly centralized black states."[107] Much of that advantage was, however, used for the enslavement of other Africans from the interior. The Ibos of Nigeria were among those who engaged in the slave trade.[108] The Ashanti on the Gold Coast (now Ghana) sold thousands of slaves to Europeans,[109] and the rise of the Ashanti marked a rise in slave-trading.[110] In general, African slaves were captured by other Africans and sold to Europeans who shipped them overseas.[111] African states that engaged in this trade achieved power and prosperity, and were bitterly discontented when the British ended the slave trade in the early nineteenth century.[112] Strange as it may seem today, for centuries the institution of slavery aroused little moral concern anywhere in the world, until an influential group of Englishmen began attacking the practice in the eighteenth century, eventually achieving an end of the trade and ultimately abolition of slavery itself.

That slavery was wrong was one of many Western ideas imported into the Third World. In centuries past, the Chinese in parts of southeast Asia traded slaves as they traded inanimate merchandise,[113] and the Arabs continued to do so well into the twentieth century.[114]

The spread of law and order under imperialist auspices had both social and economic implications. Much land that was unused before, because it was militarily vulnerable to raiding parties, could now be used for farming and grazing. Yet, at the same time, the Europeans themselves took land from the conquered peoples.[115]

The net balance of European impacts on the Third World may never be totaled in all their psychic, cultural, social, and political dimensions. The record of oppression is long and often ghastly—both before and after the imperialists came. European oppression was by no means unique in kind or degree, and the spread of this particular oppression cannot be assumed to be a net increase of oppression in the world. There was certainly no Eden before. On the central issue of economic exploitation, however, the empirical evidence is somewhat more clear. Those parts of the Third World which have had the most extensive, persuasive, and diversified contacts with the Western world have generally achieved much higher standards of living than those regions that have remained relatively untouched by Western civilization. Aborigines in the jungles and deserts of Africa, Asia, or South America have yet to approach the economic level of those native peoples who live in the ports, mining towns or cash-crop areas that developed under Western auspices.[116]

The enduring and fervent belief in imperialism as the cause of Third World poverty is difficult to understand in terms of empirical evidence. But this belief is much more readily understandable in terms of the high psychic and political costs of believing otherwise. These costs are high not only to some people in the Third World, but also to those in the West whose whole vision of the world depends upon seeing poverty as victimization and themselves as rescuers—both domestically and internationally. Many such people assume a stance of being partisans of the poor. But even to be an effective partisan of the poor, one must first be a partisan of the truth.

ECONOMIC DEVELOPMENT

Economic development is difficult to define and measure, much less plan and execute. Change may be objectively determined but progress is inherently subjective. Statistical indexes may put an imposing scientific facade on a disorderly mass of value judgments and arbitrary assumptions. But there is still no real meaning to the statement that country A has 8.5 times the income of country B, when one country's output (income) is made up of coconuts, loin cloths, fish and thatched huts in a tropical climate and the other consists of fur-lined coats, heavy boots, seal meat and igloos in the frozen north. Even among nations that are part of the same European civilization and temperate zone, there are serious comparison problems when one country's output is valued according to what people are willing to pay in a competitive market while another country's output is valued by what it cost to be produced by a government monopoly paying little attention to consumer demand. A wide range of qualitative differences in what is nominally the "same" product superimpose still another set of incommensurabilities.

Where one country is well fed, has advanced medical care widely available, and lives in homes with many amenities, it can safely be said to enjoy a higher material standard of living than another that is starving, living in shacks or shanties, and is helplessly disease-ridden. But to say that one country has an income 6.3 times as high, or 10.2 times as high as the other is to add nothing except self-deception about numerical precision. No doubt Japan and the United States do indeed have much higher standards of living than India or Ethiopia, but precisely by how much can only be a mathematical exercise based on a given set of arbitrary weights given to specific items.

These difficulties in comparing different countries apply as well to comparisons of the same country at different points in time—that is, in measuring its economic development. If a country were simply to increase its output of every product by 3 percent, there would be no problem in saying that its economic growth rate was 3 percent. But that almost never happens. More usually, it will increase its output of some item by 22 percent, another item by 1 percent, and still another will *decline* by 10 percent, etc. What the overall growth rate will be depends on how one arbitrarily chooses to add all these apples and oranges together to get a grand total of "fruit." There are various ways of coping with this problem but no way of solving it, for it is not merely a practical difficulty but a conceptual contradiction to add apples and oranges.

Statistical uncertainties, illusions, and deceptions are especially likely in measuring the economic progress of a Third World country that is in the process of shifting from agricultural to industrial output, paying market prices for services that were formerly provided outside the market (child care, for example), and channelling an increasing proportion of its resources through government monopolies of one sort or another. The fact that a rising share of the nation's goods and services now pass through statistical checkpoints does not mean that there is a correspondingly larger amount than before, when much of this same activity took place informally, without money changing hands or being recorded on the government's books. Conversely, much saving and investment by peasant farmers in Third World countries may go entirely unrecorded, either because of secretiveness on the part of peasants, or because of the practical difficulties of the government's keeping track of innumerable peasants and their many small repairs and improvements on their farms or their larger or smaller amounts of fertilizer, seeds, seedlings or other materials set aside for the coming year's crop. Investments in the form of planting materials or improved irrigation ditches may completely escape the attention of the government's statisticians in the capital city, and would be virtually impossible to quantify if they did know about them. Yet such investments may be larger in the aggregate than the steel mills or paper assets that are much easier to put into a statistical index.

The bias toward preoccupation with individually large and striking investments, to the neglect of individually small and unimpressive investments—which may in the aggregate be of far greater economic consequence—is due not only to statistical difficulties but also to political bias. As Adam Smith noted two centuries ago:

> The proud minister of an ostentatious court may frequently take pleasure in executing a work of splendour and magnificience, such as a great highway, which is frequently seen by the principal nobility, whose applauses not only flatter his vanity, but even contribute to support his interest at court. But to execute a great number of little works, in which nothing that can be done can make any great appearance, or excite the smallest degree of admiration in any traveller, and which, in short, have nothing to recommend them but their extreme utility, is a business which appears in every respect too mean and paultry to merit the attention of so great a magistrate.[117]

Those who believe in the brotherhood of man should not be surprised to find the same attitudes that Adam Smith saw in eighteenth century European governments re-appearing in twentieth century Third World governments (and non-Third World governments). Third World countries differ, however, in being (1) less able to afford large misdirections of their economic resources, and (2) often having Western-educated or Western-oriented rulers, who wish to show off not only domestically but also to Western visitors—whether in an attitude of sycophancy or of defiant pride —even at the expense of reducing their ability to feed and clothe their own people. Uneconomic steel mills built in Third World nations have become a symbol of this attitude, so are national airlines that operate in the red when there are plenty of existing international airlines capable of handling the same volume of traffic at lower cost. This approach has aptly been termed an "investment fetish."[118] It has been seconded by international organizations who have been impressed by grandiose plans, strikingly visible demon-stration projects, and rhetoric—that is, by things that impress the eye and ear, rather than things that actually produce economic results. The extent to which plausibility has replaced performance in discussions of economic development in the Third World may be illustrated by an example of successful development that should have been very unsuccessful, according to prevailing theories:

> How would you rate the economic prospects of an Asian country which has very little land (and only eroded hillsides at that), and which is indeed the most densely populated country in the world; whose popula-tion has grown rapidly, both through natural increase and large-scale immigration; which imports all its oil and raw materials, and even most of its water; whose government is not engaged in development plan-ning and operates no exchange controls or restrictions on capital ex-ports and imports; and which is the only remaining Western colony of any significance? You would think that this country must be doomed, unless it received large external donations. Or rather you would have to believe this if you went by what politicians of all parties, the United Nations and its affiliates, prominent economists and the quality press all say about less developed countries.[119]

This country is, however, the British colony of Hong Kong, which has a per capita income more than five times that of Malaysia, the Philippines, Indonesia, Burma, or Thailand—just to compare countries in the area.[120] In the post war world, Hong Kong's popu-lation increased more than seven-fold,[121] nearly half being ref-ugees.[122] Despite low tax rates—a 15 percent maximum on per-sonal income—the Hong Kong government has had budget sur-pluses in 31 of the 34 years from 1945 to 1980.[123] Hong Kong's population is 98 percent Chinese.[124] This is not only another exam-ple of the productiveness of the overseas Chinese; it also fatally undermines the "exploitation" explanation of the prosperity of the overseas Chinese because there are only 2 percent of non-Chinese who might conceivably be exploited, and many of these are the British who control the colony. More broadly, Hong Kong under-scores the point that the "human capital" in the general populace is crucial to economic development.

Economic development, whether in the Third World or else-where, depends upon many factors. Among them are geographic conditions, human capital and international transfers.

Geographic Factors

Geographic factors influence development in many ways. The more obvious influences—soil fertility, natural resources, climate—are not necessarily the most important. Often lands that are more favored in these respects—Mexico versus Japan, Ireland versus Britain—are less prosperous, and some very poorly endowed places like Switzerland, Israel, and Hong Kong are doing well.

Often geography plays its role in a more indirect but powerful way: It facilitates or restricts communication and interaction among different peoples, and therefore affects the formation of human capital. Navigable rivers, sheltered and deep harbors, and level plains, facilitate people's coming together from different places and cultures. The benefits of this extend beyond the particular goods, inventions, or discoveries, and general knowledge that are more widely shared. Interaction with different ways of life erodes insularity and provokes thinking, rather than blind repetition of the inherited formulas and framework of any given culture. The world's great centers of learning and of economic progress have been its ocean ports, its cities on great rivers, and other natural or man-made crossroads where differing peoples met. London on the Thames, New York on the Hudson, and Paris on the Seine are only the most prominent of a long list of such places.

Barriers to such communication and interaction take many forms, both natural and made-made. One of the largest areas in the world with a dearth of navigable rivers or natural harbors is Africa. As the great explorer David Livingstone said:

> The sea after all is the great civilizer of nations. If Africa, instead of simple littoral outline, had been broken up by deep indentations of glorious old ocean, how different would have been the fate of its inhabitants.[125]

Livingstone did not find the African *people* lacking—he considered them more "reasonable" than Europeans[126]—but found their geographic environment not conducive to developing their human potential.

In addition to missing communications links like harbors and rivers, or barriers like mountains and deserts, people may be separated by the occurrence of fertile land in isolated patches, as in the mountain valleys of Southern Italy[127]—a highly regionalized and disunited area that took centuries to unite into a nation.

Because geographic factors operate in part directly (by providing natural resources, fertile soil and other ingredients of economic prosperity) and partly indirectly (by affecting the development of human beings through interaction among diverse peoples), there is no simple geographic determinism. That is, "the races and peoples of mankind, ranging all the way from savagery to high civilization, make very different adjustments to similar natural environments."[128] But, at the same time, "their initiative, energy, and intelligence are products of underlying environmental factors operating upon these peoples in various places and for long ages."[129] The indigenous Indians of Brazil, the Portuguese settlers, and the later immigrants from Germany, Italy, and Japan, all confronted the same geographic reality in Brazil, but they developed the country very differently. Yet much of the attitudes, goals, skills and disciplines they brought to the situation were products of geographic conditions and historical developments that took very different courses in different parts of the world.

Human Capital

The actual material wealth brought to a region has in many cases played a relatively small role in economic development, compared to the human capital that was brought. Poverty-stricken Italians immigrated to poverty-stricken Argentina in the nineteenth century and made both the country and themselves more prosperous. Chinese immigrants with little more than the clothes on their backs have entered southeast Asia—often on foot—and proceeded to create economic advancement for both the native populations and themselves. Germans too poor to pay their passage to eighteenth century America nevertheless, after years of unpaid work as indentured servants, went out to the undeveloped frontier and built prosperous farming communities up and down the great valleys of the eastern United States.

The human capital approach conflicts sharply with the widely touted "vicious circle of poverty" approach as an explanation of both domestic and international poverty. If the vicious circle theory is correct, then adding more poor people to an already poor country only makes the situation more desperate. Yet that is by no means a foregone conclusion:

> It is a familiar phenomenon that Chinese, Lebanese and Indians arrive in what appear to be hopelessly over-populated countries such as the West Indies, make a living there, create capital and provide opportunities for the employment of others as well.[130]

Much of the poverty, stagnation, and even retrogression found in Third World countries is not the result of an inevitable vicious circle of poverty, for which dramatic aid programs or draconian domestic policies are the only cures. Indeed, a substantial part of the current efforts of the rulers and governments of such countries often consists of repressing, impeding, or even driving out of the country those who possess the human capital to develop it. The massive deaths on the high seas of southeast Asia of the "boat people" were not only a moral horror and a human catastrophe but also an economic insanity of destroying vast amounts of human capital desperately needed in that region of the world. It made sense only politically.

Less dramatic examples and policies also indicate massive destruction of, or impeding of the operation of, human capital. South Africa has, at various times in its history, forcibly forbidden various skills acquired by black Africans to be used, and has put positive barriers in the way of their further acquisition of such skills. Jews have been hounded from one country to another in Europe and the Middle East, often to the economic detriment of the country they left and the economic benefit of the country to which they went. Idi Amin's brutal expulsions of the East Indians from Uganda and the Nigerians' slaughter of the Ibos were part of a similar pattern.

Even where groups with much needed human capital are not killed or expelled, they may be impeded in applying their knowledge and skills. Some idea of the magnitude of difference that political institutions can make in economic development is indicated by the output in Shanghai under British colonial rule and the output of the same race of people—the Chinese—in the rest of China. Shanghai in 1900 produced one-fourth of the entire industrial output of China, in a city containing only one percent of its population.[131] The detrimental effect of Chinese political institutions can also be observed in a larger historical perspective. This great empire and leading civilization in the world began its decline in the Ming dynasty, when intellectuals gained unprecedented levels of power and influence. In support of various social goals, they created great bureaucratic control of business activity[132] and relegated the businessman to the lowest level in their scheme of values.[133] It was during the Ming dynasty that the large-scale emigration out of China began, creating the overseas Chinese business class throughout southeast Asia and in the Western Hemisphere. In short, China ended up exporting vast amounts of human capital, as a result of its political policies.

One form of human capital emphasized by many Third World countries and the international agencies advising them is formal education. While this can be beneficial, it by no means follows that every increment of schooling is more beneficial than alternative uses of the same resources, whether viewed economically or socially. Desperately needed technological, organizational, and entrepreneurial skills tend to be neglected in favor of literary education.

Agricultural science, for example, tends to be neglected even in predominantly agricultural nations of the Third World. In Nigeria, more than 40 percent of the jobs for senior agricultural researchers have been vacant at one time.[134] In Senegal, it was 1979—a generation after independence—before agriculture was taught at the university level, though the University of Dakar had thousands of liberal arts students.[135] In Malaysia, where the Malay college students are concentrated in the liberal arts[136]—mostly Malay studies and Islamic studies—many end up working for the government after graduation,[137] for they lack skills that would have a value in the economy. Nor is Malaysia unique. In India three-quarters of the college graduates work for the government,[138] and a leading authority on Africa describes African education as "a machine for producing graduate bureaucrats."[139] Indonesian youth likewise turn after graduation toward bureaucratic careers, despite the warning of Indonesian novelist Ananta Toer that "we must get rid of the silly idea of wanting to be government clerks."[140]

A burgeoning bureaucracy is more likely to be an impediment than a contributor to economic development. They are, for example, a major factor in many African nations' declining ability to feed themselves.[141] Yet in many Third World countries, the alternative to increasing bureaucracies to absorb college graduates without economically meaningful skills is to let them become unemployed, discontented and politically dangerous.

International Transfers of Wealth

The migration of human beings is one of the mechanisms by which wealth has been transferred internationally—perhaps the most important way. But the invisible wealth transferred inside people's heads is often overlooked, partly because it is difficult to quantify, even when its benefits are demonstrable.

Discussions of wealth transfers are usually discussions of the transfer of physical capital, consumer goods, raw material or financial paper. These transfers take place through two principal mechanisms—economic and political. Economic transfers are made by individuals and private organizations, to other individuals or organizations. Wealth transfers from one individual to another have played an important role in economic development, as well as in changing living standards directly. For example, remittances sent by Chinese Americans to their relatives in the Toishan district of Kwantung province in southern China helped make that one of the most prosperous districts in China, on into the middle of the twentieth century.[142] Remittances from Japanese Americans helped build up the Hiroshima district in Japan,[143] perhaps thereby contributing to its selection as a military target in World War II. Remittances from the United States helped pay the passage of most of those who emigrated from Ireland during the great famines of the 1840s.[144] Remittances from the overseas Chinese in southeast Asia to their families in China[145] have been not only economically but politically significant—with political leaders of southeast Asian nations accusing them of draining away their national wealth, much of which owed its existence to the Chinese.

Individuals not only remit to other individuals, but also donate through philanthropic organizations and invest through commercial businesses. Private transfers of wealth to Third World countries have often exceeded all official transfers combined, including both bilateral and multilateral transfers via international agencies such as the World Bank. Most private transfers from the West are through commercial investment and lending, which totalled more than $20 billion in 1977, compared to $18 billion in all forms of official international aid from the West.[146] Wealth transfers from Communist bloc nations to the Third world have been much smaller—less than $1.5 billion, and less than grants from private voluntary agencies in the West.[147]

Different incentives and constraints operate in directing wealth transfers through these various institutional mechanisms. Person-to-person aid is the most precisely targeted. Commercial investment is likely also to reflect considerable knowledge of the people and conditions at the location to which the resources are transferred, and the likelihood that they can in fact accomplish whatever is intended to be accomplished. Politically directed transfers of wealth are more likely to reflect immediate pressures or fashions affecting the decision-makers, rather than the long run effectiveness of the transfers in terms of achieving some economic success or failure, which is unlikely to become manifest before the next election in any case. Where politically directed economic aid is bilateral (government-to-government), it often reflects a need to shore up a particular Third World ally or to prevent chaotic breakdowns in a particular country, rather than being based on any careful calculation of its economic impact, though bilateral aid may also be given in such a way as to be spent in the donor nation to the benefit of particular special interests there.

Politically directed multilateral transfers of wealth through international organizations like the World Bank have even fewer built-in incentives or constraints to see that the resources are used in economically effective ways. The size, resources, power and visibility of the transferring organization depend primarily on the volume of wealth it dispenses, not on the long term effectiveness of its efforts. Those who constitute its leadership at any given moment have far more incentive to promote increasing wealth transfers under their administration than to be concerned with economic results that will become visible after they are gone, and will redound to the credit or discredit of their successors. Indeed, a critical evaluation of the likelihood of economic success by the agency might tend to reduce the volume of aid invested, and so reduce the organization's own importance, however much it might tend to improve the quality of investment decisions.

Against this background of incentives and constraints, it may be easier to understand various features of international wealth transfers. The very phrase "foreign aid," which has become so familiar through repetition, is one which—in the words of a distinguished development economist—"disarms criticism, prejudges the effects of the policy and also obscures its realities and results."[148] In short, whether the political process of transferring wealth from Western taxpayers to Third World government officials aids or hinders economic development in the Third World is an empirical question rather than a foregone conclusion. Using the phrase "foreign aid" is no more justified *a priori* than calling it "foreign hindrance." Whether it is an aid or a hindrance is a question of fact in each specific case. Calling the transferring organizations "development agencies" is likewise begging the central question. They are in fact transfer or donor organizations, and the actual effect of their donations is precisely what is at issue. For example, Africa has lost its historic ability to feed itself precisely during the era when the phasing out of donations to Latin America has caused donor agencies to "smother Africa with project aid."[149] Despite ever-increasing appeals for foreign aid, "technical specialists in most donor agencies will privately concede that there is currently an excess of donor funds in search of technically sound agricultural projects."[150]

"Foreign aid" is in fact often used by Third World governments to (1) acquire arms to be used principally in suppressing political critics and movements within their own country;[151] (2) persecute racial and ethnic minorities, especially those who are more economically productive or entrepreneurial, such as the overseas Chinese; (3) cover deficits caused by the inefficiency or irresponsibility of the recipient government, thereby enabling it to remain in power longer by insulating it from the consequences of its own actions. Moreover, international transferring organizations tend to want recipient governments to be more activist or *dirigiste* in planning and controlling the economy—a process which may or may not prove beneficial, in the Third World or elsewhere—and their control of vast funds enables them to impose experiments and preconceived schemes from which the aid organization officials suffer no damage if these schemes should prove catastrophic to Third World peoples. Moreover, the failure of these schemes or the waste of funds in general will not embarrass any given donor nation, since multilateral transfers are administered from a fund to which many nations contribute and for which none is responsible. The chief benefit of multilateral grants, from the standpoint of the recipient governments, is that they are less likely to carry restrictions or preconditions designed to insure economic efficiency or responsible financial policies.

Part of the international wealth transfers administered by multilateral international agencies takes the form of "soft loans"—meaning that the interest rates are lower than those prevailing in the market and the terms of re-payment more flexible. Just how flexible may be indicated by the fact that Britain alone cancelled one billion pounds sterling in debts owed by Third World governments in 1978.[152] In short, much of what is carried on the books as "loans" are in fact politically disguised gifts, concealed only from the Western taxpayers. Some loans that are unpaid are simply covered by new loans. For example the World Bank in 1980 arranged a "structural adjustment" loan of $60 million annually to Tanzania, for each of the next five years, at zero interest.[153]

Tanzania is a striking example of the effects of international wealth transfers through multilateral agencies. It has received more "foreign aid" per capita than any other nation.[154] Its output per worker has *declined* 50 percent over a period of a decade; it has turned from an exporter of maize to an importer; nearly half the more than 300 companies expropriated by the government ("nationalized") were bankrupt by 1975, with many of the remainder operating at a loss.[155] As the economy has declined, government bureaucracy has grown by 14 percent per annum, doubling in less than a decade.[156] Tanzania's ruler, Julius Nyerere, has repeatedly been unopposed in "elections,"[157] and his political prisoners run into the thousands—many tortured, according to Amnesty International.[158] International wealth transfers to the Nyerere regime have not proved to be "foreign aid" to Tanzania.

The Tanzanian example illustrates another important point—the political importance of professed *intentions,* as contrasted with demonstrable economic or other *results.* Despite a despotic rule and economic declines, Julius Nyerere remains one of the most revered African leaders, especially among Western intellectuals. Nyerere has expressed many noble intentions and humanitarian goals, even as he has jailed or executed his critics, uprooted vast portions of the Tanzanian population at gunpoint, and mismanaged nationalized industries into bankruptcy, while producing widespread hunger in a country that was once an exporter of food. Conversely, the very phrase "multinational corporation" immediately evokes negative feelings, because their *intentions*—to make a profit for themselves—are not nearly as noble as those expressed by Nyerere, and it is often the intentions rather than the results that count politically.

Multinational corporations may themselves engage in expressions of altruistic intentions toward Third World countries for public relations purposes, but no one is deceived, and such statements may in fact increase cynicism toward the multinationals. If they were in fact engaged in altruistic behavior, they would be violating the confidence of the stockholders who entrusted their savings to the corporations for the purpose of gain rather than philanthropic donation.

The real basis on which the impact of multinational corporations on Third World countries is to be judged is in terms of results. The prevalence of heated rhetoric and vague surmises in most discussions of multinational corporations suggest that their results are not nearly as vulnerable as their intentions. Often they are said to have great "power" vis-à-vis Third World governments when in fact they are reducing no one's options, but often increasing them. When the multinational corporations pay higher wages than those prevailing in a Third World country, this is criticized as promoting "the interests of the small number of modern-sector workers against the interests of the rest by widening wage differentials."[159] When multinational corporations fill some local consumer need, this is criticized because it means "inhibiting the expansion of indigenous firms" who might have served the same market, even if they have never done so before.[160] In short, multinational corporations are blamed for a pervasive reality of the human condition—that benefits have costs. Such economic *results* as higher wages for Third World workers, or new or cheaper products for Third World consumers are politically unacceptable, because the *intentions* that produced these results are morally suspect. But when looked at systemically,[161] instead of by intentions, it is hardly surprising that an economic organization like a multi-national corporation is more effective in economic decisions, while political leaders who make disastrous economic decisions are more effective in gaining political acceptance and even admiration. Conversely, the political failure of multi-national corporations is evident from the fact that their very name is anathema to many.

CHAPTER EIGHT

The Past and the Future

History is a treasure of experience, available without paying the high price often inflicted on those who lived through it. But history is not free, however. It conflicts painfully with many cherished beliefs and shatters many carefully built theories. At best it is untidy and complex, and often it is a battleground for those with differing visions of the world today. Yet history remains a massive fact and a massive influence on our lives: "We do not live in the past, but the past in us."[1]

To seek to look ahead into the future is to seek to understand the momentum of the past and the choices available to us in the present. We live in a world of options constrained by decisions already made and actions already taken—many before we were born—as well as constrained by mutually competitive and perhaps irreconcilable goals among contemporaries.

The history of racial and ethnic groups around the world is a story of the heights and depths of the human spirit—the glory of its perseverance in the face of every kind of adversity and the vileness of its brutality against the helpless. Whether the future brings great advancements or succumbs to wretched agonies, it will have ample precedents. How well we understand the past can be an important factor in decisions to shape that future.

RACIAL AND ETHNIC DIFFERENCES

The most obvious fact about the history of racial and ethnic groups is how different they have been—and still are. Sometimes there is a tendency to glide over the obvious to look for something more sophisticated. But "we need education in the obvious more than investigation of the obscure," as Oliver Wendell Holmes once said.[2] Sophistication and complexity sometimes represent attempts to reconcile the obvious facts of history with preconceptions that they contradict.

Human differences are often assumed away in social theories, either because they would needlessly complicate the exposition[3] or because they are presumed to be negligible or subject to change by "society," which takes each new individual as a blank page on which it can write its social message. But this fashionable view of society ignores the fact that groups may carry their own messages with them from country to country—a very different message from those who live cheek-by-jowl with them in the same society and sit next to them in the same school rooms or on the same factory assembly line. Germans in Australian or Brazilian society have had a distinctive social pattern more similar in many respects to that of Germans in the United States or Germany than to other Australians or Brazilians. The Chinese have likewise taken their own behavior patterns throughout southeast Asia and across the ocean to the United States and the Caribbean. The Jews have done much the same in Europe, North Africa, the Middle East, and the Western Hemisphere. So have East Indians, Armenians, and many others. If any group was ever a blank page, it has ceased to be so many centuries ago.

With the passage of time—generations or centuries—groups do interact and evolve in a given society, but in a complex manner that is difficult to follow and impossible to control. Grandiose schemes of molding a people—"Russification" under the Czars, the "cultural revolution" under Mao, or mass indoctrination and draconian relocations by Nyerere in Tanzania or Pol Pot in Cambodia—produce more agony than adaptation. No small part of the historic advantages of the United States has been that it developed at a time when it was neither constitutionally nor practically possible to control all the many peoples scattered across a vast continent in isolated settlements. The country developed on the basis of the experience of the many rather than the presumptions of the few.

A second obvious and important fact is that racial or ethnic differences have serious costs. These costs may range from difficulties of comprehension to misunderstandings of verbal or other communication[4] to outright hostility and violence. Nor are these kinds of reactions limited to racial and ethnic differences. Ironically, many people who advocate that divorce laws be made easier, because sometimes people simply cannot get along, at the same time also advocate that people of different races and ethnicity be forcibly brought together in schools and housing—or, at the very least, regard separation along racial or ethnic lines as irrational. Yet separation between people of very different values and lifestyles has often been the least costly way of dealing with such differences, whether the differences be between spouses, generations, or racial and ethnic groups.[5]

How far and in what manner groups may separate in the same society is a legitimate question. What cannot be denied, however, is that their association entails higher costs than association with people of the same backgrounds and inclinations. There are also benefits to interaction with people from different backgrounds, but how the costs compare to the benefits is something that can be determined by each individual who experiences both. Third parties are only guessing, however elegantly their guesses may be phrased.

Much discussion of racial and ethnic separation treats it as a bad thing imposed by the dominant group on a weaker group. It may in some cases be that—the Jewish ghettoes of medieval Europe or the Jim Crow laws against blacks in the United States—but the phenomenon of separation extends far beyond these kinds of examples, and includes many wholly voluntary separations. Nineteenth century native-born Americans separated themselves almost totally from neighborhoods inhabited by European immigrants,[6] even though the immigrants from various parts of Europe were not wholly separated from each other.[7] Moreover, social separation has operated even among groups not residentially separated. Even today, among Russian emigres, those from Moscow, Leningrad and

Odessa do not mix socially in the United States,[8] and Italian immigrants tend to avoid Italian Americans.[9] Internal social separation has long characterized many American ethnic groups.[10] Nor is the United States by any means unique. The overseas Chinese in southeast Asia have likewise been fragmented into Fukkienese, Hainanese, and other groups that went their separate ways socially and occupationally. In short, group separation is not something arbitrarily imposed from above by "society." It is a widespread human phenomenon throughout history and around the world. It is one way of minimizing inherent costs, not simply itself an arbitrarily created cost which can equally arbitrarily be eliminated by fiat.

Countries with relatively homogeneous populations, such as Japan or Australia, avoid many of these costs by restricting immigration—either numerically or categorically to racial or ethnic groups like those already in the country. More heterogeneous countries like the United States have at various times attempted to restrict immigration in such a way as to let in primarily those groups most readily and successfully assimilated into the existing population. In the heated controversies that have developed over restrictions based on national origins, opponents of such restrictions have depicted the issue as solely one of presuming some groups "inferior." In reality, the principle of selective immigration restriction requires only recognition of the historical fact that some groups have indeed adapted more readily than others to the existing population, culture and institutions.

The politicization of economic and social life increases the costs of intergroup differences, and tends to heighten mutual hostility: "Political competition requires the aggregation of individuals into winning coalitions; markets do not."[11] Politics offers "free" benefits for people to fight over. Markets put prices on benefits, forcing each group to limit its own use of them, thereby in effect sharing with others. A society with both Buddhist and Islamic citizens must somehow allocate its available building materials in such a way as to have these materials shared in the building of temples and mosques. If the building materials are shared through economic processes, each set of religious followers weighs costs against benefits and limits its demand accordingly. But if these same building materials are provided free or are otherwise shared through political processes, each group has an incentive to demand the lion's share—or all—of the materials for building its own place of worship, which is always more urgently needed, in more grandiose proportions, than the other.

People who will not share in the spirit of fair play under political allocation are forced to share by rising prices when they compete economically. Quite aside from more efficient economic allocation, there are fewer social frictions to the process of price competition than the process of political competition. Consensus is very costly to achieve in general;[12] where there are great disparities in values —as between racial, religious, and ethnic groups—these costs can reach very high levels, including bloodshed and the tearing apart of the whole society. Minimizing the need for consensus is one of the advantages of economic processes over political processes.

Groups that hate each other often transact peacefully in the market place but erupt into violence when their conflicting interests are at stake in political decisions. As a noted political scientist has pointed out, "given the different values of the separate races, the likelihood that each race will try to impose its values over others means that multiracial societies may be inherently prone to conflict when fighting over control of the public sector."[13] Historical evidence for this thesis includes "multiracial societies that rely chiefly on market exchange"—Hong Kong and Singapore, for example— contrasted with more politically directed economies, such as those in Guyana, South Africa or Malaysia. It is the latter that "have been the scene of extensive racial or ethnic conflict, ranging from chronic riots to full-scale civil war."[14]

HISTORY

What must be understood first about history is that it is irrevocable. Attempts to redress the wrongs of history face the intractable fact that whatever may be done will apply only to the future, not to the past. Most of history's victims or villains are beyond the reach of human power. Symbolic expiation creates new incentives and constraints for the future, and the specific consequences of this need serious consideration. Rewarding those who are adept at evoking guilt promises few benefits to anyone other than themselves— whether they be Third World rulers or domestic opportunists. To the extent that such rewards encourage the further politicization of race, they are encouraging a process that has ended in tragedy many times.

History is a bottomless pit of wrongs, and the interminable bloodshed caused by territorial irredentism offers no ground for optimism about social irredentism. We cannot simply equate past victims with current members of the same group, and the latter in turn with "those who think and act on their behalf."[15] When speaking in the name of other people becomes a well-rewarded activity, it can be expected to attract many practitioners, with varying qualifications and varying honesty. While we cannot do anything about the past, we can at least avoid jeopardizing the future with futile symbolic attempts to undo history.[16]

HUMAN CAPITAL

At various times in history, nations and peoples have recovered from economic destitution in remarkably short order. The physical devastation of German and Japanese industrial cities during World War II did not prevent either nation from rising from the rubble to become major industrial powers in the postwar world. Numerous confiscations of the wealth of Jews in Europe or of the Chinese in southeast Asia have been followed by their rising again to prosperity and wealth. In the United States, penniless refugees from Cuba, Korea, or Vietnam have begun in the most menial occupations and within one generation produced a business-owning middle class.

The key to all these phenomena is that the destruction of physical capital or financial capital—painful as this may be—does not touch a nation's or a people's human capital, which is ultimately decisive. Conversely, the transfer of vast amounts of physical capital or financial assets has failed to create prosperity in many Third World nations or among many poorer classes, races, and ethnic groups within a given country. In those cases as well, it is the human capital that is economically decisive, and the visible investment of secondary importance. Visible physical capital—factories, power dams, oil refineries—is always in a process of deterioration, whether at a slower or a faster rate. Financial assets likewise are constantly being consumed in order to live. Wealth in both forms will have to be

replaced, even in the normal course of events. What war or expro-
priation does is to speed up this process of wealth's exhaustion and
its need for replenishing. But the real source of wealth in both
normal and abnormal times is the *ability* to produce—human capital
—not the inventory of goods, equipment, or paper assets in existence at a given time.

Human capital takes many forms, of which formal schooling is
the most visible but not for that reason any more important than
skills, discipline, organizational talents, foresight, frugality, or simply good health. One of the ways in which tropical peoples are often
lacking in human capital is in having various debilitating diseases
that flourish in hot climates—in addition to the debilitation of suffocating heat and humidity in themselves. This last point is easily
overlooked by visiting "experts" who "stay in underdeveloped
countries only briefly and spend much of their visit in sheltered
conditions including air-conditioned buildings."[17] Human capital
is not all a human achievement, nor due simply to the merits of
those who happen to possess it. Climate, geography, and history
play major roles. What is economically salient is that differences in
human capital produce large differences in results, reflected in vast
gaps in standards of living, both domestically and internationally.
Politically, these vast differences promote envy, resentment, and
suspicions of exploitation among the less fortunate, and often either
arrogance or guilt among the more fortunate.

Economically, the question is how best to make the existing
human capital more widely available, so that the less fortunate have
more opportunity to achieve higher levels of productivity and consequently higher real income. Politically, the question is how to
transfer the fruits of existing human capital through redistributional
policies, both domestic and international. These two approaches
conflict sharply. Maximum utilization and dissemination of existing
human capital is achieved by incentives that reward those who have
it—however much of a windfall benefit that human capital may
have been to these individuals. This induces existing possessors of
human capital to use it more extensively for the rewards and—more
important in the long run—encourages others to acquire more
human capital in order to reap similar rewards. In both cases total
output rises, lifting the general standard of living. Redistributional
policies, on the other hand, reduce incentives to use human capital,
and especially to engage in the difficult task of acquiring it. Indeed,

such policies reduce the very awareness of its crucial economic importance—because the redistributional approach is so often accompanied by a political vision that explains wealth differences by exploitation or discrimination. If one's poverty is caused by the evil deeds of others, then rejecting, fighting, expelling, or confiscating the ill-gotten gains of others is a higher priority (and a more gratifying) endeavor than the painful and slow process of changing one's own behavior pattern.

The need to acquire human capital is likewise obscured by cultural relativism—the refusal to consider one culture as better in any way than another. Praiseworthy humanitarianism may be behind the statement that "we must not divide men into primitive and civilized,"[18] but there is nothing to be gained by pretending that the pre-Roman Britons were not primitive barbarians. How else could they have been so easily conquered by Roman legionnaires whom the British warriors outnumbered several times over? Why was the whole British economy and society developed to new heights under Roman rule? Cultural relativism, carried to its logical conclusions, becomes self-contradiction:

> If value judgments about a culture are themselves illegitimate, why are a relativistic scholar's standards to be preferred to those of a Hebrew prophet or a British district commissioner? Relativism, in other words, is liable to defeat itself for the relativist may fail, by his own standards. He must accept whatever is; he cannot condemn Hitler's Germany, Verwoerd's South Africa, or the practices of cannibalism and ritual murder.[19]

SOCIAL PROCESSES

One of the hardest realities to accept is that we cannot prescribe end results but can only initiate processes. Human beings cannot simply say, "Let there be light," and there is light. We can only initiate various processes—constructing power lines, building a hydroelectric dam, etc.—whose purpose is ultimately to produce light. This means that the specifics of the process determine the actual outcome, *regardless* of the intentions of those who created the process. For example, the purpose of employment quotas ("affirmative action") in the United States was to improve the economic condition of various racial and ethnic groups, both absolutely and relative to Americans as a whole. The actual consequences, however, have included a further falling behind in family incomes as regards Puerto Ricans and Mexican Americans, and a more mixed result among blacks as a whole, with the better-off blacks continuing to progress and the poorer blacks falling further behind.

These kinds of results are not accidental, nor merely the result of inefficiency or the flaws of a particular program. They derive from a whole vision of how the world works and how it can be made to work—a vision that applies both domestically and internationally. In this vision, "disparities" and "gaps" in incomes and occupations are evidence—or proof—of discrimination or exploitation by those with the higher incomes and occupations. Given this premise, then clearly existing institutions—including the marketplace—have failed to operate properly and must be over-ridden by political, judicial, or bureaucratic decisions. Without this arbitrary premise, however, we are simply left with the mundane conclusion that those with less human capital are less in demand in the marketplace domestically and less able to produce high standards of living internationally. When the same groups are generally found with higher and lower incomes in country after country—including countries in which they are the dominant majority—this premise at least has some factual support that is lacking for the other. When the Japanese have substantially higher standards of living than the Mexicans—both in the United States and when comparing the populations of Japan and Mexico—then it is hard to explain this by discrimination or exploitation. Japanese Americans are too small a group—less than one percent of the U.S. population—to hold down Mexican Americans' earnings or occupations. Moreover, Japanese Americans have not encountered any less discrimination than Mexican Americans, but historically more.[20] Yet the magnitude of their income difference is greater than black-white income differences in the United States.

The same kind of comparison could be made of the Germans and the Portuguese, whether in Brazil or in their respective homelands. The Chinese have likewise generally lived better than the other peoples of southeast Asia, whether in Indonesia, Malaysia, and other countries where the Chinese are a minority—or whether comparing these nations with predominantly Chinese places such as Singapore, Hong Kong, or Taiwan. China itself is an exception, for here a succession of despotic governments have stifled the creativity that only a few centuries ago had China in the forefront of human progress. Ironically, many in the Third World and in the West see despotism as the key to economic development.

In short, one vision of the world sees earnings in the marketplace as transmitting false information about intergroup differences, while the other vision sees these earnings as transmitting differences that are equally demonstrable from non-market comparisons —between nations or among self-employed farmers, for example. These are not simply different interpretations of history but have opposite policy implications for the future as well. If social processes are transmitting real differences—in productivity, reliability, cleanliness, sobriety, peacefulness—then attempts to impose politically a very different set of beliefs will necessarily backfire, for the truth remains the same, regardless of what is transmitted through social processes. If one group in fact produces less than another, then imposing minimum wages or equal pay by law simply makes employers more reluctant to hire the lower productivity group at all. If in fact some groups are more destructive as tenants and less reliable in paying the rent, then forbidding landlords from charging rent differentials that reflect these underlying realities will make landlords more reluctant to rent to such groups, and therefore will make it harder for them to find housing.

The crucial question, then, is whether the truth is more likely to emerge from the systemic effects of competition or from the beliefs of third party observers. The repeated disasters from well-intentioned "planning,"[21] both domestically and internationally, suggest that third parties are not an adequate substitute for transactors who personally suffer the consequences of being wrong and reap the benefits of being right. It is also worth noting that letting third parties decide for others means reducing freedom, in addition to its economic inefficiencies.

Freedom is a process unlikely to be tried in many Third World countries—especially recently independent former colonies, for it is a process with which they have had little experience, either during colonial times or before. Neither political freedom nor economic freedom have characterized the history of these nations. Imperialist powers have often given preferential or even monopolistic advantages to their own nationals operating in the colonial economies. Some have also imposed forced labor in various forms on the indigenous peoples. "Free enterprise" is only a mocking phrase to those on the receiving end of such treatment. Believing that they have experienced capitalism, they are understandably driven to try socialism instead. In reality, they have historically experienced one form of political control of economic processes and are now in the throes of trying an even more pervasive form of the same oppressive approach.

Much discussion of policy is not in terms of process characteristics but of noble goals—"social justice," "decent housing," "freedom from hunger," etc. The desirability of these goals is not at issue. Their emotional and political appeal makes it all the more necessary to remember that human beings can only create processes, not direct end results. The nature of these processes must therefore be scrutinized to see whether they in fact take us closer to, or further away from, humanitarian goals.

THE OPPORTUNITY AND THE DANGERS

The range of technological possibilities open to the human race today makes poverty and many diseases eradicable. Moreover, there has probably never been a period of history when humanitarian appeals on behalf of the less fortunate have found a more ready response, or when the human race has been thought of in more places as one family. Humanitarian and universalistic ideals are far from being realized, or even pervasive as ideals, but this era has moved further in that direction than those that went before. But this creates serious dangers as well as wider opportunities.

When vast resources can be tapped by invoking "social justice," many other important social phenomena that need to be dealt with in their own specific terms are likely to be transformed rhetorically into social justice issues—and therefore *not* dealt with effectively. Moreover, when costly processes created to handle these situations as misconceived turn out to be ineffective or counterproductive, the anger of those who pay these costs can jeopardize the social fabric of a nation or the cause of international understanding. Preferential treatment of various racial and ethnic groups has produced political resentments and a growing racist extremist fringe in the United

States. It has produced bloodshed in the streets in India.[22] Those who reap the political, financial or psychic benefits of advocating or administering such programs can wave these things aside as the incidental price of progress. But the politicization of race and the polarization of societies has historically been far more than an incidental cost. History shows repeated and sustained retrogressions, agonies of oppression, and trails of blood when racial animosities are stirred. The Nazi holocaust was unique in its magnitude but had many precedents around the world, in countries that lacked only the technology to vent their hatreds on such a scale.

Historically before Nazism, Germans were not more racist than many other peoples of Europe, Asia, Africa or the Western Hemisphere. Indeed, Germans tended to be *less* racist than many others. Before the rise of Hitler and the Nazis, Jews found greater acceptance in Germany than elsewhere in Europe. This was reflected not only in the economic prosperity of German Jews but also in their appointment to high positions and their high rate of intermarriage with other Germans—nearly one-half of all Jewish marriages in Germany in the 1920s. German immigrants in early America likewise acquired a reputation for their ability to get along with the American Indians.[23] Germans also held the first anti-slavery meeting in America in the eighteenth century[24] and were fervent supporters of Lincoln and the emancipation of blacks in the nineteenth century.[25] If genocidal racism could arise among Germans, it can arise anywhere.

The politicization of race, even for well-intentioned reasons, is not an incidental consideration to be waved aside. The ardent promotion of Chinese nationalism among the overseas Chinese, first by Sun Yat-sen in the early twentieth century, and then by Chiang Kai-shek and Mao Tse-tung afterwards, polarized relationships between the overseas Chinese and the indigenous populations of countries throughout southeast Asia. After decades of peaceful co-existence, there began decades of renewed discrimination, violence, and bloodshed, culminating in the massive horrors inflicted on the "boat people." Racial polarization is not a responsibility to be lightly assumed, in hopes of benefits of the moment.

Both domestically and internationally, advocates of "social justice" often ignore the prerequisites of wealth or other benefits. For example, the complex personal and social prerequisites for a prosperous level of output are often simply glided over, and material wealth treated as having been produced *somehow,* with the only real question being how to distribute it justly. This approach sidesteps the crucial issue of the effect of those processes characterized as "social justice" on the production of the benefits themselves. Many redistributive and compensatory schemes involve accepting a lower level of performance, responsibility, or plain honesty from the recipients of redistributed benefits. Indeed, sometimes those among the recipients who are *more* inept or irresponsible are rewarded with *greater* benefits, based on "need." This patronizing approach has extended from minority college students[26] to the rulers of Third World nations.[27] It rewards *not* forming human capital.

The need to form more human capital if prosperity is to be increased is not based on any belief that those who currently possess larger amounts of human capital do so as a matter of personal merit. There is no question that many—perhaps most—of the more fortunate people are recipients of windfall gains that derive from the accident of their being born where they were, if not to immediate affluence, then into families, communities, or nations where the values and patterns of life were a human capital that made economic success more readily attainable. Even those born into the wretched poverty of the nineteenth century Jewish immigrant neighborhoods on the lower east side of New York were born into a set of centuries-old traditions, attitudes, values, and habits that were tailor-made for success in American society.

But the crucial question for the future is not whether fortunate individuals are being treated fairly, considering both their windfall inheritance of human capital and their windfall losses through redistribution of income. The crucial question is whether society as a whole—or mankind as a whole—gains when the output of both the fortunate and the unfortunate is discouraged by disincentives, and when there are transfers that reduce the extent to which those with human capital can afford to have offspring and increase the extent to which those lacking human capital can afford to have offspring.

Providing children with human capital is very costly, whether these costs take the form of time and efforts required to raise the child to have discipline, intelligence, and consideration for others, or whether it takes the form of payments for high-quality schooling and health care. Parents with high levels of human capital themselves tend to want their children to have similar (or higher) levels

—which is to say, they are constrained to have only that number of children that they feel able to raise to such standards. But parents who are lacking in human capital may be unable or unwilling to provide adequate amounts of human capital to their children—or even to see the need for it, especially if others pay much of the cost of their children's later inability or unwillingness to support themselves or even to control themselves in ways that enable a society to function. Transfers from those with self-supporting levels of human capital tend to reduce the number of self-supporting members of the next generation. Transfers to non-self-supporting people tend to increase the proportion of the next generation unable to support themselves. Insofar as a given sum transferred will generally support more ill-raised children than well-raised children, it tends also to increase the total number of people, while inhibiting the production of the means to support them. It is not clear how this is either humane or just to anyone.

Even if it could be demonstrated, for example, that Jews have received economic justice in the United States on net balance—considering their windfall inheritance of human capital and their windfall losses through redistribution—the larger question would be: What of the economic losses to the American economy and society as highly skilled people like the Jews, the Chinese and the Japanese dwindle away with each passing generation? None of these groups has enough children to reproduce itself. Neither does the U.S. population as a whole. What does this imply as population soars in countries dependent upon wealth transfers from the United States and similar advanced nations, while the population declines in those nations producing the wealth?

Many of those who promote redistribution adopt the stance of looking at the world from the point of view of society as a whole, or mankind as a whole. But more fundamentally, it is a posture of partisanship to the poorer and currently less productive segments of society, or of the world community—providing incentives for them to *remain* less productive and to become a growing proportion of mankind. Political "social justice" concerns itself with immediate effects, as most political policies do. But the only clear long-run gainers from such policies are those who feel noble or who gain politically by advocating them, or who gain power and prosperity from administering them. They are not merely transferring the world's wealth; they are also in part converting what would otherwise be capital in the country that produced it into consumption in the country that receives it. Consuming the capital of mankind is hardly humanitarian in its long-run implications.

The oft-repeated demand for alternative policies ("What would you put in its place?") will not be met here. There are innumerable ways to formulate reasonable policies, or—perhaps better yet—to allow systemic processes to generate material benefits and personal freedom. What is truly needed is not a blueprint to be imposed from on high but an understanding of what does and does not produce prosperity and freedom. History can be a valuable help in this. But we must never imagine that we can either recreate or atone for yesterday. What we can do is to make its experience the basis for a better today and a better tomorrow.

NOTES

PREFACE

1. For example, Thomas Sowell, *Ethnic America* (Basic Books, Inc., 1981), Chapter 11; Thomas Sowell, *Markets and Minorities* (Basic Books, Inc., 1981), passim.

CHAPTER 1

1. Alvin Rabushka and Kenneth A. Shepsle, *Politics in Plural Societies: A Theory of Democratic Instability* (Charles E. Merrill Publishing Co., 1972), pp. 5, 124–125; L. H. Gann and Peter Duignan, *Africa South of the Sahara* (Hoover Institution Press, 1981), p. 25; David Lowenthal, *West Indian Societies* (New York: Oxford University Press, 1972), p. 169.
2 Victor Purcell, *The Chinese in Southeast Asia,* 2nd edition (Oxford University Press, 1980), pp. 148, 472–476, 478; Stanford M. Lyman, *Chinese Americans* (New York: Random House, 1974), pp. 4, 7.
3. Gunnar Myrdal, *An American Dilemma* (New York: McGraw-Hill, 1964), Vol. 1, pp. 132–133, cxiv.
4. J. C. Furnas, *The Americans* (G. P. Putnam's Sons, 1969), p. 406.
5. Alvin Rabushka and Kenneth A. Shepsle, *Politics in Plural Societies: A Theory of Democratic Instability,* p. 8.
6. Ibid., p. 186.
7. Ibid., p. 4.
8. Michael Grant, *The Fall of the Roman Empire* (The Annenberg School Press, 1976), p. 216.
9. Ibid., p. 219.
10. Ibid., p. 225.

11. Raphael Patai, *The Vanished Worlds of Jewry* (Macmillan Publishing Co., Inc., 1980), pp. 56–57.
12. Thomas Sowell, *Markets and Minorities* (New York: Basic Books, Inc., 1981), pp. 69–70.
13. Alvin Rabushka and Kenneth A. Shepsle, *Politics in Plural Societies: A Theory of Democratic Instability,* passim.
14. Ibid., p. 165.
15. C. Vann Woodward, *The Strange Career of Jim Crow* (New York: Oxford University Press, 1966), pp. 67–69.
16. Alvin Rabushka and Kenneth A. Shepsle, *Politics in Plural Societies: A Theory of Democratic Instability,* p. 95.
17. Ibid., p. 105.
18. Ibid., pp. 122–123.
19. Ibid., p. 125.
20. Ibid., pp. 126–127.

CHAPTER 2

1. Charles O. Hucker, *China's Imperial Past,* (Stanford University Press, 1975), pp. 324, 336, 349, 351, 352.
2. Ibid., p. 65.
3. Ibid., p. 336.
4. Ibid., p. 324.
5. Ibid., p. 356.
6. Ibid., pp. 2–3.
7. Ibid., p. 6. See also Charles Koppel, "The Position of the Chinese in the Philippines, Malaysia and Indonesia," *The Chinese in Indonesia, The Philippines and Malaysia,* Report No. 10 (London: Minority Rights Group, 1972), p. 18n.
8. Stanford M. Lyman, *Chinese Americans* (Random House, 1974), p. 14.
9. Victor Purcell, *The Chinese in Southeast Asia,* 2nd edition, (Oxford University Press, 1980), pp. 8–13.
10. Charles O. Hucker, *China's Imperial Past,* p. 296; Victor Purcell, *The Chinese in Southeast Asia,* 2nd edition, p. 24.
11. Victor Purcell, *The Chinese in Southeast Asia,* 2nd edition, p. 27.
12. Ibid., p. 26.
13. Ibid., p. 3.
14. Ibid., p. 30.
15. Ibid., p. 3.
16. Yuan-li Wu and Chun-hsi Wu, *Economic Development in Southeast Asia* (Hoover Institution Press, 1980), p. 133.
17. "The fact remains that whereas the colonization of the Europeans followed in the wake of their fleets and soldiers or to lands obtained by treaty from native rulers, the Chinese in the last three and a half centuries have entered Southeast Asia either as visiting merchants or as suppliants for permission to remain from the Javanese sultans,

or from the Spanish, Dutch, British, or French. They came no more as haughty emissaries of the Dragon Throne, armed to the teeth to impose the imperial will, but as humble and peaceable shiploads of traders, artisans, or coolies, waiting, like Czech or Italian peasants on Ellis Island, for permission to enter the land of promise. But their meekness and peaceableness were in the long run more forceful than the militancy of the Europeans; for where the latter came in their tens the Chinese came in their thousands, and when the Europeans had gone, they remained." Victor Purcell, *The Chinese in Southeast Asia,* 2nd edition, p. 23.

18. Ibid., p. 32.
19. Ibid., pp. 1–2; see also p. 42.
20. Yuan-li Wu and Chun-hsi Wu, *Economic Development in Southeast Asia,* pp. 29–30.
21. Ibid., p. 133.
22. Alvin Rabushka, *Race and Politics in Urban Malaysia* (Hoover Institution Press, 1973), p. 22.
23. Yuan-li Wu and Chun-hsi Wu, *Economic Development in Southeast Asia,* p. 67.
24. Ibid., pp. 84, 87.
25. Ibid., p. 74.
26. Victor Purcell, *The Chinese in Southeast Asia,* 2nd edition, p. 24.
27. Ibid., p. 26.
28. Ibid., pp. 46, 69, 92, 103–104, 115, 125, 179, 498, 538.
29. Ibid., pp. 103–104, 122.
30. Lennox A. Mills, *Southeast Asia* (University of Minnesota Press, 1964), p. 110.
31. Ibid., p. 111.
32. Ibid.
33. Victor Purcell, *The Chinese in Southeast Asia,* 2nd edition, p. 121.
34. Ibid., p. 284.
35. Yuan-li Wu and Chun-hsi Wu, *Economic Development in Southeast Asia,* p. 53.
36. Lennox A. Mills, *Southeast Asia,* pp. 111–112; see also Victor Purcell, *The Chinese in Southeast Asia,* 2nd edition, p. 548.
37. Victor Purcell, *The Chinese in Southeast Asia,* 2nd edition, p. 430.
38. Ibid., p. 450.
39. Virginia Thompson and Richard Adloff, *Minority Problems in Southeast Asia* (Russell & Russell, 1955), p. 4.
40. Ibid., p. 195.
41. Ibid., p. 540.
42. Ibid., p. 128.
43. Yuan-li Wu and Chun-hsi Wu, *Economic Development in Southeast Asia,* p. 51.
44. Ibid., p. 85.
45. Ibid., p. 71.
46. Victor Purcell, *The Chinese in Southeast Asia,* 2nd edition, p. 546.

47. Ibid., p. 514n.
48. Ibid., p. 551.
49. Ibid., pp. 120–122, 418.
50. Ibid., p. 458; Lennox A. Mills, *Southeast Asia,* p. 110; Naosaku Uchida, *The Overseas Chinese* (Stanford: The Hoover Institution Press, 1960), pp. 24–25, 28–35.
51. Lennox A. Mills, *Southeast Asia,* p. 130.
52. Victor Purcell, *The Chinese in Southeast Asia,* 2nd edition, p. 433.
53. Owen Lattimore, *The Situation in Asia* (Boston: Little, Brown and Co., 1949), p. 197.
54. Victor Purcell, *The Chinese in Southeast Asia,* 2nd edition, p. 457.
55. Yuan-li Wu and Chun-hsi Wu, *Economic Development in Southeast Asia,* p. 57.
56. Ibid., pp. 55, 57.
57. Ibid., pp. 31, 133.
58. Cynthia Enloe, *Police, Military and Ethnicity* (Transaction Books, 1980), p. 75.
59. Alvin Rabushka, *Race and Politics in Urban Malaysia,* p. 21.
60. Ibid., p. 24.
61. Victor Purcell, *The Chinese in Southeast Asia,* 2nd edition, p. 94; Lennox A. Mills, *Southeast Asia,* p. 110.
62. Ivan H. Light, *Ethnic Enterprise in America* (Berkeley: University of California Press, 1972), p. 174.
63. Victor Purcell, *The Chinese in Southeast Asia,* 2nd edition, p. 96; see also p. 220.
64. Ibid., p. 94.
65. Ibid., p. 118.
66. Ibid., p. 121.
67. Ibid., pp. 106, 418, 421.
68. Ibid., p. 433.
69. Ibid., pp. 134, 139, 147, 187–189, 216, 219, 404–405, 409n, 427, 433, 439, 487–488, 489, 516–518, 530, 544–545, 559, 564; Yuan-li Wu and Chun-hsi Wu, *Economic Development in Southeast Asia,* pp. 173–179.
70. Victor Purcell, *The Chinese in Southeast Asia,* 2nd edition, p. 101.
71. Ibid., p. 104.
72. Ibid., pp. 96, 98, 100, 101, 104.
73. Lennox A Mills, *Southeast Asia,* p. 116.
74. Victor Purcell, *The Chinese in Southeast Asia,* 2nd edition, pp. 101, 513–514, 519, 523.
75. Ibid., pp. 513–514.
76. Ibid., pp. 148, 472–476, 478.
77. Ibid., pp. 494, 496, 527.
78 Ibid., pp. 472–476; Virginia Thompson and Richard Adloff, *Minority Problems in Southeast Asia,* p. 9.
79. Stanford M. Lyman, *Chinese Americans,* p 4
80. Ibid. p. 7

81. See, for example, Victor Purcell, *The Chinese in Southeast Asia,* 2nd edition, p. 512. See also xii, 177–178, 187–189, 190, 290–291, 383, 518, 535, 536, 537.

82. Yuan-li Wu and Chun-hsi Wu, *Economic Development in Southeast Asia,* p. 59.

83. Ibid., p. 58.

84. Ibid., p. 61.

85. Ibid., p. 65.

86. Ibid., p. 71.

87. Ibid., p. 76.

88. Ibid., p. 77.

89. Ibid., p. 59.

90. Ibid., p. 88–89.

91. Milton J. Esman, "Communal Conflict in Southeast Asia," *Ethnicity: Theory and Experience,* ed. Nathan Glazer and Daniel P. Moynihan (Harvard University Press, 1981), p. 401.

92. Ibid., p. 402.

93. Victor Purcell, *The Chinese in Southeast Asia,* 2nd edition, p. 86.

94. Ibid., p. 81.

95. Ibid., p. 82.

96. Ibid., p. 90.

97. Ibid., p. 91.

98. Ibid.

99. Ibid.

100. Ibid., p. 92.

101. Ibid.

102. Ibid., pp. 92–93, 96, 124–125.

103. Ibid., p. 97.

104. Ibid., p. 107.

105. Ibid.

106. Ibid., p. 97.

107. Ibid., p. 83.

108. Ibid., p. 127.

109. Ibid., p. 129.

110. Yuan-li Wu and Chun-hsi Wu, *Economic Development in Southeast Asia,* p. 70.

111. Victor Purcell, *The Chinese in Southeast Asia,* 2nd edition, p. 261.

112. Charles O. Hucker, *China's Imperial Past,* p. 338.

113. Victor Purcell, *The Chinese in Southeast Asia,* 2nd edition, p. 272.

114. Ibid., p. 108.

115. Ibid., p. 83.

116. Ibid., p. 95.

117. Ibid., p. 114.

118. Ibid., p. 96.

119. Ibid., p. 101.

120. Ibid.

121. Ibid., pp. 100, 104.

122. Ibid., p. 107.
123. Ibid., p. 101.
124. Ibid., p. 119.
125. Ibid., p. 85.
126. Ibid., p. 125.
127. Ibid., pp. 142–143.
128. Ibid., p. 146.
129. Ibid., p. 137.
130. Ibid., p. 139.
131. Ibid., pp. 136–137.
132. Ibid., p. 147.
133. Ibid., p. 163; Yuan-li Wu and Chun-hsi Wu, *Economic Development in Southeast Asia,* p. 171.
134. Victor Purcell, *The Chinese in Southeast Asia,* 2nd edition, p. 117.
135. Ibid., p. 127.
136. Ibid., p. 128.
137. Ibid., p. 131.
138. Ibid., pp. 130–131.
139. Lennox A. Mills, *Southeast Asia,* p. 129.
140. Yuan-li Wu and Chun-hsi Wu, *Economic Development in Southeast Asia,* p. 71.
141. Lennox A. Mills, *Southeast Asia,* p. 129.
142. Victor Purcell, *The Chinese in Southeast Asia,* 2nd edition, p. 139n.
143. Lennox A. Mills, *Southeast Asia,* p. 130.
144. Victor Purcell, *The Chinese in Southeast Asia,* 2nd edition, p. 235.
145. Ibid., p. 241.
146. Ibid., p. 243.
147. Ibid.
148. Ibid., p. 245.
149. Ibid., p. 244.
150. Alvin Rabushka, *Race and Politics in Urban Malaysia,* p. 17; Lennox A. Mills, *Southeast Asia,* p. 41.
151. Victor Purcell, *The Chinese in Southeast Asia,* 2nd edition, p. 246.
152. Ibid., p. 248.
153. Ibid., p. 247.
154. Ibid., p. 248.
155. Ibid., p. 249.
156. Ibid., p. 234.
157. Ibid., pp. 251–252.
158. Ibid., pp. 282–283.
159. Ibid., p. 267.
160. Yuan-li Wu and Chun-hsi Wu, *Economic Development in Southeast Asia,* p. 53.
161. Victor Purcell, *The Chinese in Southeast Asia,* 2nd edition, p. 283n.
162. Ibid., p. 284.
163. Ibid., p. 285.
164. Ibid., p. 277.

165. Ibid., pp. 277–279.
166. Yuan-li Wu and Chun-hsi Wu, *Economic Development in Southeast Asia,* p. 57.
167. Victor Purcell, *The Chinese in Southeast Asia,* 2nd edition, p. 322.
168. Ibid., pp. 305–306.
169. Ibid., p. 305.
170. Ibid., p. 311.
171. Lennox A. Mills, *Southeast Asia,* p. 42.
172. Ibid., p. 43.
173. Ibid., p. 41.
174. Alvin Rabushka, *Race and Politics in Urban Malaysia,* p. 21.
175. Ibid., p. 22.
176. Ibid., pp. 26, 27.
177. Ibid., p. 31.
178. Ibid., p. 30.
179. Ibid., p. 33.
180. Ibid., p. 26; see also Yuan-li Wu and Chun-hsi Wu, *Economic Development in Southeast Asia,* p. 57.
181. Yuan-li Wu and Chun-hsi Wu, *Economic Development in Southeast Asia,* p. 57.
182. Robert E. Klitgaard and Ruth Katz, "Ethnic Inequalities and Public Policy: The Case of Malaysia," Mimeographed, Kennedy School of Government, Harvard University, July 1981, p. 11.
183. Alvin Rabushka, *A Theory of Racial Harmony* (University of South Carolina Press, 1974), p. 82.
184. Yuan-li Wu and Chun-hsi Wu, *Economic Development in Southeast Asia,* p. 58.
185. Victor Purcell, *The Chinese in Southeast Asia,* 2nd edition, p. 389.
186. Ibid., p. 404.
187. Ibid., p. 398.
188. Ibid., p. 394.
189. Ibid., p. 396.
190. Ibid., p. 402.
191. Ibid., p. 404.
192. Ibid., p. 406.
193. Ibid., p. 410.
194. Ibid., pp. 422–423.
195. Ibid., p. 431.
196. Ibid.
197. Ibid., p. 432.
198. Ibid., p. 469n.
199. Ibid., p. 439.
200. Ibid., p. 445.
201. Ibid., p. 449.
202. Ibid., p. 450.
203. Ibid., p. 461.
204. Ibid., p. 402.

205. Ibid., p. 457.
206. Ibid., p. 472.
207. Ibid., p. 475.
208. Ibid., pp. 474–476.
209. Ibid., p. 383.
210. Yuan-li Wu and Chun-hsi Wu, *Economic Development in Southeast Asia,* p. 61.
211. Victor Purcell, *The Chinese in Southeast Asia,* 2nd edition, p. 383.
212. Lennox A. Mills, *Southeast Asia,* p. 122.
213. Victor Purcell, *The Chinese in Southeast Asia,* 2nd edition, pp. 487–488.
214. Ibid., p. 487.
215. Yuan-li Wu and Chun-hsi Wu, *Economic Development in Southeast Asia,* p. 65.
216. Ibid., p. 63.
217. James Fallows, "Indonesia: An Effort to Hold Together," *The Atlantic,* June 1982, p. 19.
218. Joseph P. Manguno, "Suharto Angling for Political Dividends in Expansionary Budget for New Year," *The Asian Wall Street Journal Weekly,* January 12, 1981, p. 12.
219. Ibid.
220. Victor Purcell, *The Chinese in Southeast Asia,* 2nd edition, p. 508.
221. Ibid., p. 512.
222. Ibid., p. 508.
223. Ibid., p. 512.
224. Ibid., pp. 516–518, passim.
225. Ibid., p. 514.
226. Ibid., p. 515.
227. Ibid., p. 519.
228. Ibid., p. 496.
229. Ibid., pp. 538–539.
230. Ibid., p. 546.
231. Ibid., p. 536.
232. Ibid., pp. 536–537.
233. Ibid., p. 540.
234. Ibid., p. 542.
235. Ibid., pp. 542–543.
236. Ibid., pp. 544–545.
237. Ibid., p. 559.
238. Ibid., p. 564.
239. Lennox A. Mills, *Southeast Asia,* p. 124.
240. Victor Purcell, *The Chinese in Southeast Asia,* 2nd edition, p. 184.
241. Ibid., p. 187.
242. Ibid., p. 189.
243. Ibid., p. 190.
244. Ibid., p. 195.
245. Ibid., p. 199.

246. Lennox A. Mills, *Southeast Asia,* p. 132.

247. Ibid., pp. 132–133.

248. Victor Purcell, *The Chinese in Southeast Asia,* 2nd edition, pp. 219, 221.

249. Yuan-li Wu and Chun-hsi Wu, *Economic Development in Southeast Asia,* p. 85.

250. Ibid., p. 133.

251. Ibid., p. 88.

252. Ibid., p. 87.

253. *Time,* May 14, 1979, p. 15; James N. Wallace, "How Chinese Bear Big Share of Refugee Load," *U.S. News & World Report,* September 17, 1979, p. 60.

254. "Emergency," *New Republic,* June 30, 1979, p. 6.

255. Bruce Grant, *The Boat People* (New York: Penguin Books, 1979), p. 65.

256. *Time,* July 2, 1979, p. 19.

257. "A Cruise to Nowhere," *Newsweek,* November 27, 1978, p. 58.

258. "Emergency," *New Republic,* June 30, 1979, p. 7

259. Lucy Sells, "The Critical Role of Mathematics in Career Education," mimeographed, January 6, 1981, Table II.

260. Jack Chen, *The Chinese of America* (San Francisco: Harper & Row, 1980), p. 23.

261. Ibid., p. 27.

262. Ibid., p. 28.

263. Stanford M. Lyman, *The Asian in the West* (Reno: University of Nevada System, 1970), p. 66.

264. Ibid., p. 68.

265. Ibid., p. 79.

266. J. C. Furnas, *The Americans* (New York: G. P. Putnam's Sons, 1969), p. 699.

267. Stanford M. Lyman, *The Asian in the West,* pp. 59–62.

268. Betty Lee Sung, *The Story of the Chinese in America* (New York: Collier Books, 1967), pp. 30–31.

269. Ibid., p. 31.

270. J. C. Furnas, *The Americans,* p. 699.

271. Betty Lee Sung, *The Story of the Chinese in America,* pp. 35–36.

272. Jack Chen, *The Chinese of America,* p. 93.

273. Ibid., pp. 99–101.

274. Ibid., pp. 105–107.

275. Ibid., p. 109.

276. Ibid., p. 113.

277 Ibid., p. 112.

278. Betty Lee Sung, *The Story of the Chinese in America,* p. 36.

279. Jack Chen, *The Chinese of America,* p. 53.

280. Ibid., p. 18.

281. Betty Lee Sung, *The Story of the Chinese in America,* pp. 16–17.

282. Stanford M. Lyman, *Chinese Americans,* pp. 70–80.

283. Stanford M. Lyman, *The Asian in the West,* p. 79.
284. Haitung King and Frances B. Locke, "Chinese in the United States: A Century of Occupational Transition," *International Migration Review,* Spring 1980, p. 19
285. Loc. cit.
286. Stanford M. Lyman, *The Asian in the West,* p. 79.
287. Stanford M. Lyman, *Chinese Americans,* p. 92.
288. Ibid., pp. 93–96.
289. Ibid., pp. 152–153.
290. Betty Lee Sung, *The Story of the Chinese in America,* p. 56.
291. Ivan H. Light, *Ethnic Enterprise in America,* p. 87.
292. Betty Lee Sung, *The Story of the Chinese in America,* p. 259.
293. H. M. Lai, "Chinese," *Harvard Encyclopedia of American Ethnic Groups* (Cambridge: Harvard University Press, 1981), p. 223.
294. Ibid., p. 225.
295. Betty Lee Sung, *The Story of the Chinese in America,* p. 171.
296. Monica Boyd, "Oriental Immigration: The Experience of the Chinese, Japanese, and Filipino Populations in the United States," *International Migration Review,* Spring 1971, p. 59; Thomas Sowell, ed., *Essays and Data on American Ethnic Groups* (The Urban Institute, 1978), pp. 257–258.
297. Haitung King and Frances B. Locke, "Chinese in the United States: A Century of Occupational Transition," *International Migration Review,* Spring 1980, p. 23.
298. Betty Lee Sung, *The Story of the Chinese in America,* p. 322; Thomas Sowell, *Ethnic America* (New York: Basic Books, Inc., 1981), p. 5.
299. Betty Lee Sung, *The Story of the Chinese in America,* pp. 143, 150, 251.

CHAPTER 3

1. Leo Schelbert, "On Becoming an Emigrant: A Structural View of Eighteenth- and Nineteenth-Century Swiss Data," *Perspectives in American History,* Vol. VII (1973), p. 461.
2. Donald Fleming and Bernard Bailyn, "Introduction," Ibid., pp. v–vi.
3. Philip Taylor, *The Distant Magnet* (Harper & Row, 1971), p. ix.
4. Emilio Willems, "Brazil," *The Positive Contribution by Immigrants,* ed. Oscar Handlin, et. al. (United Nations Educational, Scientific and Cultural Organization), p. 121.
5. Jorge Hechen, "The Argentine Republic," Ibid., pp. 147–148.
6. Philip Taylor, *The Distant Magnet,* p. 18.
7. Ibid., p. 44.
8. Emilio Willems, "Brazil," op. cit., p. 123.
9. Charles Wagley, *An Introduction to Brazil* (New York: Columbia University Press, 1971), p. 79.
10. Emilio Willems, "Brazil," op. cit., p. 127.

11. Ibid., p. 129.
12. Ibid., p. 127.
13. Ibid., p. 124.
14. Ibid., p. 125.
15. Ibid., p. 129.
16. Ibid.
17. Ibid., p. 130.
18. Ibid.
19. Mark Jefferson, *Peopling the Argentine Pampa* (Port Washington, New York: Kennikat Press, 1971), pp. 41–42.
20. Ibid., pp. 28–29, 60, 76.
21. Ibid., pp. 24, 31, 32, 33, 50, 99.
22. Ibid., p. 76; see also p. 78.
23. Ibid., p. 137.
24. J. Halero Ferguson, *Latin America: The Balance of Race Redressed* (London: Oxford University Press, 1961), p. 56.
25. Bernard Kayser, "European Migrations: The New Pattern," *International Migration Review,* Summer 1977, p. 234.
26. Ibid., p. 233.
27. Robert F. Foerster, *The Italian Emigration of Our Times 1969),* (Arno Press, 1969), passim.
28. Wolfgang Kollman and Peter Marschalk, "German Emigration to the United States," *Perspectives in American History,* Vol. VII (1973), p. 519.
29. Ibid., p. 518.
30. Emilio Willems, "Brazil," op. cit., p. 121.
31. U.S. Bureau of the Census, *Historical Statistics of the United States, From Colonial Times to 1970* (Government Printing Office, 1975), p. 106.
32. Jorge Hechen, "The Argentine Republic," *The Positive Contribution by Immigrants,* ed. Oscar Handlin, et. al., p. 153.
33. W. D. Borrie, "Australia," Ibid., p. 79.
34. Frederick Merk, *History of the Westward Movement* (New York: Alfred A. Knopf, 1978), p. 49.
35. Ibid., p. 50.
36. Virginia Brainard Kunz, *The Germans in America* (Minneapolis: Lerner Publications Co., 1966), p. 11; Carl Wittke, *We Who Built America* (Case Western Reserve University Press, 1939), p. 198.
37. Carl Wittke, *We Who Built America,* pp. 81–82.
38. Ibid., p. 82.
39. Ibid., p. 84.
40. Ibid., p. 84.
41. Wolfgang Kollman and Peter Marschalk, "German Emigration to the United States," op. cit., p. 537.
42. Carl Wittke, *We Who Built America,* p. 215.
43. Kathleen Neils Conzen, *Immigrant Milwaukee, 1836–1860* (Harvard University Press, 1976), p. 73.

44. Virginia Yans-McLaughlin and Alice Kessler-Harris, "European Immigrant Groups," *Essays and Data on American Ethnic Groups,* ed. Thomas Sowell (The Urban Institute, 1978), p. 111.
45. Thomas Sowell, *Ethnic America* (Basic Books, 1981), pp. 21–22.
46. Carl Wittke, *We Who Built America,* p. 195.
47. Ibid., pp. 200, 201, 226.
48. Ibid., p. 240.
49. E. V. Smalley, "The German Element in the United States," *The Ordeal of Assimilation,* ed. Stanley Feldstein and Lawrence Costello (Anchor Books, 1974), p. 105.
50. Kathleen Neils Conzen, "Germans," *Harvard Encyclopedia of American Ethnic Groups,* ed. Stephan Thernstrom, et al., (Belknap Press, 1980), p. 425.
51. Emilio Willems, "Brazil," op. cit., pp. 120, 123.
52. Charles Wagley, *An Introduction to Brazil* (New York: Columbia University Press, 1971), p. 78.
53. Emilio Willems, "Brazil," op. cit., p. 124.
54. "Introduction," *The Positive Contribution by Immigrants,* ed. Oscar Handlin, et. al., p. 13.
55. Emilio Willems, "Brazil," Ibid., p. 134.
56. Ibid., p. 141.
57. Ibid., p. 140.
58. Ibid., p. 121.
59. Ibid., p. 123.
60. Ibid., p. 124.
61. Ibid., p. 125.
62. Ibid., p. 127.
63. Ibid.
64. Ibid., p. 129.
65. Ibid., p. 133.
66. W. D. Borrie, "Australia," Ibid., p. 87.
67. Ibid., p. 88.
68. W. D. Borrie, *Italians and Germans in Australia* (Melbourne: The Australian National University, 1934), p. 157.
69. W. D. Borrie, "Australia," *The Positive Contribution by Immigrants,* ed. Oscar Handlin, pp. 90–91.
70. Ibid., p. 91; W. D. Borrie, *Italians and Germans in Australia,* p. 173.
71. W. D. Borrie, "Australia," *The Positive Contribution by Immigrants,* ed. Oscar Handlin, p. 92; J. Lyng, *Non-Britishers in Australia* (Melbourne: Melbourne University Press, 1935), p. 40.
72. Ibid., p. 93.
73. W. D. Borrie, *Italians and Germans in Australia,* p 182.
74. Ibid., p. 184.
75. Ibid., p. 188.
76. Ibid., pp. 193, 210.
77. Ibid., p. 211.

78. Ibid., p. 93.
79. Ibid., p. 94.
80. Ibid.
81. Ibid.; J. Lyng, *Non-Britishers in Australia*, pp. 34, 46.
82. Gustave de Beaumont, *Ireland: Social, Political, and Religious*, Vol. II (Rich and Bentley, 1839), p. 17.
83. Maire and Conor Cruise O'Brien, *A Concise History of Ireland* (New York: Beckman House, 1972), p. 47.
84. Arthur Young, *A Tour in Ireland 1776–1779*, Vol. II (Shannon: Irish University Press, 1970), p. 54.
85. Loc. cit.
86. James G. Leyburn, *The Scotch-Irish* (University of North Carolina Press, 1962), p. 125.
87. George Potter, *To the Golden Door: The Story of the Irish in Ireland and America* (Greenwood Press, 1960), p. 22.
88. Ibid., p. 23.
89. Ibid.
90. Maire and Conor Cruise O'Brien, *A Concise History of Ireland*, p. 68.
91. Patrick J. Blessing, "Irish," *Harvard Encyclopedia of American Ethnic Groups*, ed. Stephan Thernstrom, et. al. (Belknap Press, 1980), p. 525.
92. Gustave de Beaumont, *Ireland: Social, Political, and Religious*, Vol. I, (Rich and Bentley, 1839), pp. 122–123.
93. Ibid., p. 124.
94. Ibid., pp. 127–128.
95. Ibid., p. 130.
96. Ibid., p. 135.
97. Arthur Young, *A Tour in Ireland 1776–1779*, Vol. I, pp. 82–83.
98. Ibid., p. 83.
99. George Potter, *To the Golden Door*, pp. 102–109.
100. Quoted in Andrew M. Greeley, *That Most Distressed Nation* (New York: Quadrangle Books, 1972), pp. 34–35.
101. Robert W. Fogel and Stanley L. Engelman, *Time on the Cross* (Little, Brown and Co., 1974), p. 125; Maldwyn Allen Jones, *American Immigration* (University of Chicago Press, 1960) p. 133.
102. Carl Wittke, *We Who Built America*, p. 125
103. Oliver MacDonagh, "The Irish Famine Emigration to the United States," *Perspectives in American History*, Vol. X (1976), p. 366.
104. Eugene D. Genovese, *Roll, Jordan, Roll* (New York: Pantheon Books, 1974), p. 525.
105. Oliver MacDonagh, "The Irish Famine Emigration to the United States," op. cit., p. 367. See also Arthur Young, *A Tour in Ireland 1776–1779*, Vol. II, pp. 85, 100–102.
106. Eugene D. Genovese, *Roll, Jordan, Roll*, p. 530.
107. Oliver MacDonagh, "The Irish Famine Emigration to the United States," op. cit., p 367.

108. W.E.B. DuBois, *The Philadelphia Negro* (Schocken Books, 1967), p. 387; see also Russell Kirk, *John Randolph of Roanoke* (Indianapolis: Liberty Press, 1978), pp. 158–159.

109. Gustave de Beaumont, *Ireland: Social, Political, and Religious,* Vol. I, p. 270.

110. Oliver MacDonagh, "The Irish Famine Emigration to the United States," op. cit., p. 368.

111. Gustave de Beaumont, *Ireland: Social, Political, and Religious,* Vol. I, p. 267.

112. Ibid., p. 267.

113. Oliver MacDonagh, "The Irish Famine Emigration to the United States," op. cit., p. 367.

114. W. E. Vaughan and A. J. Fitzpatrick, *Irish Historical Statistics* (Dublin: Royal Irish Academy, 1978), pp. 260–261.

115. Winston S. Churchill, *A History of the English Speaking Peoples,* Vol. II (New York: Bantam Books, 1961), pp. 223–226.

116. Arthur Young, *A Tour In Ireland 1776–1779,* Vol. II, pp. 5–6.

117. Ibid., Vol. I, pp. 378–379.

118. Ibid., Vol. I, p. 20.

119. See, for example, George Potter, *To the Golden Door,* p. 47; Lynn Holleen Lees, *Exiles of Erin* (Ithaca: Cornell University Press, 1979), p. 71; Kevin O'Connor, *The Irish in Britain* (London: Sidgwick & Jackson, 1972), p. 11.

120. Arthur Young, *A Tour in Ireland 1776–1779,* Vol. II, p. 147.

121. George Potter, *To the Golden Door,* p. 44.

122. Maire and Conor Cruise O'Brien, *A Concise History of Ireland,* p. 25.

123. Nathan Glazer and Daniel Patrick Moynihan, *Beyond the Melting Pot* (Cambridge, Mass.: M.I.T. Press, 1966), p. 232.

124. George Potter, *To the Golden Door,* p. 94.

125. Ibid., p. 86.

126. Andrew M. Greeley, *That Most Distressful Nation,* p. 129.

127. Ibid., p. 132.

128. Ibid., p. 134.

129. George Potter, *To the Golden Door,* p. 93.

130. Ibid., p. 101; see also Andrew M. Greeley, *That Most Distressful Nation,* pp. 52–57.

131. George Potter, *To the Golden Door,* p. 84.

132. Ibid., p. 85.

133. Loc. cit.

134. Oscar Handlin, *Boston's Immigrants* (New York: Atheneum, 1970), p. 42.

135. George Potter, *To the Golden Door,* p. 38.

136. Nicholas Flood Davin, *The Irishman in Canada* (London: Sampson Low, Marston & Co., 1877), p. 245.

137. Robert E. Kennedy, Jr., *The Irish: Emigration, Marriage, and Fertility* (Berkeley: University of California Press, 1975), p. 27.

138. Ibid., p. 74.

139. W. E. Vaughn and A. J. Fitzpatrick, eds., *Irish Historical Statistics* (Dublin: Royal Irish Academy, 1978), p. 3.
140. *The World Almanac & Book of Facts, 1981,* pp. 547, 589.
141. Loc. cit.; U.S. Bureau of the Census, *Current Population Reports,* Series P-20, No. 249 (Washington: U.S. Government Printing Office, 1972), p. 11.
142. Kevin O'Connor, *The Irish in Britain,* p. 2.
143. Ibid., p. 9.
144. Ibid., p. 10.
145. Frederick Engels, *The Condition of the Working Class in England in 1844* (London: George Allen and Unwin, Ltd., 1952), pp. 90–94.
146. Ibid., p. 91.
147. Ibid., p. 93.
148. Ibid., p. 92.
149. Ibid., p. 93.
150. Lynn Hollen Lees, *Exiles of Erin,* p. 42.
151. Ibid., p. 43.
152. Ibid., p. 44.
153. Ibid., p. 63.
154. Ibid., p. 71
155. Ibid., p. 72.
156. Ibid., p. 79.
157 Kevin O'Connor, *The Irish in Britain,* p. 13.
158 Ibid., p. 14.
159. Lynn Hollen Lees, *Exiles of Erin,* p. 92.
160. Ibid., p. 93.
161. Ibid., pp. 97–98.
162. Kevin O'Connor, *The Irish in Britain,* p. 14.
163. Ibid., p. 15.
164. See, for example, Ibid., pp. 16–18.
165. W. E. Vaughn & A. J. Fitzpatrick, *Irish Historical Statistics,* p. 264.
166. Kevin O'Connor, *The Irish in Britain,* p. 20.
167. W. E. Vaughn & A. J. Fitzpatrick, *Irish Historical Statistics,* p. 264
168. Kevin O'Connor, *The Irish in Britain,* p. 25.
169. Ibid., p. 26.
170. Ibid., pp. 33–34.
171. Ibid., p. 48.
172. Ibid., p. 54.
173. Ibid., p. 83
174. Ibid., p. 86
175. Ibid., p. 96.
176. Ibid., p. 118.
177. Ibid., p. 137
178. Carl Wittke, *We Who Built America,* p. 129.
179. Thomas Sowell, *Ethnic America,* pp. 23–25.
180. Carl Wittke, *We Who Built America,* p. 130.
181. Ibid., p. 133

182 Maldwyn Allen Jones, *American Immigration* (Chicago: University of Chicago Press, 1970), p. 130.
183. Carl Wittke, *We Who Built America*, p. 133.
184. Ibid., p. 134; Oscar Handlin, *Boston's Immigrants*, Chapter IV; Diane Ravitch, *The Great School Wars* (New York: Basic Books, 1974), pp. 27–28.
185. Thomas Sowell, *Ethnic America*, p. 26.
186. Carl Wittke, *We Who Built America*, p. 134.
187. James McCague, *The Second Rebellion* (New York: The Dial Press, Inc., 1968), p. 25.
188. James McCague, *The Second Rebellion* (New York: The Dial Press, Inc., 1968), p. 21.
189. Oscar Handlin, *Boston's Immigrants*, p. 114.
190. Ibid., p. 121.
191. George Potter, *To the Golden Door*, p. 169.
192. Carl Wittke, *We Who Built America*, p. 135.
'93. Jacob Riis, *How the Other Half Lives* (Harvard University Press, 1970), p. 18; George Potter, *To the Golden Door*, p. 169; Carl Wittke, *We Who Built America*, p. 137; J. C. Furnas, *The Americans* (G. P. Putnam's Sons, 1969), pp. 386, 705; Nathan Glazer and Daniel Patrick Moynihan, *Beyond the Melting Pot*, p. 240.
194. Robert Ernst, "The Economic Status of New York City Negroes, 1850–1863," *The Making of Black America*, eds. August Meir and Elliott Rudwick, Vol. I (New York: Atheneum, 1969), p. 255.
195. Carl Wittke, *We Who Built America*, p. 145.
196. Stephen Steinberg, *The Ethnic Myth* (New York: Atheneum, 1981), p. 154.
197. Patrick J. Blessing, "Irish," op. cit., p. 531.
198. Oscar Handlin, *Boston's Immigrants*, p. 253.
199. Carl Wittke, *We Who Built America*, pp. 146–150.
200. Ibid., p. 131.
201. Carl Wittke, *The Irish in America* (Russell & Russell, 1970), p. 37.
202. Carl Wittke, *We Who Built America*, p. 157.
203. Ibid., pp. 156–161; Carl Wittke, *The Irish in America*, pp. 103–113; George Potter, *To the Golden Door*, pp. 217–241.
204. George Potter, *To the Golden Door*, p. 218.
205. Ibid., p. 235.
206. Carl Wittke, *The Irish in America*, pp. 103–113; Nathan Glazer and D. P. Moynihan, *Beyond the Melting Pot*, pp. 221–229.
207. Nathan Glazer and D. P. Moynihan, *Beyond the Melting Pot*, p. 226; Humbert Nelli, *Italians in Chicago, 1880–1930* (New York: Oxford University Press, 1970), Chapter 4.
208. Carl Wittke, *The Irish in America*, p. 23.
209. Stephan Thernstrom, *The Other Bostonians* (Cambridge, Mass: Harvard University, 1973), pp. 130–142, passim.
210. Patrick J. Blessing, "Irish," op. cit., p. 538.

211. Stephan Thernstrom, *The Other Bostonians*, p. 137; Nathan Glazer and D. P. Moynihan, *Beyond the Melting Pot*, p. 255.
212. Patrick J. Blessing, "Irish," op. cit., p. 540.
213. Robert F. Foerster, *The Italian Emigration of Our Times* (Arno Press, 1969), p. 3.
214. Ibid., pp. 4, 6.
215. Ibid., p. 14.
216. Ibid., p. 28.
217 Ibid., p. 32.
218. Ibid., p. 42.
219. Leonard Covello, *The Social Background of the Italo-American School Child* (Totowa, N.J.: Rowman and Littlefiel 1972), p. 25.
220. Ibid., pp. 161.
221. Ibid., pp. 186, 188, 190.
222. Ibid., p. 191.
223. Ibid., pp. 229–231.
224. Ibid., p. 230.
225. Ibid., pp. 254–274.
226. Robert F. Foerster, *The Italian Emigration of Our Times*, p. 226.
227. Ibid., p. 227.
228. Ibid., p. 253.
229. Jorge Hechen, "The Argentine Republic," op. cit., p. 149.
230. Ibid., p. 150.
231. Robert F. Foerster, *The Italian Emigration of Our Times*, p. 228.
232. Ibid., p. 228.
233. Ibid., p. 227; Jorge Hechen, "The Argentine Republic," op. cit., pp. 150–151.
234. Robert F. Foerster, *The Italian Emigration of Our Times*, pp. 228–229.
235. Jorge Hechen, "The Argentine Republic," op. cit., p. 151.
236. Leonard Covello, *The Social Background of the Italo-American School Child* (Rowan and Littlefield, 1972), p. 223; Thomas Sowell, "Ethnicity in a Changing America," *Daedalus*, Winter 1978, p. 217.
237. Robert F. Foerster, *The Italian Emigration of Our Times*, p. 230.
238 Ibid., pp. 237–239.
239 Mark Jefferson, *Peopling the Argentine Pampa*, p. 42.
240. Robert F. Foerster, *The Italian Emigration of Our Times*, p. 235.
241. Ibid., p. 238.
242. Ibid., p. 239.
243. Ibid., p. 238.
244. Ibid., p. 257.
245. Ibid., p. 227.
246. Ibid., p. 243.
247. Mark Jefferson, *Peopling the Argentine Pampa*, p. 183.
248 Robert F. Foerster, *The Italian Emigration of Our Times*, p. 252.
249. Ibid., p. 201.
250. Ibid., p. 256.

251. Ibid., p. 253.
252. Ibid., pp. 255–257.
253. Mark Jefferson, *Peopling the Argentine Pampa*, p. 74.
254. Robert F. Foerster, *The Italian Emigration of Our Times*, p. 262.
255. Samuel L. Baily, "The Italians and the Development of Organized Labor in Argentina, Brazil and the United States," *Journal of Social History*, Winter 1969–70, pp. 124–125.
256. Robert F. Foerster, *The Italian Emigration of Our Times*, p. 273.
257. Mark Jefferson, *Peopling the Argentine Pampa*, p. 120.
258. Ibid., p. 2.
259. Ibid., p. 120.
260. Samuel L. Baily, "The Role of Two Newspapers in the Assimilation of Italians in Buenos Aires and São Paulo, 1893–1913," *International Migration Review*, Fall 1978, p. 339.
261. James Bruce, *Those Perplexing Argentines* (New York: Longmans, Green and Co., 1953), p. 101.
262. Ibid., p. 102.
263. Mark Jefferson, *Peopling the Argentine Pampa*, p. 121.
264. Emilio Willems, "Brazil," op. cit., p. 121.
265. Robert F. Foerster, *The Italian Emigration of Our Times*, p. 279.
266. Ibid., p. 287.
267. Ibid., p. 289.
268. Ibid., pp. 289–290.
269. Ibid., p. 290.
270. Ibid.
271. Ibid., p. 295.
272. Ibid., p. 296.
273. Ibid., p. 297.
274. Ibid., p. 298.
275. Samuel L. Baily, "The Role of Two Newspapers in the Assimilation of Italians in Buenos Aires and São Paulo, 1893–1913," op. cit., p. 324.
276. Emilio Willems, "Brazil," op. cit., p. 133.
277. Ibid., p. 124.
278. Ibid., p. 131.
279. W.P.A. Writers' Project, *The Italians of New York* (ew York: Random House, 1938), p. 3.
280. Ibid.
281. Humbert S. Nelli, "Italians," *Harvard Encyclopedia of American Ethnic Groups,* ed. Stephan Thernstrom, et al., p. 547.
282. Robert F. Foerster, *The Italian Emigration of Our Times,* p. 325.
283. Humbert S. Nelli, *Italians in Chicago, 1880–1930* (Oxford University Press, 1970), pp. 50–51.
284. Robert F. Foerster, *The Italian Emigration of Our Times,* p. 393; Joseph Lopreato, *Italian Americans* (Random House, 1970), pp. 41–42; Humbert S. Nelli, "Italians in Urban America," in *The*

Italian Experience in the United States, edited by Silvano M. Tomasi and Madeline H. Engel (Center for Migration Studies, 1970), pp. 79, 91; William H. Whyte, *Street Corner Society* (Chicago: University of Chicago Press, 1955), pp. xvii, p. 201; Nathan Glazer and D. P. Moynihan, *Beyond the Melting Pot,* p. 186; Luciano J. Iorizzo and Salvatore Mondello, *The Italian Americans* (Twayne Publishers, Inc., 1971), pp. 88–89; Robert F. Foerster, *The Italian Emigration of Our Times,* p. 393.

285. Humbert S. Nelli, *The Italians in Chicago,* pp. 195–196; Thomas Sowell, *The Golden Door* (New York: Oxford University Press, 1977), pp. 195–196.

286. Robert F. Foerster, *The Italian Emigration of Our Times,* p. 393; Humbert S. Nelli, "Italians in Urban America," *The Italian Experience in the United States,* ed. S. M. Tomasi and M. H. Engel, p. 91; William H. Whyte, *Street Corner Society,* p. xviii.

287. Samuel L. Baily, "Italians and Organized Labor in the United States and Argentina, 1880–1910," *The Italian Experience in the United States,* ed. S. M. Tomasi and M. H. Engel, p. 119; Robert F. Foerster, *The Italian Emigration of Our Times,* pp. 272, 317.

288. Richard Gambino, *Blood of My Blood* (New York: Anchor Books, 1974), p. 86.

289. Ibid., p. 87.

290. Humbert S. Nelli, "Italians," *The Harvard Encyclopedia of American Ethnic Groups,* ed. Stephan Thernstrom, et. al., p. 548.

291. Carl Wittke, *We Who Built America,* p. 444.

292. Luciano J. Iorizzo, "The Padrone and Immigrant Distribution," *The Italian Experience in the United States,* edited by Silvano M. Tomasi and Madeline H. Engel (Center for Migration Studies, 1970), p. 57. See also Robert F. Foerster, *The Italian Emigration of Our Times,* pp. 380, 381, 407.

293. Thomas Kessner, *The Golden Door* (New York: Oxford University Press, 1977), p. 162.

294. Robert F. Foerster, *The Italian Emigration of Our Times,* pp. 36, 362; Luciano J. Iorizzo, "The Padrone and Immigrant Distribution," *The Italian Experience in the United States,* ed. T. M. Tomasi and M. H. Engel, p. 20.

295. Thomas Sowell, *Ethnic America,* pp. 104–105, 113.

296. Nathan Glazer and D. P. Moynihan, *Beyond the Melting Pot,* pp. 257–258.

297. Humbert S. Nelli, "Italians," *The Harvard Encyclopedia of American Ethnic Groups,* ed. Stephan Thernstrom, et. al., p. 545.

298. Thomas Sowell, *Ethnic America,* p. 112.

299. Ibid., p. 112.

300. Humbert S. Nelli, "Italians," op. cit., p. 549.

301. Ibid., p. 551.

302. Ibid., p. 557.

303. Ibid., p. 554.
304. Leonard Covello, *The Social Background of the Italo-American School Child* (Rowan and Littlefield, 1972), pp. 282–310.
305. U.S. Bureau of the Census, *Current Population Reports*, Series P-20, No. 220 (Washington: Government Printing Office, 1971), p. 1.
306. Thomas Kessner, *The Golden Door*, p. 81.
307. U.S. Bureau of the Census, *Current Population Reports*, Series P-20, No. 221 (Washington: Government Printing Office, 1971), p. 19.
308. Richard Gambino, *Blood of My Blood*, p. 87; U. S. Bureau of the Census, Series P-20, No. 221, op. cit., p. 22.
309. J. Lyng, *Non-Britishers in Australia* (Melbourne University Press, 1935), p. 94.
310. Loc. cit.
311. Ibid., pp. 98, 103.
312. W. D. Borrie, *The Italians and Germans in Australia*, p. 147. See also J. Lyng, *Non-Britishers in Australia*, p. 105.
313. W. D. Borrie, *The Italians and Germans in Australia*, p. 147.
314. J. Lyng, *Non-Britishers in Australia*, p. 95.
315. Ibid., p. 96.
316. W. D. Borrie, *The Italians and Germans in Australia*, p. 104. See also Ibid., p. 142; W.D. Borrie, "Australia," *The Positive Contribution by Immigrants*, edited by Oscar Handlin (Unesco, 1955), pp. 91, 99.
317. W.D. Borrie, *The Italians and Germans in Australia*, p. 132.
318. Loc. cit.
319. Ibid., p. 137.
320. Ibid., p. 135.
321. Ibid., p. 136.
322. Ibid., pp. 145, 150.
323. Ibid., p. 145; W.D. Borrie, "Australia," *The Positive Contribution by Immigrants*, edited by Oscar Handlin, p. 103.
324. W.D. Borrie, *The Italians and Germans in Australia*, p. 144.
325. Ibid., pp. 141, 143.
326. Ibid., p. 135.
327. Ibid., p. 134.
328. Ibid., p. 141.
329. Ibid., p. 142.
330. Raphael Patai, *The Vanished Worlds of Jewry* (New York: Macmillan Publishing Co., Inc., 1980), pp. 86, 142.
331. Ibid., pp. 77, 82, 83, 88, 97, 112, 121, 149, 151.
332. Ibid., p. 101.
333. Louis Wirth, *The Ghetto* (Chicago: University of Chicago Press, 1956), p. 70n.
334. Raphael Patai, *The Vanished Worlds of Jewry*, p. 12.
335. Ibid., p. 14.
336. Ibid., p. 27.
337. Ibid., p. 11
338. Ibid., pp 66, 80

339 Ibıd., p. 143.
340. Ibid., p. 145.
341. Ibid., p. 178.
342. "Election: But No Mandate," *Time,* July 13, 1981, p. 27.
343. Solomon Grayzel, *A History of the Jews* (Mentor Books, 1968), pp 265, 270.
344. Ibid., p. 266.
345. Ibid., p. 271.
346. Ibid., pp. 271, 272.
347. Louis Wirth, *The Ghetto,* p. 14.
348. Ibid., p. 17.
349. Raphael Patai, *The Vanished Worlds of Jewry,* p. 165.
350. Louis Wirth, *The Ghetto,* p. 30.
351. Ibid., p. 32.
352. Louis Wirth, *The Ghetto,* p. 32.
353. Solomon Grayzel, *A History of the Jews,* pp. 342, 343.
354. Ibid., p. 412.
355. Raphael Patai, *The Vanished Worlds of Jewry,* p. 165.
356. Ibid., p. 167.
357. Solomon Grayzel, *A History of the Jews,* pp. 271, 272.
358. Ibid., p. 271.
359. Bernard S. Bachrach, "A Reassessment of Visigothic Jewish Policy, 589–711," *American Historical Review,* February 1973, p. 13.
360. Ibid.
361. Solomon Grayzel, *A History of the Jews,* p. 270.
362. Bernard S. Bachrach, "A Reassessment of Visigothic Jewish Policy, 589–711," op. cit., p. 19.
363. Solomon Grayzel, *A History of the Jews,* p. 290.
364. Ibid., p. 291.
365. Ibid., p. 291–292; Stephen H. Haliczer, "The Castilian Urban Patriciate and the Jewish Expulsions of 1480–92," *American Historical Review,* February 1973, p. 39.
366. Stephen H. Haliczer, "The Castilian Urban Patriciate and the Jewish Expulsions of 1480–92," op. cit., p. 39.
367. Ibid., p. 38n.
368. Ibid., pp. 39–40.
369. Raphael Patai, *The Vanished Worlds of Jewry,* p. 12.
370. Stephen H. Haliczer, "The Castilian Urban Patriciate and the Jewish Expulsions of 1480–92," op. cit., p. 42.
371. Nathan Glazer, *American Judaism* (Chicago: University of Chicago Press, 1957), p. 13.
372. Raphael Patai, *The Vanished Worlds of Jewry,* p 73
373. Ibid., p. 117
374. Ibid., p. 90.
375. Solomon Grayzel, *A History of the Jews* p. 305.
376. Ibid., p. 306.
377. Raphael Patai, *The Vanishea Worlds of Jewry,* p. 50.

378. Louis Wirth, *The Ghetto,* p. 50.
379. Raphael Patai, *The Vanished Worlds of Jewry,* p. 52.
380. Ibid., p. 51.
381. Ibid.
382. Ibid., pp. 53–55.
383. Solomon Grayzel, *A History of the Jews,* p. 551.
384. Raphael Patai, *The Vanished Worlds of Jewry,* p. 56.
385. Ibid., p. 57.
386. Thomas Sowell, *Ethnic America,* p. 97.
387. Raphael Patai, *The Vanished Worlds of Jewry,* p. 56.
388. Ibid., p. 57.
389. Solomon Grayzel, *A History of the Jews,* p. 390.
390. Raphael Patai, *The Vanished Worlds of Jewry,* p. 19.
391. Solomon Grayzel, *A History of the Jews,* pp. 394–395.
392. Raphael Patai, *The Vanished Worlds of Jewry,* p. 18.
393. Ibid., p. 20.
394. Arthur A. Goren, "Jews," *Harvard Encyclopedia of American Ethnic Groups,* Stephen Thernstrom, et. al., p. 572.
395. Louis Wirth, *The Ghetto,* p. 91.
396. Ibid., p. 92.
397. Ibid., pp. 93–94.
398. Solomon Grayzel, *A History of the Jews,* pp. 518–519.
399. Ibid., p. 549.
400. Irving Howe, *World of Our Fathers* (Harcourt, Brace, Jovanovich, 1976), p. 2.
401. Simon Kuznets, "Immigration of Russian Jews to the United States: Background and Structure," *Perspectives in American History,* Vol. IX (1975), p. 48.
402. Ibid., p. 39.
403. Raphael Patai, *The Vanished Worlds of Jewry,* pp. 32–33.
404. Ibid., p. 33.
405. Louis Wirth, *The Ghetto,* p. 133.
406. Ibid., p. 136.
407. Arthur A. Goren, "Jews," op. cit., p. 581.
408. Irving Howe, *World of Our Fathers,* p. 148.
409. Philip Taylor, *The Distant Magnet,* p. 168.
410. Irving Howe, *World of Our Fathers,* p. 157.
411. Philip Taylor, *The Distant Magnet,* p. 168.
412. Irving Howe, *World of Our Fathers,* p. 67.
413. Thomas Kessner, *The Golden Door,* p. 33.
414. Ibid., p. 37.
415. Virginia Yans-McLaughlin and Alice Kessler-Harris, "European Immigrants," *Essays and Data on American Ethnic Groups,* ed. Thomas Sowell (Washington: The Urban Institute, 1978), p. 116.
416. Thomas Kessner, *The Golden Door,* p. 98.
417. Arthur A. Goren, "Jews," op. cit., p. 589.

CHAPTER 4

1. L. H. Gann and Peter Duignan, *Burden of Empire* (Hoover Institution Press, 1977), p. 150.
2. Ray H. Whitbeck and Olive J. Thomas, *The Geographic Factor: Its Role in Life and Civilization* (Port Washington, N.Y.: Kennikat Press, 1970), p. 234.
3. L. H. Gann and Peter Duignan, *Burden of Empire,* pp. 150–151.
4. Ibid., p. 136.
5. Ibid., p. 150.
6. Ibid., pp. 293–294.
7. Philip D. Curtin, *The Atlantic Slave Trade* (University of Wisconsin Press, 1969), p. 18.
8. A.J.R. Russell-Wood, "Colonial Brazil," *Neither Slave Nor Free,* David W. Cohen and Jack P. Greene, eds. (Johns Hopkins University Press, 1972), p. 120.
9. Philip D. Curtin, *The Atlantic Slave Trade,* p. 19.
10. See, for example, Frank Tannenbaum, *Slave & Citizen* (Vintage Books, 1946), passim.
11. Gwendolyn Midlo Hall, *Social Control in Slave Plantation Societies* (Baltimore: Johns Hopkins University Press, 1971), pp. 13–15.
12. Carl N. Degler, *Neither Black Nor White* (New York: MacMillan Publishing Co., 1971), pp. 67–75; Gwendolyn Midlo Hall, *Social Control in Slave Plantation Societies,* pp. 15–20; Stanley M. Elkins, *Slavery* (Chicago: University of Chicago Press, 1969), pp. 51n, 78; Ulrich B. Phillips, *American Negro Slavery* (Baton Rouge: Louisiana State University, 1969), p. 52; Lewis C. Gray, *History of Agriculture in the Southern United States* vol. 2 (Washington, D.C.: Carnegie Institution of Washington, 1933), p. 519; David Lowenthal, "Race and Color in the West Indies," *Daedalus,* Spring 1967, pp. 610–611. See also David Brion Davis, *The Problem of Slavery in Western Culture* (Ithaca, N.Y.: Cornell University Press, 1960), Chapter 8.
13. Frank Tannenbaum, *Slave & Citizen* (Vintage Books, 1946), p. 64.
14. Carl N. Degler, *Neither Black Nor White,* p. 67.
15. Ibid., p. 66.
16. Ibid., p. 64.
17. Ibid., p. 65.
18. Ibid., p. 66.
19. Ibid., p. 72.
20. Gwendolyn Midlo Hall, *Social Control in Slave Plantation Societies,* Chapter II.
21. Frank Tannenbaum, *Slave & Citizen,* pp. 6–7.
22. Ibid., p. 8.
23. J. C. Furnas, *The Americans* (G. P. Putnam's Sons, 1969), p. 406.
24. Carl N. Degler, *Neither Black Nor White,* p. 102.
25. Gunnar Myrdal, *An American Dilemma* (McGraw-Hill, 1964), pp. 132–133.

26. Newton E. Morton, Chin S. Chung and Ming-Pi Mi, *Genetics of Interracial Crosses in Hawaii* (Basel, Switzerland: S. Krager, 1967), p. 78.
27. Ira Berlin, *Slaves Without Masters* (Pantheon, 1974), pp. 114, 116.
28. See, for example, David Lowenthal, *West Indian Societies* (New York: Oxford University Press, 1972), pp. 14–25, 93–100, 250–264; Ruth Glass, *London's Newcomers* (Cambridge, Mass: Harvard University Press, 1961), p. 65.
29. E. Franklin Frazier, *Black Bourgeoisie* (The Free Press, 1962), pp. 18–19.
30. A.J.R. Russell-Wood, "Colonial Brazil," *Neither Slave Nor Free*, eds. David W. Cohen and Jack P. Greene, p. 97.
31. Jerome S. Handler, *The Unappropriated People: Freedmen in the Slave Society of Barbados* (Baltimore: Johns Hopkins University Press, 1974), p. 21.
32. David Lowenthal, *West Indian Societies*, p. 46.
33. David W. Cohen and Jack P. Greene, "Introduction," *Neither Slave Nor Free*, p. 7; Frederick P. Bowser, "Colonial Spanish America," op. cit., p. 31; H. Hoetink, "Surinam and Curacao," op. cit., p. 62; Jerome S. Handler and Arnold A. Sio, "Barbados," op. cit., pp. 221, 229; Franklin W. Knight, "Cuba," op. cit., p. 286; Herbert S. Klein, "Nineteenth Century Brazil," op. cit., pp. 317–318.
34. Stephen Birmingham, *Certain People* (Little, Brown and Co., 1970), pp. 62, 69, 70. See also pp. 130–131, 160–161.
35. David W. Cohen and Jack P. Greene, "Introduction," *Neither Slave Nor Free*, p. 3; U.S. Bureau of the Census, "The Social and Economic Status of the Black Population of the United States: An Historical View, 1790–1978," *Current Population Reports*, Series P-23, No. 80 (Government Printing Office), p. 11.
36. David W. Cohen and Jack P. Greene, "Introduction," *Neither Slave Nor Free*, p. 3.
37. Frederick P. Browser, "Colonial Spanish America," op. cit., p. 19.
38. Donald Pierson, *Negroes in Brazil* (Southern Illinois University Press, 1967), p. 73.
39. Ibid., pp. 104–107.
40. Herbert S. Klein, "Nineteenth Century Brazil," op. cit., p. 319.
41. Robert W. Fogel and Stanley L. Engerman, *Time on the Cross* (Little, Brown and Co., 1974), pp. 23–24.
42. Carl N. Degler, *Neither Black Nor White*, pp. 67–75.
43. A.J.R. Russell-Wood, "Colonial Brazil," *Neither Slave Nor Free*, eds. David W. Cohen & Jack P. Greene, p. 131.
44. Ibid., pp. 84–85.
45. Ibid., p. 97.
46. Donald Pierson, *Negroes in Brazil*, p. 129.
47. Ibid., p. lvii.
48. Ibid., p. 126.

49. Florestan Fernandes, *The Negro in Brazilian Society* (Columbia University Press, 1969), p. 9.
50. A.J.R. Russell-Wood, "Colonial Brazil," op. cit., p. 86.
51. Ibid., p. 94.
52. Ibid., pp. 89–90.
53. Mavis C. Campbell, "The Price of Freedom: On Forms of Manumission," *Revista/Review Interamericana*, Summer 1976, p. 249 (see also p. 245).
54. Herbert S. Klein, "Nineteenth Century Brazil," op. cit., p. 325–326.
55. A.J.R. Russell-Wood, "Colonial Brazil," op. cit., p. 108.
56. Carl N. Degler, *Neither Black Nor White*, p. 44.
57. Herbert S. Klein, "Nineteenth Century Brazil," op. cit., p. 331.
58. A.J.R. Russell-Wood, "Colonial Brazil," op. cit., p. 115.
59. Ibid., p. 113.
60. Charles Wagley, ed., *Race and Class in Rural Brazil* (United Nations Educational, Scientific and Cultural Organization, 1952), p. 37.
61. Carl N. Degler, *Neither Black Nor White*, p. 30.
62. Charles Wagley, *An Introduction to Brazil* (New York: Columbia University Press, 1971), p. 123.
63. Charles Wagley, ed., *Race and Class in Rural Brazil*, p. 145.
64. Ibid., pp. 7–9.
65. Ibid., p. 143.
66. Donald Pierson, *Negroes in Brazil*, pp. xlvii, lvii, 150, 152.
67. Charles Wagley, ed., *Race and Class in Rural Brazil*, p. 143.
68. Herbert S. Klein, "Nineteenth Century Brazil," op. cit., p. 332.
69. Charles Wagley, ed., *Race and Class in Rural Brazil*, pp. 144–145.
70. Ibid., p. 145.
71. Ibid., p. 69.
72. Carl N. Degler, *Neither Black Nor White*, pp. 282, 285.
73. Ibid., p. 280.
74. Charles Wagley, *An Introduction to Brazil*, pp. 123–124. See also Florestan Fernandes, *The Negro in Brazilian Society*, (New York: Columbia University Press, 1969), pp. 239–243.
75. Donald Pierson, op. cit., p. lxvi.
76. Ibid., p. 176.
77. The term "West Indies" has various definitions. It is used here to refer to Jamaica, Barbados, Trinidad and other islands historically part of the British West Indies. The term is defined more broadly by some other writers—for example, David Lowenthal, *West Indian Societies*, pp. 2–4, 78–79; Ira Reid, *The Negro Immigrant* (New York: AMS Press, 1970), pp. 45–66, passim.
78. Frank Wesley Pitman, "Slavery on British West India Plantations in the Eighteenth Century," *Journal of Negro History*, October 1926, pp. 630, 637; David Lowenthal, *West Indian Societies*, p. 42. See also

Gwendolyn Midlo Hall, *Social Control in Slave Plantation Societies*, pp. 13–20, 24–25.

79. Philip D. Curtin, *The Atlantic Slave Trade*, pp. 52–53.

80. Ulrich B. Phillips, *American Negro Slavery* (Baton Rouge: Louisiana State University Press, 1969), p. 52; David Lowenthal, *West Indian Societies*, pp. 41–43.

81. Frank Wesley Pitman, "Slavery on British West India Plantations in the Eighteenth Century," op. cit., pp. 595, 632; Ulrich B. Phillips, *American Negro Slavery*, pp. 53–54; Gwendolyn Midlo Hall, *Social Control in Slave Plantation Societies*, p. 13.

82. Frank Wesley Pitman, "Slavery on British West India Plantations in the Eighteenth Century," op. cit., p. 608. See also Claude Levy, "Slavery and the Emancipation Movement in Barbados, 1650–1833," *Journal of Negro History*, January 1970, p. 6.

83. Jerome S. Handler, *The Unappropriated People*, p. 128.

84. Thomas Sowell, *Ethnic America* (New York: Basic Books, Inc., 1981), p. 187.

85. Kenneth M. Stampp, *The Peculiar Institution* (New York: Vintage Books, 1956), p. 354.

86. Eugene D. Genovese, *Roll, Jordan, Roll* (New York: Pantheon Books, 1974), p. 421; Charles H. Wesley, "The Negro in the West Indies, Slavery and Freedom," *Journal of Negro History*, January 1932, pp. 56–57; Douglas Hall, "Jamaica," *Neither Slave Nor Free*, eds. David W. Cohen & Jack P. Greene (The Johns Hopkins University Press, 1972), pp. 208–209; Philip D. Curtin, *Two Jamaicas* (Atheneum, 1970), pp. 14, 15.

87. Philip D. Curtin, *Two Jamaicas*, p. 18; Douglas Hall, "Jamaica," op. cit., pp. 208–209; Eric Williams, *The Negro in the Caribbean* (Negro Universities Press, 1971), p. 57; Frank Wesley Pitman, "The Emancipation of the Free Colored Population in the British Empire," *Journal of Negro History*, April 1934, pp. 138–139.

88. Frank Wesley Pitman, "Slavery on British West Indian Plantations in the Eighteenth Century," *Journal of Negro History*, October 1926, p. 635; Jerome S. Handler, *The Unappropriated People*, pp. 137, 149–150. A similar pattern existed in Latin slave societies. See Gwendolyn Midlo Hall, *Social Control in Slave Plantation Societies*, pp. 90–92.

89. Ibid., p. 636.

90. Philip D. Curtin, *Two Jamaicas*, pp. 45–46; David Lowenthal, *West Indian Societies*, pp. 72n, 308.

91. Douglas Hall, "Jamaica," op. cit., pp. 195–196; David Lowenthal, *West Indian Societies*, p. 95.

92. Douglas Hall, "Jamaica," op. cit., p. 202; Jerome S. Handler & Arnold A. Sio, "Barbados," op. cit., p. 241; David Lowenthal, *West Indian Societies*, pp. 46–47; Jerome S. Handler, *The Unappropriated People*, pp. 117–138.

93. Jerome S. Handler & Arnold A. Sio, "Barbados," op. cit., p. 245;

Jerome S. Handler, *The Unappropriated People,* pp. 146–153; David Lowenthal, *West Indian Societies,* p. 46.

94. Jerome S. Handler and Arnold A. Sio, "Barbados, ' op. cit., p. 250.
95. Ibid., p. 256; pp. 305–308.
96. Douglas Hall, "Jamaica," op. cit., p. 194. See also David Lowenthal, *West Indian Societies,* pp. 305–306.
97. Douglas Hall, "Jamaica," op. cit., p. 194.
98. Ibid.
99. Jerome S. Handler & Arnold A. Sio, "Barbados," op. cit., p. 220.
100. Ibid., p. 221.
101. Ibid., p. 229.
102. Philip P. Curtin, *Two Jamaicas.* pp. 107–109, 127.
103. Virginia R. Dominguez, *From Neighbor to Stranger: The Dilemma of Caribbean Peoples in the United States* (Antilles Research Program, Yale University, 1975), p. 70.
104. Ira Reid, *The Negro Immigrant* (A.M.S. Press, 1970), pp. 239–240; U.S. Bureau of the Census, *Historical Statistics of the United States, From Colonial Times to 1970* (Government Printing Office, 1975).
105. Ira Reid, *The Negro Immigrant,* p. 81.
106. Virginia R. Dominguez, *From Neighbor to Stranger: The Dilemma of Caribbean Peoples in the United States,* op. cit., p. 72.
107. Reed Ueda, "West Indians," *Harvard Encyclopedia of American Ethnic Groups,* ed. Stephan Thernstrom, et al. (Belknap Press, 1980), p. 1022.
108. Ira Reid, *The Negro Immigrant,* pp. 226–227.
109. Thomas Sowell, "Three Black Histories," *Essays and Data on American Ethnic Groups,* ed. Thomas Sowell (The Urban Institute, 1978), pp. 42, 44.
110. Reed Ueda, 'West Indians," op. cit., p. 1026.
111. Nancy Foner, "West Indians in New York City and London: A Comparative Analysis," *International Migration Review,* Summer 1979, p. 285
112. David Lowenthal, *West Indian Societies,* p. 321.
113. Ibid., pp. 284–297.
114. Jaime Santiago, "One Step Forward," *Wilson Quarterly,* Spring 1980, p. 138.
115. L. H. Gann and Peter Duignan, *South Africa* (Hoover Institution Press, 1978), p. 10; See also George M. Frederickson, *White Supremacy* (Oxford University Press, 1981), p. 3; W. H. Hutt, *The Economics of the Colour Bar* (The Institute of Economic Affairs, 1964), p. 14; Pierre L. van den Berghe, *South Africa* (University of California Press, 1965), pp. 13, 87.
116. George M. Frederickson, *White Supremacy,* p. 64.
117. Ibid., pp. 64–65.
118. Ibid., p. 58
119. Ibid., p. 65
120. Ibid., p. 126.

121. Ibid., pp. 96–97, 108–112, 117, 128.
122. Ibid., pp. 87–88.
123. Ibid., pp. 96–97.
124. Ibid., p. 116n.
125. Ibid., p. 36.
126. Ibid., p. 48.
127. Ibid., p. 129.
128. Ibid., pp. 82–83.
129. Ibid., pp. 138–139.
130. Ibid., p. 167n.
131. Pierre L. van den Berghe, *South Africa*, p. 30.
132. W. H. Hutt, *The Economics of the Colour Bar*, pp. 18–19.
133. George M. Frederickson, *White Supremacy*, p. 231.
134. W. H. Hutt, *The Economics of the Colour Bar*, p. 35.
135. George M. Frederickson, *White Supremacy*, p. 67; See also W. H. Hutt, *The Economics of the Colour Bar*, p. 35; Pierre L. van den Berghe, *South Africa*, p. 14.
136. George M. Frederickson, *White Supremacy*, p. 206.
137. Ibid., p. 267n.
138. Pierre L. van den Berghe, *South Africa*, p. 19.
139. W. H. Hutt, *The Economics of the Colour Bar*, p. 61.
140. George M. Frederickson, *White Supremacy*, pp. 228–229.
141. Pierre L. van den Berghe, *South Africa*, p. 196.
142. W. H. Hutt, *The Economics of the Colour Bar*, p. 62.
143. Ibid., p. 63.
144. George M. Frederickson, *White Supremacy*, pp. 231–232.
145. W. H. Hutt, *The Economics of the Colour Bar*, pp. 68–69.
146. George M. Frederickson, *White Supremacy*, pp. 232–233.
147. Ibid., p. 233.
148. T.R.H. Davenport, *South Africa*, 2nd edition (University of Toronto Press, 1977), p. 209.
149. W. H. Hutt, *The Economics of the Colour Bar*, pp. 60, 62, 68, 69, 174; Pierre L. van den Berghe, *South Africa*, p. 205; L. H. Gann and Peter Duignan, *South Africa*, p. 41.
150. W. H. Hutt, *The Economics of the Colour Bar*, p. 80.
151. Pierre L. van den Berghe, *South Africa*, p. 192; W. H. Hutt, *The Economics of the Colour Bar*, p. 49.
152. George M. Frederickson, *White Supremacy*, pp. 181–182.
153. W. H. Hutt, *The Economics of the Colour Bar*, pp. 36, 56, 77, 82, 84, 108–109, 129.
154. W. H. Hutt, *The Economics of the Colour Bar*, pp. 72, 75, 79.
155. George M. Frederickson, *White Supremacy*, p. 229.
156. Ibid., p. 276.
157. W. H. Hutt, *The Economics of the Colour Bar*, p. 98; Pierre L. van den Berghe, *South Africa*, p. 71.
158. Pierre L. van den Berghe, *South Africa*, p. 186.
159. W. H. Hutt, *The Economics of the Colour Bar*, pp. 21–22, 158, 159.

160. George M. Frederickson, *White Supremacy*, p. xii; see also pp. 228–229.
161. Ibid., p. 240.
162. Pierre L. van den Berghe, *South Africa*, p. 138.
163. George M. Frederickson, *White Supremacy*, p. 279.
164. W. H. Hutt, *The Economics of the Colour Bar*, p. 42.
165. Ibid., p. 113.
166. Pierre L. van den Berghe, *South Africa*, p. 138.
167. W. H. Hutt, *The Economics of the Colour Bar*, pp. 29, 127; see also Pierre L. van den Berghe, op. cit., p. 46.
168. Pierre L. van den Berghe, *South Africa*, p. 288.
169. Ibid., p. 289; W. H. Hutt, *The Economics of the Colour Bar*, p. 181.
170. Pierre L. van den Berghe, *South Africa*, p. 195.
171. Ibid., p. 91.
172. Study Commission on U.S. Policy Toward South Africa, *South Africa: Time Running Out* (Berkeley: University of California Press, 1981), p. 43.
173. George M. Frederickson, *White Supremacy*, p. 119; See also Pierre L. van den Berghe, *South Africa*, p. 56.
174. George M. Frederickson, *White Supremacy*, p. 310.
175. Pierre L. van den Berghe, *South Africa*, p. 56.
176. Ibid., p. 60.
177. Ibid., p. 61.
178. Cynthia Enloe, *Police, Military and Ethnicity* (Transaction Books, 1980), p. 56; L. H. Gann and Peter Duignan, *South Africa*, p. 34.
179. Cynthia Enloe, *Police, Military and Ethnicity*, p. 51.
180. Ibid., p. 56.
181. Pierre L. van den Berghe, *South Africa*, pp. 60–61.
182. Joseph Lloyd, "Anxiety Over Apartheid," *New York Times Magazine*, April 19, 1981, p. 22.
183. W. H. Hutt, *The Economics of the Colour Bar*, p. 182; Pierre L. van den Berghe, *South Africa*, pp. 303, 304.
184. W. H. Hutt, *The Economics of the Colour Bar*, p. 81.
185. Pierre L. van den Berghe, *South Africa*, p. 57.
186. Ibid., p. 187.
187. Ibid., pp. 90, 91.
188. Ibid., p. 184.
189. W. H. Hutt, *The Economics of the Colour Bar*, p. 81; Pierre L. van den Berghe, *South Africa*, p. 303.
190. L. H. Gann and Peter Duignan, *South Africa*, p. 9.
191. Ibid., p. 42.
192. "Education for Blacks," *South African Digest*, August 1, 1980, Supplement between pp. 14 and 15.
193. *South African Digest*, October 3, 1980, p. 1.
194. Pierre L. van den Berghe, *South Africa*, p. 46.
195. Ibid., p. 67.
196. Ibid., p. 71.

197. Study Commission on U.S. Policy Toward Southern Africa, *South Africa: Time Running Out*, p. 42.
198. George M. Frederickson, *White Supremacy*, p. 255.
199. Ibid., p. 38.
200. Pierre L. van den Berghe, *South Africa*, p. 40.
201. Ibid.
202. George M. Frederickson, *White Supremacy*, p. 272; Pierre L. van den Berghe, *South Africa*, p. 151.
203. Ibid., pp. 132–133.
204. Ibid., p. 265.
205. Ibid., p. 279.
206. W. H. Hutt, *The Economics of the Colour Bar*, p. 81; see also Pierre L. van den Berghe, *South Africa*, p. 184.
207. Pierre L. van den Berghe, *South Africa*, p. 307.
208. George M. Frederickson, *White Supremacy*, p. 255.
209. Pierre L. van den Berghe, *South Africa*, pp. 64–65, 229.
210. Thomas Sowell, *Ethnic America*, pp. 196, 205–206; Stephen Birmingham, *Certain People*, pp. 70, 71, 130–131, 160; Gunnar Myrdal, *An American Dilemma*, pp. 695–705.
211. E. Franklin Frazier, *Black Bourgeoisie*, Chapters VIII, IX, X; Stephen Birmingham, *Certain People* (Little, Brown and Co., 1977), Chapters 1, 11, 14, 17.
212. Pierre L. van den Berghe, *South Africa*, pp. 65, 160, 178, 229.
213. Ibid., p. 160; W. H. Hutt, *The Economics of the Colour Bar*, p. 28.
214. Pierre L. van den Berghe, *South Africa*, p. 234.
215. Ibid., pp. 168–169.
216. Ibid., p. 169; W. H. Hutt, *The Economics of the Colour Bar*, pp. 122–123.
217. Alvin Rabushka and Kenneth A. Shepsle, *Politics in Plural Societies: A Theory of Democratic Instability* (Charles E. Merrill Publishing Co., 1972), p. 167; Pierre L. van den Berghe, *South Africa*, p. 167.
218. Pierre L. van den Berghe, *South Africa*, pp. 103–104.
219. Alvin Rabushka and Kenneth A. Shepsle, *Politics in Plural Societies: A Theory of Democratic Instability*, pp. 164–165.
220. L. H. Gann and Peter Duignan, *South Africa*, p. 11.
221. Ibid., p. 9.
222. Ibid., p. 25.
223. Joseph Lloyd, "Anxiety Over Apartheid," *New York Times Magazine*, April 19, 1981, p. 18ff.
224. George M. Frederickson, *White Supremacy*, pp. 76–79.
225. Thomas C. Holt, "Afro-Americans," *Harvard Encyclopedia of American Ethnic Groups*, Stephan Thernstrom, et al. (Belknap Press, 1980), p. 7.
226. Ibid., p. 6.
227. Ibid.
228. Ibid.

229. U.S. Bureau of the Census, *Current Population Reports,* Series P-23, No. 80 (Government Printing Office), p. 9.
230. Thomas C. Holt, "Afro-Americans," p. 6.
231. Robert W. Fogel and Stanley L. Engerman, *Time on the Cross* (Boston: Little, Brown and Co., 1974), pp. 23–24.
232. Ibid., pp. 21–22.
233. Ibid., pp. 23–24.
234. Thomas C. Holt, "Afro-Americans," p. 6.
235. U.S. Bureau of the Census, *Current Population Reports,* Series P-23, No. 80, p. 11.
236. Ibid., p. 11.
237. Ulrich B. Phillips, *The Slave Economy of the Old South* (Baton Rouge: Louisiana State University Press, 1968), pp. 4–5; Thomas Sowell, *Markets and Minorities* (Basil Blackwell, 1981), p. 90.
238. U.S. Bureau of the Census, "The Social and Economic Status of the Black Population of the United States: An Historical View, 1790–1978," op. cit., p. 11.
239. Ira Berlin, "Time, Space and the Evolution of Afro-American Society on British Mainland North America," *American Historical Review,* February 1980, p. 49.
240. Ibid., p. 49.
241. Robert W. Fogel and Stanley L. Engerman, *Time on the Cross,* pp. 29–30.
242. Kenneth M. Stampp, *The Peculiar Institution,* pp. 19–20.
243. U.S. Bureau of the Census, *Current Population Reports,* Series P-23, No. 80, p. 12.
244. George M. Frederickson, *White Supremacy,* p. 105.
245. Ibid., pp. 108–124.
246. Ira Berlin, "Time, Space and the Evolution of Afro-American Society on British Mainland North America," op. cit., p. 69.
247. Ibid.
248. George M. Frederickson, *White Supremacy,* pp. 102–103.
249. Ibid., pp. 101–108.
250. Ibid., pp. 102–103, 127.
251. Ibid., p. 105.
252. U.S. Bureau of the Census, *Current Population Reports,* Series P-23, No. 80, p. 13.
253. Carl Kelsey, "The Evolution of Negro Labor," *The Annals of the American Academy,* Vol. XXI (January 1903–June 1903), pp. 68–73; Frederick Law Olmsted, *The Cotton Kingdom* (Modern Library, 1969), pp. 28, 32, 42, 100, 101, 102–103, 104–105, 143–146, 254, 402–403, 564, 565; Eugene D. Genovese, *Roll, Jordan, Roll,* pp. 295–309.
254. Thomas Sowell, *Ethnic America,* p. 197.
255. U.S. Bureau of the Census, *Historical Statistics of the United States, From Colonial Times to 1970* (Government Printing Office, 1975), p. 297.

256. Alexis de Tocqueville, *Democracy in America* (Alfred Knopf, 1945), p. 361.
257. Ibid., p. 363.
258. Ibid., p. 362.
259. Frederick Law Olmsted, *The Cotton Kingdom*, p. 305.
260. Ibid., pp. 29, 38, 43, 44, 126, 152, 158, 168, 177, 186, 212, 214, 220, 232, 258–259, 294, 307, 317–318, 330, 374, 423, 425, 427.
261. Ulrich B. Phillips, *The Slave Economy of the Old South* (Louisiana State University, 1968), p. 273.
262. W. J. Cash, *The Mind of the South* (Vintage Press, 1967), p. viii.
263. Ibid., p. 274.
264. U.S. Bureau of the Census, "The Social and Economic Status of the Black Population of the United States: An Historical View, 1790–1978," op. cit., p. 13.
265. Robert W. Fogel and Stanley L. Engerman, *Time on the Cross*, Chapter 4.
266. Herbert G. Gutman, *The Black Family in Slavery and Freedom, 1750–1925* (New York: Vintage Books, 1977), p. 147.
267. Leon F. Litwack, *Been in the Storm So Long* (Alfred A. Knopf, 1979), p. 232.
268. Herbert G. Gutman, op. cit., p. 12.
269. Ibid., pp. 32, 45.
270. U.S. Bureau of the Census, "The Social and Economic Status of the Black Population of the United States: An Historical View, 1790–1978," op. cit., p. 11.
271. U.S. Bureau of the Census, *Current Population Reports*, Series P-23, No. 80 (Government Printing Office, no date), p. 11.
272. Bureau of the Census, *Negro Population, 1790–1915* (Washington: Government Printing Office, 1918), p. 57.
273. Robert W. Fogel and Stanley L. Engerman, *Time on the Cross*, pp. 38, 64; Wilbur Zelinsky, "The Population Geography of the Free Negro in Ante-Bellum America," *Population Studies*, March 1950, p. 387.
274. Thomas Sowell, *Race and Economics* (David McKay Co., 1975), p. 37.
275. Thomas Sowell, "Three Black Histories," pp. 10–11, 16–17, 21.
276. Horace Mann Bond, "The Negro Scholar and Professional in America," *The American Negro Reference Book*, ed., John P. Davis (Prentice-Hall, 1970), p. 551.
277. Thomas Sowell, "Three Black Histories," op. cit., pp. 15–17.
278. Ibid., p. 21.
279. E. Franklin Frazier, *The Negro in the United States* (The MacMillan Co., 1971), p. 70.
280. Ira Berlin, *Slaves Without Masters*, p. 244.
281. Ibid., pp. 244–245.
282. See Ira Berlin, *Slaves Without Masters*, Chapter 4.

283. James E. Winston, "The Free Negro in New Orleans, 1803–1860," *Louisiana Historical Quarterly,* October 1938, p. 1080.

284. Ira Berlin, *Slaves Without Masters,* p. 245.

285. E. Franklin Frazier, *The Negro in the United States,* pp. 73–74.

286. Carter G. Woodson, *The Education of the Negro Prior to 1961* (Arno Press, 1968), Chapter IX.

287. E. Horace Fitchett, "The Origin and Growth of the Free Negro Population of Charleston, South Carolina," *Journal of Negro History,* October 1941, p. 423.

288. David C. Rankin, "The Impact of the Civil War on the Free Colored Community of New Orleans," *Perspectives in American History,* Vol. XI (1977–1978), p. 381.

289. Computed from *The Seventh Census of the United States: 1850* (Robert Armstrong, Public Printer, 1853), pp. xliii, lxi.

290. U.S. Bureau of the Census, *Historical Statistics of the United States, Colonial Times to 1970,* p. 382.

291. Wilbur Zelinsky, "The Population Geography of the Free Negro in Ante-Bellum America," p. 387; U.S. Bureau of the Census, *Historical Statistics of the United States, Colonial Times to 1970,* p. 14.

292. Ira Berlin, *Slaves Without Masters,* p. 385.

293. Ibid., p. 386n.

294. Ibid., p. 396.

295. E. Franklin Frazier, "Race Contacts and the Social Structure," *E. Franklin Frazier on Race Relations,* ed. G. Franklin Edwards (Chicago: University of Chicago Press, 1968), p. 54.

296. Thomas Sowell, "Three Black Histories," op. cit., p. 12.

297. Thomas Sowell, "Patterns of Black Excellence," *The Public Interest,* Spring 1976, p. 29.

298. Thomas Sowell, "Three Black Histories," pp. 11–13, 19, 22.

299. Benjamin Brawley, *A Social History of the American Negro* (Collier Books, 1970), p. 269.

300. U.S. Bureau of the Census, *Historical Statistics of the United States, Colonial Times to 1970,* p. 422.

301. Gilbert Osofsky, *Harlem: The Making of a Ghetto* (New York: Harper and Row, 1966), p. 12; St. Clair Drake and Horace B. Cayton, *Black Metropolis,* Vol. I (New York: Harcourt, Brace and World, 1970), p. 176n; Allen H. Spear, *Black Chicago* (Chicago: University of Chicago Press, 1967), Chapter 1; David M. Katzman, *Before the Ghetto* (Urbana: University of Illinois Press, 1975), p. 73; W.E.B. DuBois, *The Philadelphia Negro* (New York: Schocken Books, 1967), p. 7; Kenneth L. Kusmer, *A Ghetto Takes Shape* (Urbana: University of Illinois Press, 1978), pp. 12–13, 42.

302. David M. Katzman, *Before the Ghetto,* p. 138.

303. W.E.B. DuBois, *The Philadelphia Negro,* pp. 33, 34–35.

304. Thomas Sowell, "Three Black Histories," op. cit., p. 35.

305. Thomas Sowell, *Markets and Minorities,* p. 86; Kenneth L. Kusmer, *A Ghetto Takes Shape,* p. 64.

306. Thomas Sowell, "Three Black Histories," op. cit., p. 36.
307 Karl E. Taeuber, "The Negro Population in the United States," *The American Negro Reference Book*, ed. John P. David (Prentice-Hall, 1970), p. 110.
308. Kenneth L. Kusmer, *A Ghetto Takes Shape*, p. 157.
309 Thomas Sowell, *Ethnic America*, p. 39.
310. Florette Henri, *Black Migration: Movement North, 1900–1920* (New York: Anchor Books, 1976), pp. 17, 86.
311. St. Clair Drake and Horace B. Cayton, *Black Metropolis*, Vol. I, p. 64; Benjamin Brawley, *Social History of the American Negro*, pp. 347–349.
312. Stephen Birmingham, *Certain People*, p. 186. See also Jeffrey S. Gorock, *When Harlem Was Jewish, 1870–1930* (New York: Columbia University Press, 1979).
313. Kenneth L. Kusmer, *A Ghetto Takes Shape*, p. 161.
314. Ibid., p. 162.
315. Ibid., p. 16.
316. Thomas Sowell, *Markets and Minorities*, pp. 66–73, passim; Florette Henri, *Black Migration: Movement North, 1900–1920* pp. 188–189.
317. Florette Henri, *Black Migration: Movement North, 1900–1920*, p. 71.
318. Thomas Sowell, "Three Black Histories," op. cit., pp. 32–34.
319. Emma Lou Thornbrough, "Introduction," *Booker T. Washington* (Prentice-Hall, Inc., 1969), p. 22. See also Louis R. Harlan, *Booker T. Washington* (Oxford University Press, 1972), pp. 81–85, 100, 102, 119, 122, 198–201.
320. Elliot M. Rudwick, *W.E.B. DuBois* (New York: Atheneum, 1969), p. 132. See also pp. 118–119.
321. Booker T. Washington, et. al., *Three Negro Classics* (New York: Avon Books, 1969), p. 149.
322. Ibid., p. 141.
323. Thomas Sowell, "Three Black Histories," op. cit., pp. 32–33; Elliot M. Rudwick, *W.E.B. DuBois*, p. 82.
324. Stephen Birmingham, *Certain People*, p. 144.
325. U.S. Bureau of the Census, *Historical Statistics of the United States, Colonial Times to 1970*, p. 382.
326. Thomas Sowell, *Ethnic America*, p. 212.
327. Daniel O. Price, *Changing Characteristics of the Negro Population* (Washington: U.S. Government Printing Office, 1969), p. 45.
328. Philip M. Hauser, "Demographic Factors in the Integration of the Negro," *Daedalus*, Fall 1965, p. 859.
329. U.S. Bureau of the Census, *Historical Statistics of the United States, Colonial Times to 1970*, p. 45.
330. Thomas Sowell, "Three Black Histories," op. cit., p. 39.
331. Ben J. Wattenberg, *The Real America* (New York: Doubleday, 1974), p. 117.

332. Thomas Sowell, ed., *Essays and Data on American Ethnic Groups*, pp. 257–258; U.S. Bureau of the Census, *Current Population Reports*, Series P-20, No. 224 (Government Printing Office, 1971), p. 14.

CHAPTER 5

1. Carrol C. Calkins, ed. *The Story of America* (The Reader's Digest Association, 1975), p. 238.
2. Virginia Brainard Kunz, *The Germans in America* (Minneapolis: Lerner Publications Co., 1966), p. 11; Daniel Boorstin, *The Americans*, Vol. I (New York: Random House, 1958), p. 225.
3. Emilio Willems, "Brazil," *The Positive Contribution of Immigrants* (Paris: United Nations Educational, Scientific and Cultural Organization, 1955), pp. 124, 125, 127, 129.
4. Pierre L. van den Berghe, *South Africa* (University of California Press, 1965), p. 10.
5. U.S. Bureau of the Census, *Current Population Reports*, Series P-20, No. 213 (Government Printing Office, 1971), p. 35; Leo A. Grebler, et. al., *The Mexican American People* (New York: The Free Press, 1970), pp. 423–428.
6. Yuan-li Wu and Chun-hsi Wu, *Economic Development in Southeast Asia* (Hoover Institution Press, 1980), pp. 55–57.
7. National Research Council, *Science, Engineering, and Humanities Doctorates in the United States* (National Academy of Sciences, 1980), p. 39.
8. Ibid., p. 13.
9. Carey McWilliams, "The Borderlands are Invaded," *The Mexican Americans: An Awakening Minority*, ed. Manual P. Servin (Glencoe Press, 1970), p. 157.
10. National Research Council, *Science, Engineering, and Humanities Doctorates in the United States* (National Academy of Sciences, 1980), p. 39.
11. Ibid., p. 13.
12. National Research Council, *Summary Report: 1980 Doctorates from United States Universities* (National Academy Press, 1981), pp. 26, 29.
13. William H. Whyte, Jr., *The Organization Man* (New York: Simon & Schuster, 1956), pp. 83–84.
14. National Research Council, *Summary Report: 1980 Doctorate Recipients From United States Universities*, pp. 26, 29.
15. See, for example, loc. cit.; Yuan-li Wu and Chun-hsi Wu, *Economic Development in Southeast Asia*, pp. 54, 57; Thomas Sowell, *Affirmative Action Reconsidered* (American Enterprise Institute, 1975), pp. 18–20; Jessie Bernard, *Academic Women* (Pennsylvania State University Press, 1964), p. 126.
16. College Entrance Examination Board, *Profiles, College-Bound Seniors, 1981* (College Entrance Examination Board, 1982), passim. See

also Lucy W. Sells, "Leverage for Equal Opportunity Through Mastery of Mathematics," *Women and Minorities in Science,* edited by Sheila M. Humphreys (Westview Press, 1982), pp. 11, 12, 14, 16, 20, 21.

17. "Race, Class, and Scores," *New York Times,* October 24, 1982, Section 4, p. 9. College Entrance Examination Board, *Profiles, College-Bound Seniors,* 1981 (College Entrance Examination Board, 1982), pp. 27, 36, 45, 55.

18. College Entrance Examination Board, *Profiles, College-Bound Seniors,* pp. 60, 79.

19. Pierre L. van den Berghe, *Race and Racism* (New York: John Wiley & Sons, 1978), p. 67. See also Carl N. Degler, *Neither Black Nor White* (Macmillan Publishing Co., Inc., 1971), p. 245.

20. George M. Frederickson, *White Supremacy* (Oxford University Press, 1981), p. 69; see also Pierre L. van den Berghe, *Race and Racism* (University of California Press, 1965), p. 98.

21. Frederick Law Olmsted, *The Cotton Kingdom* (Modern Library, 1969), p. 19.

22. Edward C. Banfield, *The Unheavenly City* (Little, Brown and Co., 1970), pp. 105, 110, 112; Carl Kelsey, "The Evolution of Negro Labor," *The Annals of the American Academy of Political and Social Science,* Vol. XXI (January–June, 1903), pp. 68, 69–70, 71–72; W.E.B. DuBois, *The Philadelphia Negro* (Schocken Books, 1967), pp. 111, 316, 395; Booker T. Washington, *The Future of the American Negro* (Boston: Small, Maynard & Company, 1900), pp. 88–90.

23. Florestan Fernandes, *The Negro in Brazilian Society* (New York: Columbia University, 1969), pp. 35–36; Carl Kelsey, op. cit., pp. 67, 68, 71–72.

24. E. Franklin Frazier, *Black Bourgeoisie* (The Free Press, 1962), Ch. IX, pp. 12–13, 35, 36, 38.

25. Florestan Fernandes, *The Negro in Brazilian Society,* p. 13.

26. Ira Reid, *The Negro Immigrant* (A.M.S. Press, 1970), p. 229.

27. Florestan Fernandes, *The Negro in Brazilian Society,* p. 40; W.E.B. DuBois, *The Philadelphia Negro* (New York: Schocken Books, 1967), pp. 192–193, 321–322.

28. Florestan Fernandes, *The Negro in Brazilian Society,* pp. 37, 38.

29. Stephen Birmingham, *Certain People* (Little, Brown and Co., 1977), pp. 5, 56, 58, 177.

30. Thomas Sowell, "Three Black Histories," *Essays and Data on American Ethnic Groups,* ed. Thomas Sowell (The Urban Institute, 1978), pp. 12–13; Audrey M. Schvey, *The Testing of Negro Intelligence,* 2nd edition (New York: Social Science Press, 1966), pp. 489–490.

31. Pierre L. van den Berghe, *Race and Racism,* p. 94.

32. Pierre L. van den Berghe, *South Africa,* p. 155.

33. George M. Frederickson, *White Supremacy* (Oxford University Press, 1981), pp. 76–85.

34. Carl N. Degler, *Neither Black Nor White,* p. 86.

35. William L. Westermann, *The Slave Systems of Greek and Roman Antiquity* (Philadelphia: The American Philosophical Society, 1955).

36. Arthur R. Jensen, "Selection of Minority Students in Higher Education," *University of Toledo Law Review*, Spring–Summer 1970, p. 436; Arthur R. Jensen, *Straight Talk About Mental Tests* (New York: The Free Press, 1981), pp. 258–259.

37. Arthur R. Jensen, "How Much Can We Boost I.Q. and Scholastic Achievement," *Harvard Educational Review*, Winter 1969, pp. 115–117.

38. Sandra Scarr and Richard A. Weinberg, "I.Q. Test Performance of Black Children Adopted by White Families," *American Psychologist*, October 1976, pp. 726–739. See also critique by Arthur R. Jensen, *Straight Talk About Mental Tests*, pp. 223–224.

39. Thomas Sowell, "Race and I.Q. Reconsidered," *Essays and Data on American Ethnic Groups* (Washington: The Urban Institute, 1978), pp. 207–208, 210–211.

40. Ibid., p. 210.

41. Technically, "overlap" refers to the proportion of one group whose scores exceed the median score of the other group. By this definition, two groups with *identical* distributions of scores would have only 50 percent "overlap."

42. Carl Brigham, *A Study of American Intelligence* (Princeton: Princeton University Press, 1923), p. 190.

43. Thomas Sowell, "Race and I.Q. Reconsidered," op. cit., pp. 209–210.

44. Richard Lynn, "I.Q. in Japan and the United States Shows a Growing Disparity," *Science*, May 20, 1982, p. 223.

45. Thomas Sowell, "Assumptions versus History in Ethnic Education," *Teachers College Record*, Fall 1981, pp. 42–45, 46.

46. John C. Leohlin, Gardner Lindzey and J. N. Spuhler, *Race Differences in Intelligence* (San Francisco: W. H. Freeman and Co., 1975), pp. 177–185.

47. Philip Taylor, *The Distant Magnet* (Harper & Row, 1971), p. 66.

48. Kathleen Neils Conzen, *Immigrant Milwaukee 1836–1860* (Harvard University Press, 1976), pp. 40–41.

49. Yasuo Wakatsuki, "Japanese Emigration to the United States, 1866–1924," *Perspectives in American History*, Vol. XII (1979), p. 429.

50. Ibid., pp. 428, 429.

51. Ibid., p. 429.

52. Ibid., p. 428.

53. Jack Chen, *The Chinese of America* (San Francisco: Harper & Row, 1980), p. 18.

54. Victor Purcell, *The Chinese in Southeast Asia*, 2nd edition (Oxford University Press, 1980), p. 174.

55. Yuan-li Wu and Chun-hsi Wu, *Economic Development in Southeast Asia* (Hoover Institution Press, 1980), pp. 134–136.

56. Victor Purcell, *The Chinese in Southeast Asia*, 2nd edition, p. 176.

57. Yuan-li Wu and Chun-hsi Wu, *Economic Development in Southeast Asia* (Hoover Institution Press, 1980), p. 84.
58. Victor Purcell, *The Chinese in Southeast Asia*, p. 656.
59. Robert F. Foerster, *The Italian Emigration of Our Times* (Arno Press, 1969), p. 393; Joseph Lopreato, *Italian Americans* (Random House, 1970), pp. 41–42; Humbert S. Nelli, "Italians in Urban America," *The Italian Experience in the United States*, ed. S. M. Tomasi and M. H. Engel, p. 91; William Foote Whyte, *Street Corner Society* (University of Chicago Press, 1955), ch. xvii, p. 201; Nathan Glazer and Daniel Patrick Moynihan, *Beyond the Melting Pot* (M.I.T. Press, 1963), p. 186; Luciano J. Iorizzo and Salvatore Mondello, *The Italian Americans* (Twayne Publishers, Inc., 1971), pp. 88–89.
60. Philip Taylor, *The Distant Magnet*, Chapter 4.
61. Ibid., pp. 81–82.
62. Victor Purcell, *The Chinese in Southeast Asia*, 2nd edition, p. 26; Chitoshi Yanaga, *Japan Since Perry* (Hamden, Ct.: Archon Books, 1966), p. 428.
63. Philip Taylor, *The Distant Magnet*, p. 81.
64. Ibid., p. 85.
65. Ibid., pp. 85–86.
66. Ibid., p. 86.
67. Maldwyn Allen Jones, *American Immigration* (University of Chicago Press, 1960), p. 100.
68. Marcus Lee Hansen, *The Atlantic Migration* (Cambridge, Mass.: Harvard University Press, 1957), pp. 153–154.
69. Philip Taylor, *The Distant Magnet*, pp. 102, 104.
70. Ibid., p. 102.
71. Oliver MacDonagh, "The Irish Famine Emigration to the United States," *Perspectives in American History*, Vol. X (1976), pp. 394–395.
72. Philip Taylor, *The Distant Magnet*, pp. 86–88; Maldwyn Allen Jones, *American Immigration*, pp. 100, 134.
73. Maldwyn Allen Jones, *American Immigration*, p. 100.
74. Ibid., p. 134.
75. W.E.B. DuBois, *The Philadelphia Negro* (Schocken Books, 1967), p 178.
76. Philip Taylor, *The Distant Magnet*, p. 148.
77. Abbot Emerson Smith, *Colonists in Bondage* (Magnolia, Maine: Peter Smith, 1965), pp. 3–4.
78. Jack Chen, *The Chinese of America*, p. 25.
79. Maldwyn Allen Jones, *American Immigration*, p. 184.
80. Ibid., p. 179.
81. Ibid.
82. Oscar Handlin, *Race and Nationality in American Life*, Chapter V.
83. Philip Taylor, *The Distant Magnet*, p. 62.
84. Karl E. Taeuber and Alma F. Taeuber, "The Negro Population in the United States," *The American Negro Reference Book*, ed. John P. Davis (Prentice-Hall, Inc., February, 1970), pp. 112–113.

85. Oliver MacDonagh, "The Irish Famine Emigration to the United States," *Perspectives in American History*, Vol. X (1976), p. 403.
86. Stanley Feldstein and Lawrence Costello, *The Ordeal of Assimilation* (Anchor Books, 1974), p. 39.
87. Ibid., p. 41.
88. Ibid., pp. 46–48, passim.
89. Philip Taylor, *The Distant Magnet*, p. 62.
90. Ibid.
91. William Petersen, "Chinese Americans and Japanese Americans," *Essays and Data on American Ethnic Groups*, ed. Thomas Sowell, p. 72.
92. Karl E. Taeuber and Alma F. Taeuber, "The Negro Population in the United States," op. cit., p. 113.
93. L. H. Gann and Peter Duignan, *South Africa: War, Revolution, or Peace?* (Stanford: Hoover Institution Press, 1978), p. 7.
94. Charles S. Johnson, "How Much Is the Migration a Flight from Persecution?" *The Black Community in Modern America*, eds. A. Meier and E. Rudwick, Vol. II (New York: Atheneum, 1969), p. 182.
95. See, for example, Maldwyn Allen Jones, *American Immigration*, p. 12.
96. Philip Taylor, *The Distant Magnet*, p. 46.
97. Ibid., p. 65.
98. Maldwyn Allen Jones, *American Immigration*, p. 187.
99. Oscar Handlin, *The Newcomers* (Garden City: Anchor Books, 1962), pp. 56–57.
100. Lennox A. Mills, *Southeast Asia* (Minneapolis: University of Minnesota Press, 1964), p. 110.
101. Jack Chen, *The Chinese of America*, p. 15.
102. Robert F. Foerster, *The Italian Emigration of Our Times*, Chapter II.
103. Philip Taylor, *The Distant Magnet*, p. 90.
104. Joseph Lopreato, *Italian Americans*, pp. 158–159.
105. Robert F. Foerster, *The Italian Emigration of Our Times*, p. 297.
106. Solomon Grayzel, *A History of the Jews* (New York: New American Library, 1968), pp. 365–366.
107. Victor Purcell, *The Chinese in Southeast Asia*, 2nd edition, p. 120.
108. Ibid., pp. 104, 115, 116, 117, 122, 201.
109. Lennox A. Mills, *Southeast Asia*, p. 112.
110. U.S. Bureau of the Census, *Current Population Reports*, Series P-20, No. 213 (Government Printing Office, 1971), p. 10.
111. Thomas Sowell, *Ethnic America* (Basic Books, Inc., 1981), p. 265.
112. Joseph Lopreato, *Italian Americans*, p. 56.
113. Maldwyn Allen Jones, *American Immigration*, p. 297.
114. Barry Chiswick, "The Economic Progress of Immigrants: Some Apparently Universal Patterns," *Contemporary Economic Problems*, ed. William Fellner (American Enterprise Institute, 1979), pp. 368, 368n.
115. Ibid., pp. 373–374.
116. Ibid., pp. 390–391.

117. Ibid., p. 392.
118. Ibid., p. 397.
119. Victor Purcell, *The Chinese in Southeast Asia*, 2nd edition, p. 116.
120. Ibid., pp. 116–117.
121. Stephen H. Haliczer, "The Castilian Urban Patriciate and the Jewish Expulsions in 1492," *American Historical Review*, February 1973, pp. 49, 52, 57.
122. Ibid., pp. 41–42.
123. See Victor Purcell, *The Chinese in Southeast Asia*, 2nd edition, p. 498.
124. Quoted in Ibid., p. 538.
125. Ibid., p. 546.
126. Solomon Grayzel, *A History of the Jews*, p. 320.
127. Ibid., p. 606.
128. Joseph P. Fitzpatrick, *Puerto Rican Americans* (Englewood Cliffs: Prentice-Hall, Inc., 1971), p. 61.
129. Stephan Thernstrom, *The Other Bostonians* (Harvard University, 1973), p. 121.
130. Thomas Sowell, *Ethnic America*, p. 262.
131. Kenneth L. Kusmer, *A Ghetto Takes Shape* (University of Illinois Press, 1973), p. 234n.
132. Yuan-li Wu and Chun-hsi Wu, *Economic Development in Southeast Asia*, pp. 58, 59, 65, 71; Thomas Sowell, *"Weber* and *Bakke* and the Presuppositions of Affirmative Action," *Wayne Law Review*, July 1980, pp. 1309–1336.
133. Edward C. Banfield, *The Moral Basis of a Backward Society* (The Free Press, 1958), passim.
134. F. Ray Marshall, Allan M. Cartter, and Allan G. King, *Labor Economics* (Homewood: Richard D. Irwin, Inc., 1976), pp. 229–230.
135. P. T. Bauer, "Regulated Wages in Underdeveloped Countries," *The Public Stake in Union Power*, ed. Philip D. Bradley (Charlottesville: University of Virginia Press, 1959), p. 346.
136. L. H. Gann and Peter Duignan, *South Africa* (Hoover Institute Press, 1979), p. 7.
137. David Caplovitz, *The Poor Pay More* (The Free Press, 1967), passim.
138. See Thomas Sowell, *Race and Economics* (New York: David McKay Co., 1975), pp. 173–178; Walter E. Williams, "Why the Poor Pay More: An Alternative Explanation," *Social Science Quarterly*, September 1973, pp. 375–379.
139. Thomas Sowell, "Ethnicity in a Changing America," *Daedalus*, Winter 1978, pp. 213–237, passim.
140. Allan Nevins and Henry Steele Commager, *A Short History of the United States* (Modern Library, 1969), p. 195.
141. George M. Frederickson, *White Supremacy*, pp. 46, 50, 51.
142. Thomas Sowell, "Three Black Histories," *Essays and Data on American Ethnic Groups*, p. 21; Carter G. Woodson, *The Education of the Negro Prior to 1860* (New York: Arno Press, 1968), Chapter VII.

See also Leon F. Litwack, *North of Slavery* (Chicago: University of Chicago Press, 1961), passim.

143. John Hope Franklin, *From Slavery to Freedom* (Vintage Books, 1969).

144. Lennox A. Mills, *Southeast Asia*, p. 116; Victor Purcell, *The Chinese in Southeast Asia*, 2nd edition, chapter xiv, pp. 156–165, 216, 219, 220, 221, 311, 322, 346, 474, 475, 476, 478, 487–491, 559, 564.

145. Thomas Sowell, *Knowledge and Decisions* (New York: Basic Books, Inc., 1980), pp. 127–129.

146. Alec Nove, *The Soviet Economy* (New York: Frederick A. Praeger, 1961), p. 234.

147. Thomas Sowell, *Knowledge and Decisions*, pp. 127–129.

148. See Thomas Sowell, *Knowledge and Decisions*, pp. 41–42.

149. Robert F. Foerster, *The Italian Emigration of Our Times*, p. 262.

150. U.S. Bureau of the Census, *Historical Statistics of the United States: Colonial Times to 1957* (Government Printing Office, 1960), p. 218; Victor Purcell, *The Chinese in Southeast Asia*, 2nd edition, pp. 406, 514, 519, 527. Note also Ibid., pp. 91–92, 97, 101, 474, 475, 476, 478.

151. Nathan Glazer and Daniel Patrick Moynihan, *Beyond the Melting Pot*, p. 213.

152. Thomas Sowell, *Ethnic America*, p. 99.

153. Victor Purcell, *The Chinese in Southeast Asia*, 2nd edition, p. 94; Lennox A. Mills, *Southeast Asia*, p. 110; Betty Lee Sung, *The Story of the Chinese in America* (Collier Books, 1967), p. 278.

154. Thomas Sowell, *Ethnic America*, pp. 59, 64.

155. Lennox A. Mills, *Southeast Asia*, pp. 113–114; Victor Purcell, *The Chinese in Southeast Asia*, 2nd edition, p. 21.

156. Victor Purcell, *The Chinese in Southeast Asia*, second edition, p. 545n.

157. *Daedalus*, 1978, pp. 220–235.

158. Lennox A. Mills, *Southeast Asia*, p. 130.

159. Ivan H. Light and Charles Choy Wong, "Protest or Work: Dilemmas of the Tourist Industries in Chinatown," *American Journal of Sociology*, May 1975, p. 1355, 1360.

160. Victor Purcell, *The Chinese in Southeast Asia*, 2nd edition, p. 556; Lennox A. Mills, *Southeast Asia*, Chapter 5.

161. Robert Higgs, "Landless by Law: Japanese Immigrants in California Agriculture to 1941," *Journal of Economic History*, March 1978, p. 209.

162. Indeed, Milton Friedman has argued against altruism by businessmen. See Milton Friedman, *Capitalism and Freedom* (Chicago: University of Chicago Press, 1962), Chapter VIII.

163. Adam Smith, *The Wealth of Nations* (New York: Modern Library, 1937), pp. 128, 249–250, 402–403, 429, 438, 579.

164. Louis Wirth, *The Ghetto* (Chicago: University of Chicago Press, 1956), p. 229.

165. Robert Higgs, *Competition and Coercion* (Cambridge University Press, 1977), pp. 117, 146.

166. Ibid., p. 41.
167. Thomas Sowell, *Ethnic America,* pp. 200–201.
168. Robert Higgs, *Competition and Coercion,* pp. 47–48.
169. Ibid., pp. 45, 49–55.
170. Ibid., Chapter 3.
171. George M. Frederickson, *White Supremacy,* pp. 236, 237.
172. Ibid., Chapter VI, passim.
173. See, for example, Albert D. Kirwan, *Revolt of the Rednecks* (New York: Harper & Row, 1965).
174. Jack Chen, *The Chinese of America,* pp. 108–110, 145; Roger Daniels, *The Politics of Prejudice* (Berkeley: University of California Press, 1962), p. 30.
175. W. H. Hutt, *The Economics of the Colour Bar* (The Institute of Economic Affairs, 1964), pp. 60, 62–63.
176. Pierre L. van den Berghe, *South Africa,* p. 205.
177. W. H. Hutt, *The Economics of the Colour Bar,* p. 44.
178. J. C. Furnas, *The Americans* (G. P. Putnam's Sons, 1969), p. 382.
179. Robert F. Foerster, *The Italian Emigration of Our Times,* pp. 393–394.
180. Douglas Henry Daniels, *Pioneer Urbanites* (Philadelphia: Temple University Press, 1980), Chapter 10.
181. See, for example, John Stephens Durham, "The Labor Unions and the Negro," *The Atlantic Monthly,* February 1898, pp. 228–229.
182. W. H. Hutt, *The Economics of the Colour Bar,* p. 29.
183. See, for example, Gunnar Myrdal, *An American Dilemma,* pp. 593–594; Walter White, *A Man Called White* (Bloomington: Indiana University Press, 1948), p. 5.
184. W. H. Hutt, *The Economics of the Colour Bar,* p. 58.
185. Ibid., p. 59.
186. Ibid., Ch. 7.
187. Ibid., p. 63.
188. Douglas Henry Daniels, *Pioneer Urbanites,* p. 165.

CHAPTER 6

1. U.S. Bureau of the Census, *1970 Census of Population,* PC(1)-B1 (Washington: U.S. Government Printing Office, 1972), p. 1–262.
2 Richard A. Easterlin, "Immigration: Social Characteristics," *Harvard Encyclopedia of American Ethnic Groups,* ed. Stephan Thernstrom, et. al. (Belknap Press, 1980), p. 479.
3. David Ward, "Immigration: Settlement Patterns," *Harvard Encyclopedia of American Ethnic Groups,* ed. Stephan Thernstrom, et. al. (Belknap Press, 1980), pp. 502–503.
4. U.S. Bureau of the Census, *Current Population Reports* P-20, No. 249 (U.S. Government Printing Office, 1973), p. 19; *Reflections of America: Commemorating the Statistical Abstract Centennial* (Washington: U.S. Government Printing Office, 1980), p. 147.

5. U.S. Bureau of the Census, *Current Population Reports* P-23, No. 116 (U.S. Government Printing Office), p. 7.
6. Lack of knowledge is not a small factor. For example, while only seven percent of American Negroes report themselves as being of multiple ancestry, numerous historical, biological and other studies show that *most* American Negroes are of mixed ancestry, though usually far too far in the past for present day "blacks" to know specifically about it.
7. U.S. Bureau of the Census, *Current Population Reports,* Series P-23, No. 116, p. 7.
8. Carl Wittke, *We Who Built America* (The Press of Case Western Reserve University, 1967), chapters 6, 9, passim; Thomas Sowell, *Ethnic America* (New York: Basic Books, Inc., 1981), chapters 3, 4, 7, passim.
9. Nathan Glazer and Daniel Patrick Moynihan, *Beyond the Melting Pot* (M.I.T. Press, 1963), pp. 221–229.
10. Thomas Sowell, *Ethnic America,* p. 5.
11 Thomas Sowell, "Race and IQ Reconsidered," *Essays and Data on American Ethnic Groups* (Washington, D.C.: The Urban Institute, 1978), pp. 214, 217.
12. Thomas Sowell, ed., *Essays and Data on American Ethnic Groups,* (Washington, D.C.: The Urban Institute, 1978), pp. 257–258.
13. Ibid., pp. 283, 385.
14. Andrew M. Greeley, *That Most Distressful Nation* (Quadrangle Books, 1972), p. 132.
15. U.S. Bureau of the Census, *Current Population Reports,* Series P-20, No. 224 (Government Printing Office, 1971), p. 13.
16. 1977 data are from U.S. Bureau of the Census, *Statistical Abstract of the United States* (Washington: U.S. Bureau of the Census, 1980), p. 35; U.S. Bureau of the Census, *Current Population Reports,* Series P-20, No. 339, (Government Printing Office), cover; U.S. Bureau of the Census, *Social Indicators III* (Washington: U.S. Government Printing Office, 1980), p. 485. 1969 data are derived in various ways for different groups. The specific incomes are all listed in Thomas Sowell, ed. *Essays and Data on American Ethnic Groups* (Washington, D.C.: The Urban Institute, 1978), pp. 266, 284, 302, 320, 333, 337, 341, 350, 362, 374, 376, 386, 404. Income percentages for Japanese, Chinese, Filipino, West Indian, Puerto Rican, black, and American Indian families were based on 1969 incomes calculated from the 1970 Census Public Use Sample, using the U.S. national average as derived from the same source by the same definitions. Percentages for Jewish families were calculated from raw data supplied by the National Jewish Population Survey, tabulated using the same definitions as those of the groups listed above and of the U.S. national average. No 1969 income data were available for Polish, Italian, German, Irish or Mexican families, but 1968 and 1970 income data were available from the Census Bureau's *Current*

Population Reports (Series P-20, Nos. 213, 221, 224, and 249). Family income percentages for these five groups were calculated using the U.S. national average family income as reported in the same respective Census publications as the group incomes. An average of the 1968 and 1970 percentages was used as an estimate of the 1969 family income percentages for these five groups.

17. U.S. Bureau of the Census, *Current Population Reports,* Series P-20, No. 224 (Government Printing Office, 1971), p. 5; U.S. Bureau of the Census, *Current Population Reports,* Series P-23, No. 38 (Government Printing Office, 1971), p. 27.

18. Thomas Sowell, "Three Black Histories," *Essays and Data on American Ethnic Groups,* ed. Thomas Sowell (The Urban Institute, 1978), p. 44.

19. Jack Chen, *The Chinese of America* (San Francisco: Harper & Row, 1980), pp. 137, 140, 144; Roger Daniels, *Concentration Camps: U.S.A.* (New York: Holt, Rinehart and Winston, Inc., 1972), pp. 4, 9–21.

20. Thomas Sowell, ed., *Essays and Data on American Ethnic Groups,* pp. 257–258. See also Family Income Table above.

21. Ibid., pp. 386, 404.

22. Harold J. Laski, *The American Democracy* (New York: Viking Press, 1949), p. 479.

23. Everett C. Ladd, Jr. and Seymour Martin Lipset, *The Divided Academy* (New York: McGraw-Hill, 1975), pp. 170–171.

24. Harry H. L. Kitano, *Japanese Americans* (Englewood Cliffs: Prentice-Hall, Inc. 1969), p. 42.

25. Thomas Sowell, "Ethnicity in a Changing America," *Daedalus,* Winter 1978, pp. 213, 218–220.

26. Akemi Kihumura and Harry H.L. Kitano, "Interracial Marriage: A Picture of the Japanese Americans," *Journal of Social Issues,* Vol. 29, No. 2 (1973), pp. 69, 73.

27. David M. Heer, "Intermarriage," *Harvard Encyclopedia of American Ethnic Groups,* ed. Stephan Thernstrom, et. al. (Belknap Press, 1980), p. 519.

28. Akemi Kihumura and Harry H.L. Kitano, "Interracial Marriage: A Picture of the Japanese Americans," op. cit.

29. Gene N. Levine and Darrel M. Montero, "Socioeconomic Mobility among Three Generations of Japanese Americans," Ibid., pp. 44–45.

30. Betty Lee Sung, *The Story of the Chinese in America* (Collier Books, 1967), pp. 250, 251.

31. David M. Heer, "Intermarriage," op. cit., p. 518.

32. Nathan Glazer, *Affirmative Discrimination* (New York: Basic Books, 1975), p. 155.

33. Stanley Lieberson, *Ethnic Patterns in American Cities* (Glencoe: The Free Press, 1963), p. 127.

34. Oscar Handlin, *Boston's Immigrants* (Atheneum, 1970), p. 259.

35. U.S. Bureau of the Census, *Current Population Reports,* Series P-20, No. 221 (U.S. Government Printing Office, 1971), p. 7.

36. Thomas Sowell, ed., *Essays and Data on American Ethnic Groups,* p. 302.

37. Ibid., p. 386.

38. Ibid.

39. U.S. Bureau of the Census, *Current Population Reports,* Series P-20, No. 224 (Government Printing Office, 1971), p. 9.

40. Data for American Indians, Blacks, Chinese, and Japanese are from *U.S. Census of Population, 1970, Subject Reports,* PC(2) IF, IB, IG, respectively. Puerto Rican and Mexican data are from the Census Bureau's *Current Population Reports,* P-20, No. 213. Other data from "Entire Group" are from *Current Population Reports,* P-20, No. 221, the "Russian" ancestry data in the latter being used as a proxy for Jewish. Data for "Income Earners" and "Family Heads" are from 1970 U.S. Census Public Use Sample, and are published in Thomas Sowell, ed., *Essays and Data on American Ethnic Groups,* pp. 262, 269, 280, 287, 298, 305, 316, 323, 365, 382, 389, 400, 407.

41. 1970 U.S. Census, Public Use Sample.

42. Thomas Sowell, ed., *Essays and Data on American Ethnic Groups,* pp. 365, 368, 389, 392.

43. U.S. Bureau of the Census, *Current Population Reports,* Series P-23, No. 38, (Government Printing Office, 1971), p. 31; Series P-23, No. 42 (Government Printing Office, 1972), p. 35.

44. U.S. Bureau of the Census, *Current Population Reports,* Series P-23, No. 42, p. 35.

45. U.S. Bureau of the Census, *Current Population Reports,* Series P-23, No. 46, p. 22.

46. U.S. Bureau of the Census, *Historical Statistics of the United States, From Colonial Times to 1970* (Government Printing Office, 1974), p. 297.

47. Thomas Sowell, *Ethnic America,* p. 237.

48. Ibid., pp. 10–13.

49. U.S. Bureau of the Census, *1970 Census of Population: Subjects Reports* PC(2)-1F (Washington: U.S. Government Printing Office, 1973), pp. 3, 18, 19.

50. U.S. Bureau of the Census, *Current Population Reports,* Series P-23, No. 80, (Government Printing Office), p. 36.

51. Thomas Sowell, "Assumptions versus History in Ethnic Education," *Teachers College Record,* Fall 1981, pp. 42–45, 46; see also Diane Ravitch, *The Great School Wars* (New York: Basic Books, 1974), p. 178.

52. Moses Rischin, *The Promised City* (Cambridge, Mass.: Harvard University Press, 1967), p. 61.

53. Ira Reid, *The Negro Immigrant* (A.M.S. Press, 1970), pp. 138–140.

54. Andrew M. Greeley, *That Most Distressful Nation.*

55. Peter Uhlenberg, "Demographic Correlates of Group Achievement: Contrasting Patterns of Mexican-Americans and Japanese-

Americans," *Race, Creed, Color, or National Origin*, ed. Robert K. Yin (F. E. Peacok Publishers, 1973), p. 91.

56. Thomas Sowell, *Markets and Minorities* (New York: Basic Books, 1981), p. 10.

57. U.S. Bureau of the Census, *Current Population Reports*, Series P-20, No. 224 (Government Printing Office, 1971), p. 15.

58 William G. Bowen and T. Aldrich Finegan, *The Economics of Labor Force Participation* (Princeton: Princeton University Press, 1969), pp. 40–49. See also *Employment and Training Report of the President* (Washington: U.S. Government Printing Office, 1980), pp. 278–279.

59. These data from highly heterogeneous sources are suggestive rather than definitive. Data for the Germans, Irish, Italians, and Poles are from U.S. Bureau of the Census, *Current Population Reports*, Series P-20, No. 249 (U.S. Government Printing Office, 1973), p. 21. Data for the blacks, Mexicans, and Puerto Ricans are from U.S. Bureau of the Census, *Current Population Reports*, Series P-20, No. 224 (Government Printing Office, 1971), p. 14. Data for American Indians is from U.S. Bureau of the Census, *1970 Census of Population: Subject Reports*, PC(2)-1F (Washington: U.S. Government Printing Office, 1973), p. 111. Data for the Chinese and Japanese are from U.S. Bureau of the Census, *1970 Census of Population: Subject Reports*, PC(2)-1G, pp. 38, 97, 156. Data for Jews and West Indians are computed from Thomas Sowell, ed., *Essays and Data on American Ethnic Groups*, pp. 365, 405.

60. U.S. Bureau of the Census, *Current Population Reports*, Series P-20, No. 372 (U.S. Government Printing Office, 1982), pp. 28, 29.

61. U.S. Bureau of the Census, *Social Indicators III* (Washington: U.S. Government Printing Office, 1980), p. 485.

62. Richard B. Freeman, *Black Elite* (New York: McGraw-Hill, 1976), Chapter 4.

63. See, for example, Stephen Steinberg, *The Ethnic Myth*, (Atheneum, 1981), pp. 66–67.

64. Leo Grebler, Joan W. Moore, Ralph C. Guzman, *The Mexican-American People* (The Free Press, 1970), p. 144.

65. Loc. cit.

66. Thomas Sowell, "Three Black Histories," p. 29.

67. Thomas Sowell, ed., *Essays and Data on American Ethnic Groups*, p 393.

68. See data for women in 35–44 year old bracket. Ibid., p. 394.

69. Ibid., p. 291.

70. Ibid., p. 393.

71. U.S. Bureau of the Census, *Current Population Reports*, P-20, No. 226 (U.S. Government Printing Office, 1971), p. 20; 1970 U.S. Census Public Use Sample.

72. Robert Higgs, "Race, Skills and Earnings: American Immigrant in 1909," *Journal of Economic History*, June 1971.

73. U.S. Senate Commission on Immigration, *The Children of Immigrants in Schools* (Government Printing Office, 1911), p. 78.

74. Diane Ravitch, *The Great School Wars*, p. 178.

75. Thomas Sowell, "Assumptions versus History in Ethnic Education," op. cit., pp. 42–45, 46.

76. U.S. Bureau of the Census, *Current Population Reports*, Series P-20, No. 46, p. 63.

77. Loc. cit.

78. Thomas Sowell, "Ethnicity in a Changing America," *Daedalus*, Winter 1978, p. 232.

79. Stanford M. Lyman, *Chinese Americans* (Random House, 1974), pp. 133, 137.

80. Thomas Sowell, *Affirmative Action Reconsidered* (American Enterprise Institute, 1975), pp. 16–21.

81. Thomas Sowell, *Black Education: Myths and Tragedies* (David McKay Co., 1972), p. 256.

82. E. Franklin Frazier, *Black Bourgeoisie* (The Free Press, 1962), pp. 73–76; Christopher Jencks and David Riesman, "The American Negro College," *Harvard Educational Review*, Winter 1967, pp. 3–60; Thomas Sowell, *Black Education: Myths and Tragedies*, Chapter 10.

83. Clifford A. Hauberg, *Puerto Rico and the Puerto Ricans* (New York: Hippocrene Books, Inc., 1974), pp. 120–121; Thomas Sowell, *Ethnic America*, pp. 234–235, 261.

84. Joseph P. Fitzpatrick, *Puerto Rican Americans* (Englewood Cliffs: Prentice-Hall, 1971), p. 133.

85. Thomas Sowell, *Affirmative Action Reconsidered*, pp. 15–17.

86. National Research Council, *Summary Report 1980: Doctorate Recipients from United States Universities* (National Academy Press, 1981), pp. 26–29.

87. Ibid., pp. 17–23.

88. Ibid., p. 21.

89. U.S. Bureau of the Census, *1970 Census of Population: Subject Reports*, PC(2)-1G, p. 68.

90. Ibid., p. 93

91. 1970 Census Public Use Sample.

92. Thomas Sowell, *Markets and Minorities*, pp. 24–26.

93. Thomas Sowell, *Ethnic America*, pp. 90–91.

94. Thomas Sowell, "Three Black Histories," op. cit., p. 43.

95. Harry H. L. Kitano, *Japanese Americans*, pp. 71, 72.

96. Ibid., pp. 23, 76n; Irving Howe, *World of Our Fathers* (Harcourt, Brace, Jovanovich, 1976), p. 273; Betty Lee Sung, *The Story of the Chinese in America*, p. 171.

97. Thomas Sowell, "Patterns of Black Excellence," *The Public Interest*, Spring 1976, pp. 54–55.

98. Thomas Sowell, *Ethnic America*, p. 266.

99. Ibid., p 221.

100. Betty Lee Sung, *The Story of the Chinese in America,* p. 125.
101. Thomas Sowell, *Ethnic America,* passim.
102. Daniel P. Moynihan, "Employment, Income, and the Ordeal of the Negro Family," *Daedalus,* Fall 1965, p. 752.
103 U.S. Bureau of the Census, *Current Population Reports,* Series P-23, No. 80 (Government Printing Office), p. 156.
104. Thomas Sowell, *"Weber* and *Bakke,* and the Presuppositions of 'Affirmative Action,'" *Wayne Law Review,* July 1980, p. 1309.
105. See Table 6-2.
106. U.S. Bureau of the Census, *Current Population Reports,* Series P-23, No. 80, p. 31.
107. See Table 6-2.
108. Finis Welch, "Economics of Affirmative Action," *The American Economic Review,* May 1981, p. 132.
109. U.S. Bureau of the Census, *Current Population Reports,* Series P-20, No. 366 (U.S. Government Printing Office, 1981), pp. 182, 184.
110. Thomas Sowell, *Affirmative Action Reconsidered,* p. 15.
111. Martin Kilson, "Black Social Classes and Intergenerational Policy," *The Public Interest,* Summer 1981, p. 63.
112. Lennox A. Mills, *Southeast Asia* (University of Minnesota Press, 1964), p. 130.
113. James P. Smith and Finis Welch, *Race Differences in Earnings: A Survey and New Evidence* (Santa Monica: The Rand Corporation, 1978), p. 19.
114. Ibid., p. viii.
115. Thomas Sowell, *Knowledge and Decisions* (Basic Books, Inc., 1980), pp. 142, 230, 265–266.
116. U.S. Bureau of the Census, *Statistical Abstract of the United States, 1981* (U.S. Government Printing Office, 1981), p. 84.
117. Ibid.
118. Ibid., p. 87.
119. Ibid., p. 192.
120. Danie Kubat, *The Politics of Immigration Policies* (New York: Center for Migration Studies, 1979), p. 23.
121. Ibid., p. 3.

CHAPTER 7

1. Peter T Bauer, *Equality, The Third World, and Economic Delusion* (Cambridge, Mass: Harvard University Press, 1981), p. 88.
2. *The World Almanac and Book of Facts, 1981* (Newspaper Enterprise Association, Inc., 1981), p. 442.
3. Ibid., p. 697.
4. Maldwyn Allen Jones, *American Immigration* (University of Chicago Press, 1970), pp. 212–213.
5. Mark Jefferson, *Peopling the Argentine Pampa* (Port Washington N.Y.: Kennikat Press, 1971), pp. 155–156.

5. Carl Wittke, *We Who Built America* (The Press of Case Western Reserve University, 1967), p. 191.

7. Peter T. Bauer, *Equality, The Third World, and Economic Delusion,* p. 49.

8. Ibid., p. 45.

9. Peter T. Bauer, loc. cit.

10. Peter T. Bauer, *Equality, The Third World, and Economic Delusion,* p. 43.

11 U.S. Bureau of the Census, *Historical Statistics of the United States, From Colonial Times to 1970* (Government Printing Office, 1975), p. 593.

12. John Stuart Mill, *Autobiography of John Stuart Mill* (New York: Columbia University Press, 1944), p. 102.

13. See Thomas Sowell, *Ethnic America* (Basic Books, Inc., 1981), Chs. 7, 10.

14. Paul R. Ehrlich, *The Population Bomb* (New York: Ballatine Books, 1978), front cover

15. Gertrude Himmelfarb, 'Introduction," Thomas Robert Malthus, *On Population* (New York: Modern Library, 1960), p. xiv. The first U.S. Census was in 1790.

16. Peter T. Bauer, *Equality, The Third World, and Economic Delusion,* p. 53; L. H. Gann and Peter Duignan, *Burden of Empire* (Hoover Institution Press, 1977), p. 227; Victor Purcell, *The Chinese in Southeast Asia,* 2nd edition (Oxford University Press, 1980), pp. 3n, 85, 170, 362.

17. John Stuart Mill, *Principles of Political Economy,* ed. W. J. Ashley (London: Longmans, Green, and Co., 1909), p. 161.

18. See, for example, Peter T. Bauer, op. cit., p. 43; W. Howard and James F. Guyot, *Population, Politics and the Future of Southern Asia* (New York: Columbia University Press, 1973), pp. 53, 54, 365n60. Throughout this latter book, the *facts* about food and population are almost uniformly optimistic; the interpretations and forecasts uniformly pessimistic—a common pattern in this literature.

19. Paul R. Ehrlich, *The Population Bomb,* p. 19.

20. Michael P. Todaro, *Economic Development in the Third World* (New York: Longman, Inc., 1981), pp. 166–167.

21. See, for example, Thomas Sowell, *Knowledge and Decisions* (Basic Books, 1980), pp. 352–368.

22. Peter T. Bauer, *Equality, The Third World, and Economic Delusion,* p. 65.

23. Ken Adelman, "The Great Black Hope," *Harper's Magazine,* July 1981, pp. 16–17.

24. Peter T. Bauer, *Equality, The Third World, and Economic Delusion,* p. 51.

25. Robert L. Schuettinger, *Forty Centuries of Wage and Price Controls* (Washington, D.C.: The Heritage Foundation, 1979), pp. 33–34.

26. Ibid., p. 34.

27. L. H. Gann and Peter Duignan, *Burden of Empire,* p. 128.

28. Victor Purcell, *The Chinese in Southeast Asia,* 2nd edition, p. 513.
29. Adam Smith, *The Wealth of Nations* (New York: Modern Library, 1937), p. 325.
30. Ibid., p. 900.
31. Ibid., p. 872.
32. Ibid., p. 900.
33. Ibid., p. 582.
34. David S. Landes, "Some Thoughts on the Nature of Economic Imperialism," *Journal of Economic History,* December 1961, p. 505.
35. Ibid.
36. Ibid., p. 498.
37. Karl Marx and Friedrich Engels, *Basic Writings on Politics and Philosophy,* ed. Lewis S. Feuer (Anchor Books, 1959), p. 479.
38. Ibid., p. 480.
39. Loc. cit.
40. Ibid., p. 475.
41. Ibid., p. 450.
42. Ibid., p. 451.
43. Ibid.
44. See, for example, Horace B. Davis, "Nations, Colonies and Social Classes: The Position of Marx and Engels," *Science and Society,* Winter 1965, pp. 26–43.
45. See, for example, Karl Marx, *Capital: A Critique of Political Economy, Volume I: The Process of Capitalist Production* (Charles H. Kerr & Company, 1919), p. 15; Karl Marx and Friedrich Engels, *Basic Writings on Politics and Philosophy,* pp. 230, 232, 235, 350, 476; Karl Marx and Frederick Engels, *Selected Correspondence 1846–1895,* trans. Dona Torr (International Publishers, 1942), pp. 58, 181.
46. See, for example, Karl Marx and Friedrich Engels, *Basic Writings on Politics and Philosophy,* pp. 107–108, 199; Karl Marx and Frederick Engels, *Selected Correspondence 1846–1895: With Explanatory Notes,* p. 58.
47. Karl Marx and Frederick Engels, *Selected Correspondence 1846–1895: With Explanatory Notes,* pp. 60, 399.
48. V. I. Lenin, *Imperialism: The Highest Stage of Capitalism* (New York: International Publishers, 1963), pp. 13–14.
49. Ibid., p. 29.
50. Ibid., pp. 16–17, 18, 22–23.
51. Ibid., pp. 31, 32, 38.
52. Ibid., pp. 34, 35, 60.
53. U.S. Bureau of the Census, *Historical Statistics of the United States, From Colonial Times to 1970,* p. 870.
54. Kwame Nkrumah, *Neo-Colonialism: The Last Stage of Imperialism* (New York: International Publishers, 1980), p. ix.
55. Ibid., p. 22.
56. Harry Magdoff, *The Age of Imperialism* (New York· Monthly Review Press, 1969), pp. 47, 97, 100.

57. Ibid., pp. 74, 75.
58. Ibid., p. 16.
59. Ibid., p. 9.
60. Ibid., p. 12.
61. Ibid., p. 61.
62. Kwame Nkrumah, *Neo-Colonialism: The Last Stage of Imperialism,* p. xvii.
63. Ibid., p. 6.
64. Ibid., p. 9.
65. Ibid., p. 32.
66. Ibid., pp. 35–36.
67. Ibid., p. 38.
68. Ibid., p. 39.
69. Karl Marx and Friedrich Engels, *Basic Writings on Politics and Philosophy,* p. 399.
70. Kwame Nkrumah, *Neo-Colonialism: The Last Stage of Imperialism,* p. xiv.
71. Ibid., p. xx.
72. Edward Gibbon, *The Decline and Fall of the Roman Empire,* Vol. I (Modern Library), p. 19.
73. Winston Churchill, *A History of the English-Speaking Peoples,* Vol. I: *The Birth of Britain,* (New York: Bantam Books, 1974), p. 9.
74. Ibid., p. 3.
75. John Wacher, *The Coming of Rome,* (New York: Charles Scribner's Sons, 1980), pp. 12–13, 17.
76. Ibid., p. 39.
77. Winston Churchill, *A History of the English-Speaking Peoples,* Vol. I: *The Birth of Britain,* p. 10.
78. "This active, alert, conquering, and ruling race established themselves wherever they went with ease and celerity, and might have looked forward to a long dominion. But the tramp of the legions had followed hard behind them, and they must soon defend the prize they had won against still better men and higher systems of government and war." Ibid., p. 9.
79. Ibid., p. 2.
80. John Wacher, *The Coming of Rome,* pp. 1–7.
81. Winston Churchill, *A History of the English-Speaking Peoples,* Vol. I: *The Birth of Britain,* p. 12.
82. Ibid., pp. 19–20.
83. Ibid., p. 17.
84. Barry Cunliffe, *Rome and Her Empire* (New York: McGraw-Hill Book Co., 1978), p. 240.
85. William H. Harris and Judith S. Leven, eds., *The New Columbia Encyclopedia* (New York: Columbia University Press, 1975), p. 1128.
86. John Wacher, *The Coming of Rome,* p. 39.
87. Ibid., p. 72.

88. Ibid., p. 76.
89. Ibid., p. 79.
90. Ibid., p. 101.
91. Winston Churchill, *A History of the English-Speaking Peoples,* Vol. I: *The Birth of Britain,* p. 25.
92. Ibid., p. 28.
93. Ibid., p. 26.
94. Ibid., pp. 25–26.
95. L. H. Gann and Peter Duignan, *Africa South of the Sahara* (Stanford: Hoover Institution Press, 1981), p. 2.
96. Loc. cit.
97. Ibid., p. 3.
98. Harold E. Driver, *Indians of North America* (Chicago: University of Chicago Press, 1975), p. 77.
99. Ibid., p. 212.
100. Ibid., pp. 324–325.
101. Ibid., p. 327.
102 L. H. Gann and Peter Duignan, *Burden of Empire,* p. 140.
103. Ibid., p. 160.
104. Seymour Martin Lipset, "Racial and Ethnic Tensions in the Third World," *The Third World,* ed. W. Scott Thompson (San Francisco: Institute for Contemporary Studies, 1978), p. 129.
105. Jane Pinchot, *The Mexicans in America* (Minneapolis: Lerner Publications, 1973), p. 12.
106. Seymour Martin Lipset, op. cit.
107. L. H. Gann and Peter Duignan, *Burden of Empire,* p. 156.
108. Ibid., p. 155.
109. Thomas Sowell, *Ethnic America,* p. 185.
110. Philip D. Curtin, *The Atlantic Slave Trade* (Madison: University of Wisconsin Press, 1969), p. 227.
111. Peter Duignan, *Africa South of the Sahara,* pp. 3–4.
112. Ibid., p. 4.
113. Victor Purcell, *The Chinese in Southeast Asia,* 2nd edition, p. 427.
114. Robert W. Fogel and Stanley L. Engelman, *Time on the Cross* (Boston: Little, Brown and Co., 1974), p. 13.
115. L. H. Gann and Peter Duignan, *Burden of Empire,* p. 248.
116. Peter T. Bauer, *Equality, The Third World, and Economic Delusion,* p. 70.
117. Adam Smith, *The Wealth of Nations,* p. 687.
118. Peter T. Bauer, *Equality, The Third World, and Economic Delusion,* p. 251.
119. Ibid., p. 185.
120. *Hong Kong: Teacher's Guide for the Film* (Liberty Fund, Inc.), p. 3; *The World Almanac and Book of Facts 1981,* pp. 521, 545, 557, 569, 582.
121. Alvin Rabushka, *Hong Kong: A Study in Economic Freedom* (Chicago: University of Chicago Press, 1979), p. 11.
122. *Hong Kong: Teacher's Guide for the Film,* p. 3.

123. Loc. cit.
124. Alvin Rabushka, *Hong Kong: A Study in Economic Freedom,* p. 11.
125. David Livingstone, *Livingstone's African Journal 1853–1856,* ed. I. Schapera (London: Chatto & Windus, 1963), Vol. II, p. 287.
126. Ibid.
127. Thomas Sowell, *Ethnic America,* p. 127.
128. Ray H. Whitbeck and Olive J. Thomas, *The Geographic Factor* (Port Washington, N.Y.: Kennikat Press, 1970), p. 398.
129. Ibid., p. 399.
130. Peter T. Bauer and Basil S. Yamey, *The Economics of Under-Developed Countries* (Chicago: The University of Chicago Press, 1963), p. 61.
131. Paul Craig Roberts and Alvin Rabushka, "A Diagrammatic Exposition of an Economic Theory of Imperialism," *Public Choice,* Spring 1973, p. 105.
132. Charles O. Hucker, *China's Imperial Past* (Stanford: Stanford University Press, 1975), Chapters 11, 12, passim.
133. Ibid., p. 334.
134. Carl K. Fisher, "Facing up to Africa's Food Crisis," *Foreign Affairs,* Fall 1982, p. 166.
135. Ibid., p. 170.
136. Yuan-li Wu and Chun-hsi Wu, *Economic Development in Southeast Asia* (Hoover Institution Press, 1980), p. 57.
137. Gordon P. Means, *Malaysian Politics* (New York: New York University Press, 1970), p. 20; See also Bee-Lan Wang, "Government Intervention in Ethnic Stratification: Effects on the Distribution of Students Among Fields of Study," *Comparative Education Review,* Vol. 21 (1977), p. 123; Victor Purcell, *The Chinese in Southeast Asia,* 2nd edition, p. 227.
138. Derek T. Healey, "Development Policy: New Thinking About an Interpretation," *Journal of Economic Literature,* September 1972, p. 771.
139. Ibid., p. 771n.
140. James Fallows, "Indonesia: An Effort to Hold Together," *The Atlantic,* June 1982, p. 22.
141. Carl K. Fisher, "Facing up to Africa's Food Crisis," *Foreign Affairs,* Fall 1982, pp. 150–174, passim.
142. Betty Lee Sung, *The Story of the Chinese in America* (New York: Collier Books, 1967), pp. 16–17.
143. Yasua Wakatsuki, "Japanese Emigration to the United States, 1866–1924," *Perspectives in American History,* Vol. XII (1979), pp. 451–452.
144. Oliver MacDonagh, "The Irish Famine Emigration to the United States," *Perspectives in American History,* Vol. X (1976), pp. 394–395.
145. Victor Purcell, *The Chinese in Southeast Asia,* 2nd edition, pp. 121, 123, 134–135, 200, 256, 282, 300–301, 410, 457.
146. Michael P. Todaro, *Economic Development in the Third World,* 2nd edition (New York: Longman, Inc., 1977), p. 409.

147. Ibid., pp. 409, 411.
148. Peter T. Bauer, *Equality, The Third World, and Economic Delusion,* p 86.
149. Carl K. Fisher, "Facing up to Africa's Food Crisis," *Foreign Affairs,* Fall 1982, p. 172.
150. Ibid., p. 174.
151. Ibid., p. 94.
152. Ibid., p. 96.
153. Ken Adelman, "The Great Black Hope," *Harper's Magazine,* July 1981, p. 18.
154. Ibid., p. 17.
155. Ibid., p. 16.
156. Ibid., p. 17.
157. Ibid., p. 15.
158. Ibid., p. 16.
159. Michael P. Todaro, *Economic Development in the Third World,* 2nd edition, p. 405.
160. Ibid., p. 404.
161. Thomas Sowell, *Knowledge and Decisions,* pp. 98–100, 153–154.

CHAPTER 8

1. Ulrich B. Phillips, *The Slave Economy of the Old South* (Baton Rouge: Louisiana State University Press, 1968), p. 269.
2. Oliver Wendell Holmes, "Law and the Courts," Speech at the Dinner of the Harvard Law School Association of New York on February 15, 1913.
3. See, for example, Thomas Sowell, *Markets and Minorities* (New York: Basic Books, 1981), p. 35.
4. Gerald D. Suttles, *The Social Order of the Slum* (Chicago: University of Chicago Press, 1973), pp. 62, 63, 66, 103, 128; Stephen Birmingham, *Certain People* (Boston: Little, Brown and Co., 1977), p. 67; Richard Gambino, *Blood of My Blood* (New York: Anchor Books, 1974), pp. 235–236.
5. See, for example, Thomas Sowell, *Knowledge and Decisions* (New York: Basic Books, 1980), pp. 83–93.
6. Maldwyn Allen Jones, *American Immigration* (Chicago: University of Chicago Press, 1970), p. 225.
7. See Stanley Lieberson, *Ethnic Patterns in American Cities* (Glencoe: The Free Press, 1963), passim.
8. Thomas Kessner and Carol Boyd, *Today's Immigrants, Their Stories: A New Look at the Latest Americans* (New York: Oxford University Press, 1981), p. 139.
9. Ibid., pp. 168, 169, 173, 175.
10. Thomas Sowell, *Ethnic America* (New York: Basic Books, 1981), pp. 287–288.

11. Alvin Rabushka, *A Theory of Racial Harmony* (Columbia, S.C.: University of South Carolina Press, 1974), p. 70.
12. Thomas Sowell, *Knowledge and Decisions,* pp. 43–44.
13. Alvin Rabushka, *A Theory of Racial Harmony,* p. 68.
14. Ibid., pp. 95–96.
15. Gunnar Myrdal, *Asian Drama* (New York: Vintage Books, 1972), p. 4.
16. See, for example, Thomas Sowell, *Knowledge and Decisions,* pp. 108–109, 267–269.
17. Peter T. Bauer, "Development Economics: The Spurious Consensus and Its Background," *Roads to Freedom: Essays in Honour of Freidrich A. von Hayek* (London: Routledge & Kegan Paul, 1969), p. 30.
18. L. H. Gann and Peter Duignan, *Burden of Empire* (Hoover Institution Press, 1977), p. 317.
19. Ibid., p. 130.
20. See Thomas Sowell, *Ethnic America,* Chapters 7, 10.
21. For an exploration of this concept, see Thomas Sowell, *Knowledge and Decisions,* pp. 213ff.
22. "Special to the New York Times," *New York Times,* February 2, 1981, p. 4.
23. See, for example, Joseph Wandel, *The German Dimension of American History* (Nelson-Hall, 1979), pp. 15, 16, 51, 65; Theodore Huebner, *The Germans in America* (Chilton Company, 1962), pp. 24, 84, 85, 109, 110; Paul A. Wallace, *The Muhlenbergs of Pennsylvania* (University of Pennsylvania Press, 1950), pp. 161, 182, 257–259.
24. Theodore Huebner, *The Germans in America,* p. 13.
25. Ibid., p. 103.
26. Thomas Sowell, *Black Education: Myths and Tragedies* (David McKay Co., 1972), pp. 133–136; David Hapgood, "The Competition for Africa's Students," *The Reporter,* September 12, 1963, pp. 43–49.
27. Peter T. Bauer, *Equality, the Third World, and Economic Delusion* (Cambridge, Massachusetts: Harvard University Press, 1981), pp. 96–97.

INDEX